Economic Commission for Europe
Geneva

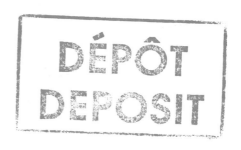

ECONOMIC SURVEY
OF EUROPE

2004 No. 2

Prepared by the
SECRETARIAT OF THE
ECONOMIC COMMISSION FOR EUROPE
GENEVA

UNITED NATIONS
New York and Geneva, 2004

NOTE

The present *Survey* is the fifty-seventh in a series of annual reports prepared by the secretariat of the United Nations Economic Commission for Europe to serve the needs of the Commission and of the United Nations in reporting on and analysing world economic conditions.

The Survey is published on the sole responsibility of the Executive Secretary of the ECE and the views expressed in it should not be attributed to the Commission or to its participating governments.

The designations employed and the presentation of the material in this publication do not imply the expression of any opinion whatsoever on the part of the Secretariat of the United Nations concerning the legal status of any country, territory, city or area, or of its authorities, or concerning the delimitation of its frontiers or boundaries.

The analysis in this issue is based on data and information available to the secretariat in mid-June 2004.

UNITED NATIONS PUBLICATION
Sales No. E.04.II.E.21
ISBN 92-1-116911-9 ISSN 0070-8712

CONTENTS

LIST OF TABLES

LIST OF CHARTS

LIST OF BOXES

EXPLANATORY NOTES

The following symbols have been used throughout this *Survey*:

  .. = not available or not pertinent

  – = nil or negligible

  * = estimate by the secretariat of the Economic Commission for Europe

  | = break in series

In referring to a combination of years, the use of an oblique stroke (e.g. 1998/99) signifies a 12-month period (say, from 1 July 1998 to 30 June 1999). The use of a hyphen (e.g. 1999-2001) normally signifies either an average of, or a total for, the full period of calendar years covered (including the end-years indicated).

Unless the contrary is stated, the standard unit of weight used throughout is the metric ton. The definition of "billion" used throughout is a thousand million. The definition of "trillion" used throughout is a thousand billion. Minor discrepancies in totals and percentages are due to rounding.

References to dollars ($) are to United States dollars unless otherwise specified.

The membership of the United Nations Economic Commission for Europe (UNECE) consists of all the states of western Europe, eastern Europe, the Commonwealth of Independent States (CIS), North America and Israel.

The term EU-15 refers to the aggregate of the following 15 member states of the European Union: Austria, Belgium, Denmark, Finland, France, Germany, Greece, Ireland, Italy, Luxembourg, Netherlands, Portugal, Spain, Sweden and the United Kingdom.

EU-25 refers to the 15 above-mentioned member states plus the 10 countries which have joined the European Union in May 2004, i.e. Cyprus, Czech Republic, Estonia, Hungary, Latvia, Lithuania, Malta, Poland, Slovakia and Slovenia.

WECEE comprises the EU-25 plus the countries of Iceland, Norway and Switzerland.

CEBS-8 (central Europe and Baltic states) includes the new member states listed above excluding Cyprus and Malta.

For the convenience in presentation, the countries of eastern Europe and the CIS are sometimes grouped into subregions based on geographical proximity.

The group of countries denoted as Eastern Europe comprises the following subregions:

- Baltic states (BS-3): Estonia, Latvia and Lithuania;

- Central Europe (CE-5): Czech Republic, Hungary, Poland, Slovakia and Slovenia;

- South-east Europe (SEE-7): Albania, Bosnia and Herzegovina, Bulgaria, Croatia, Romania, Serbia and Montenegro and The former Yugoslav Republic of Macedonia.

The Commonwealth of Independent States comprises the Russian Federation and the following subregions:

- Caucasian CIS (CCIS-3): Armenia, Azerbaijan and Georgia;

- Central Asian CIS (CACIS-5): Kazakhstan, Kyrgyzstan, Tajikistan, Turkmenistan and Uzbekistan;

- European CIS, excluding Russia (ECIS-3): Belarus, Republic of Moldova and Ukraine.

ABBREVIATIONS

c.i.f.	cost, insurance, freight
CIS	Commonwealth of Independent States
CMEA	(former) Council for Mutual Economic Assistance
CPI	consumer price index
DIW	Deutsches Institut für Wirtschaftsforschung (German Institute for Economic Research)
EBRD	European Bank for Reconstruction and Development
ECB	European Central Bank
ECE	Economic Commission for Europe
EMU	Economic and Monetary Union
EPO	European Patent Office
ERM-2	Exchange Rate Mechanism-2 (of the EU)
EU	European Union
EURIBOR	euro interbank offered rate
FDI	foreign direct investment
FOMC	Federal Open Market Committee
G-7	Group of Seven
GDP	gross domestic product
GDR	(former) German Democratic Republic
GERD	gross domestic expenditure on R&D
HICP	Harmonized Index of Consumer Prices
HWWA	Hamburgisches Welt-Wirtschafts-Archiv (Hamburg Institute of International Economics)
ICT	information and communication technologies
IEA	International Energy Agency
ILO	International Labour Office
IMF	International Monetary Fund
ISCED	International Standard Classification of Education
ISI	Institute for Scientific Information Citation Indexes
ITU	International Telecommunication Union
LFS	labour force survey
mb/d	million barrels per day
NIC	newly industrializing country
NMP	net material product
OECD	Organisation for Economic Co-operation and Development
OLS	Ordinary Least Squares
OPEC	Organization of the Petroleum Exporting Countries
OPT	outward processing trade
p/b	price per barrel
PPI	producer price index
PPP	purchasing power parity
R&D	research and development
S&T	science and technology
SAAR	seasonally adjusted annual rates
SARS	severe acute respiratory syndrome

SGP	Stability and Growth Pact
SITC	Standard International Trade Classification
ULC	unit labour costs
UNCTAD	United Nations Conference on Trade and Development
UNECE	United Nations Economic Commission for Europe
UNESCO	United Nations Educational, Scientific and Cultural Organization
USAID	United States Agency for International Development
USPTO	United States Patent and Trademark Office
USSR	(former) Union of Soviet Socialist Republics
VAT	value added tax
WTO	World Trade Organization

FOREWORD

The world economy strengthened in the first half of 2004 and the consensus of current forecasts is for the global recovery to continue in the second half of this year and into 2005. There remain important risks and uncertainties, however, that could trigger a cyclical setback. Higher oil prices have so far had little if any noticeable impact on the pace of the global growth, but any further large increases – as a result, for example, of continuing or intensified geopolitical uncertainties – could very well jeopardize the recovery. Another important downside risk is whether the rapid closing of the global output gap will lead to stronger than expected inflationary pressures which could result in a more pronounced tightening of monetary policy than is currently anticipated. The possibility of disruptions in the pattern of capital flows and exchange rates arising from abrupt changes in market sentiment and investor confidence about the sustainability of the twin deficits of the United States also remains a major downside risk.

Against this background, macroeconomic policy makers are faced with important challenges. The surge in global liquidity resulting from the considerable easing of monetary policy in recent years in the major industrialized countries carries risks of higher rates of inflation and the creation or intensification of asset price bubbles. The difficult task is to return to a broadly neutral monetary policy stance without endangering the sustainability of the global recovery. The decision of the Federal Reserve to raise its key interest rate in late June 2004 is a key turning point for monetary policy in both the United States and the rest of the world. But the expected further tightening of monetary policy will need to be accompanied by a more prudent fiscal policy to restore the internal and external balance of the United States economy.

In the euro area, the strength of the recovery remains relatively moderate, relying largely on the stimulus from foreign demand. In view of moderate rates of inflation, monetary policy can remain on hold until the recovery is more broadly based. This requires a sustained strengthening of domestic demand. Due to the recent deterioration of public finances, however, the scope for fiscal policy to stimulate economic activity in the three largest member states of the euro area has been reduced to the operation of automatic stabilizers, as is now also the case in the United States. This is partly the price being paid for not having pursued fiscal consolidation when the economic situation was more favourable. A major challenge is therefore to design consolidation strategies that will ensure fiscal sustainability in the medium and longer term without limiting the operation of the built-in stabilizers in the short run. This underlines the important role of monetary policy in contributing to a supportive policy mix that will keep the European economy on a sustained and, eventually, more dynamic growth path.

A better balance of macroeconomic policies needs to be complemented by structural reforms if the improvement is to be sustainable. The "conventional wisdom" is that there is a need for more structural reforms in labour markets and further deregulation in product markets if the growth potential of the European economy is to be increased. But the reform agenda is often too narrowly conceived in terms of making it easier for firms to hire and fire employees: it should comprise much more than that, including reforms in the sectors providing services of general interest as well as education and training, research and development, and health care. There is also the need to improve labour market flexibility by raising labour skills and matching them more closely to the changing requirements of the economy. Improving the incentives to work, particularly on the part of older workers, can also contribute to meeting the challenge of coping with the adjustment pressures created by population ageing and the associated problems of financing retirement pensions in the medium to longer term.

Structural reforms frequently involve adjustment costs, which generally appear before the benefits of the reform; the population naturally tends to resist such adjustments in times of cyclical weakness and crisis. Such adjustment costs can be more easily absorbed in a context of sustained economic growth, supported by adequate macroeconomic policies. It is therefore important that policy makers better exploit the opportunity for structural reforms and fiscal consolidation provided by a growing economy and expanding employment. This is a lesson that applies equally to the countries of eastern Europe and the CIS, all of which are still facing difficult structural adjustment problems.

For the eastern European countries that joined the EU at the beginning of May 2004 an immediate policy challenge is to develop a coherent strategy for achieving the nominal convergence targets (the Maastricht criteria), without at the same time jeopardizing further progress in real convergence. The timing of the obligatory entry into the EMU is a key element in such a strategy. An important intermediate step is the decision as to when to join the new European Exchange Rate Mechanism (ERM-2), which is the antechamber to the EMU. The precise timing will have to reflect the specific economic circumstances in the individual countries. Three economies – Estonia, Lithuania and Slovenia – joined the ERM-2 after only two months of EU membership. For those countries that have not yet followed a fixed exchange rate regime – Estonia and Lithuania have maintained their currency boards – joining ERM-2 will reduce the scope for using monetary policy as an instrument of macroeconomic policy. Given the potential conflicts between the EMU targets for inflation and exchange rate stability that may arise in the process of economic catch-up, this will require skilful management. In the presence of volatile and often speculative capital flows, there is an increased risk of currency crises that should not be underestimated.

Another major preoccupation of governments in many of the new EU member states is the fiscal adjustment required by the rules of the EU's fiscal policy framework. Many of the new member states have budget deficits that are significantly above the threshold of 3 per cent of national GDP. These countries face major structural adjustments, including the urgent need to rehabilitate and enhance their infrastructures, which, for reasons of intergenerational equity and political feasibility, will have to be financed by government borrowing. This is a transitory process but it will require a flexible interpretation of the Stability and Growth Pact (SGP), in order to avoid a counterproductive fiscal tightening. The crisis of the SGP in 2003 has, in any case, accentuated the need for a more flexible interpretation of the fiscal rules. The recent proposals made by the European Commission go in the right direction, but any modifications should explicitly take into account the specific circumstances of the new member states.

In oil-exporting CIS countries, especially Russia, the sharp rise in oil prices has led to a large and progressive real appreciation of their national currencies in the past few years, with adverse effects on their domestic manufacturing sectors. One of the current policy challenges for these economies is thus to prevent a possible overshooting of the real exchange rate. If the increased oil revenues, however, are used efficiently to enhance productive capacities and promote economic diversification, the growth potential of these economies can be increased and their dependence on natural resources reduced.

All of the UNECE economies continue to face increasing pressures from the forces of globalization and technological progress. In order to ensure that these forces are exploited to enhance rather than diminish the welfare of their populations it is up to governments to design policies and institutions that create an environment that will encourage both the necessary structural changes in the patterns of specialization and ensure that the costs and benefits of such change are equitably distributed.

Brigita Schmögnerová
Executive Secretary
United Nations Economic Commission for Europe

CHAPTER 1

THE ECE ECONOMIES AT MID-2004

1.1 The global context

A strong recovery of world output...

In mid-2004, the global recovery, which started in the second half of 2003, appears to be well established. Economic activity continues to be stimulated by very relaxed monetary policy and associated interest rates at very low levels. In many regions, fiscal policy is also supporting domestic demand. Against this backdrop, economic activity is strengthening in all the major regions of the world. In the spring 2004, forecasts of global economic growth in 2004 were raised by 0.6 percentage points above those made in the autumn of 2003.[1] World output is now expected to increase by 4.6 per cent this year, the largest annual increase since 2000.[2]

This optimistic outlook extends to 2005, when the same average annual rate of global growth is expected to be maintained, although this masks a gradual slowdown in the course of the year. At the same time, however, there are lingering concerns about important downside risks associated with the necessary adjustments of global external imbalances, high levels of public sector debt and, in some countries, bubbles in housing markets. A major feature of economic developments in the first half of 2004 was the surge in international commodity prices, especially crude oil prices (see below). While higher oil prices will tend to restrain economic activity somewhat in the course of 2004, there has so far been no noticeable adverse effect on the pace of the global recovery. Given their greater dependence on oil imports and their lower levels of energy efficiency, net oil importers among the emerging market and developing economies will be more affected by the rise in oil prices than the advanced industrialized countries.

The cyclical momentum in the global economy in the early months of 2004 has indeed been remarkable. In the United States, economic activity grew at an annual rate of about 4 per cent in both the final quarter of 2003 and the first of 2004. Short-term economic indicators suggest that the upswing continued strongly in the second quarter, underpinned by a significant rise in employment and higher rates of capacity utilization.[3] Official concerns about the potential risks of deflation have been replaced by worries about risks of higher inflation, although this has so far remained relatively moderate (see section 1.2 below).

There was also continuing strong growth in Japan and the other Asian economies. In China, real GDP rose by 9.8 per cent in the first quarter of 2004 compared with the same period of the previous year. Economic growth has also remained relatively strong in central and eastern Europe and in the CIS. The latter region, especially Russia, has been benefiting from high prices for oil and other raw materials, which are boosting export revenues and economic growth.

The euro area continues to lag behind in the international growth cycle, largely reflecting the weakness of domestic demand. Exports are leading the recovery, supported by growing international demand, which has helped to offset the restraining effects of the appreciation of the euro and the rise in oil prices. The spillovers from stronger exports should stimulate domestic demand in the second half of the year, but the overall cyclical momentum is likely to remain moderate, especially given the relatively depressed spending propensity of private households.

In the major seven economies (G7) combined, real GDP rose by 1 per cent in the first quarter of 2004 (chart 1.1.1), bringing aggregate output to 3¾ per cent above its level in the same quarter of 2003. This was the strongest year-over-year rate of growth since the peak of the previous global growth cycle in the second quarter of 2000.

...and world trade

The pervasive strengthening of economic activity is also reflected in the expansion of international trade. The volume of world merchandise trade rose by some 2 per cent in the first quarter of 2004 compared with the preceding quarter, and was about 9.5 per cent higher than

---

[1] IMF, *World Economic Outlook* (Washington, D.C.), April 2004.

[2] Calculated by the IMF using Purchasing Power Parity (PPP) based GDP weights for aggregating the growth rates of individual countries. The use of PPP-based weights for calculating world output growth instead of market exchange rate-based GDP weights, however, is controversial. Using the latter yields a forecast of aggregate output growth of some 3¾ per cent for 2004. Consensus Economics, *Consensus Forecasts*, May 2004. The difference is due to the fact that some developing countries with growth rates significantly above the average, especially China, have a smaller weight when GDP is based on market exchange rates.

[3] The Federal Reserve Board, *The Beige Book*, 16 June 2004 [www.federalreserve.gov].

CHART 1.1.1

Quarterly changes in real GDP in the euro area and the G7 economies, 1998-2004

(Percentage change over the previous quarter, SAAR)

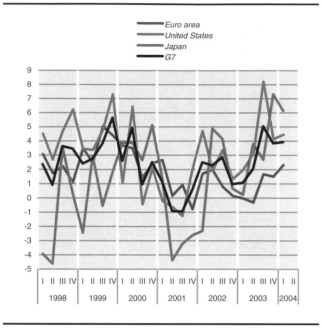

Source: National statistics.

Note: Growth rates are seasonally adjusted and expressed at annual rates (SAAR). The G7 economies are Canada, France, Germany, Italy, Japan, the United Kingdom and the United States.

a year earlier.[4] Forecasts for the annual increase in the volume of goods and services in 2004 range from 6.8 per cent[5] to 8.6 per cent,[6] up from 4.5 per cent in 2003.

Equity markets stabilize...

International equity markets continued to rise in the first quarter of 2004, sustained by the positive prospects for economic growth and corporate earnings as well as a renewed appetite of investors for risk-taking. In the second quarter, however, equity prices levelled off and became more volatile, reflecting investor concern about the anticipated rise in short-term interest rates in the United States (and possibly China), compounded by lingering geopolitical uncertainties and developments in the oil markets.

...but financial conditions for emerging markets turn somewhat less favourable

The financial conditions facing emerging markets remained relatively favourable in the first half of 2004, given the continuing low level of United States interest rates, notably a federal funds rate at 1 per cent, its lowest

---

[4] CPB Netherlands Bureau for Economic Policy Analysis, *CPB Memo: World Trade Monitor*, 24 May 2004 [www.cpb.nl].

[5] IMF, op. cit.

[6] *OECD Economic Outlook*, No. 75 (Paris), May 2004 (Preliminary edition). OECD expects a further strengthening of world trade in 2005 (an increase of 10.2 per cent), whereas the IMF forecasts a mild slowdown to 6.6 per cent.

---

level since 1958. The search for higher yields and an increased willingness of investors to accept higher risk, led to a strong recovery in net private capital flows to emerging markets in 2003, when they reached $194 billion, an increase of some 50 per cent compared with 2002. These inflows have been projected to increase further in 2004.[7] The increase in international capital flows, which was also stimulated by the improved economic outlook for the emerging market economies, has led to a marked narrowing of interest rate spreads on emerging market bonds,[8] which fell to a record low of 384 basis points in January 2004. But emerging markets are vulnerable to rising interest rates in the major industrialized countries, especially the United States.[9] It is generally expected that higher interest rates will lead to widening spreads and a more than proportionate deterioration in the financing conditions for emerging markets. In April 2004, expectations of a rise in United States interest rates led to a sharp fall in the prices of treasury bills and a concomitant surge in the yield on 10-year bonds. This drove speculators to reduce significantly their exposure to emerging markets, and the strong selling pressure on emerging market bonds led to a substantial widening of yield spreads. In early May 2004, spreads over the United States treasury bills had risen to 478 basis points, but these were still low by historical standards. In mid-June 2004, the spread over United States treasuries had risen a little more to 499 basis points.

The dollar depreciation appears to have bottomed out...

In the foreign exchange markets, the marked depreciation of the dollar in 2002 and 2003 was partly reversed in the first five months of 2004 (chart 1.1.2). The strengthening of the dollar was probably driven by the strong recovery of the United States economy and, as a result, investors' expectations of higher yields on dollar-denominated assets. In nominal effective terms, the dollar appreciated against a basket of major currencies (including the euro, yen and UK sterling) by 5 per cent between January and May 2004. Compared with its recent peak in February 2002, however, there was still a nominal effective depreciation of 20.5 per cent in May 2004. In contrast, a broader measure of the nominal effective exchange rate of the dollar fell by only 10.6 per cent over the same period, a reflection of the efforts made in Asian economies to stabilize their exchange rates against the dollar. The recent statement of G7 Finance

---

[7] Institute of International Finance, *Capital Flows to Emerging Market Economies,* 15 April 2004 [www.iif.com].

[8] As measured by JP Morgan, Emerging Markets Bond Index Plus (EMBI+).

[9] There has been a large increase in the so-called "carry trade" which involves short-term borrowing at low interest rates in the United States and long-term investing in high-yield assets in emerging markets. The unwinding of these positions in reaction to expected increases in interest rates in the United States creates a risk of destabilizing outflows of capital from the emerging markets.

CHART 1.1.2

Bilateral exchange rates of the dollar, January 1999-June 2004
(Indices, January 1999=100)

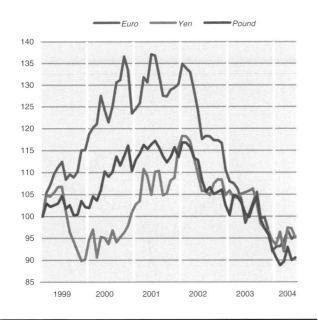

Source: United States Federal Reserve Board.

Note: National currency units per dollar. Average monthly data; June 2004: average of daily data for 1-15 June.

Ministers[10] about exchange rates does not appear to have had any visible impact on the foreign exchange markets.

...but the pattern of exchange rates among major currencies remains fragile

A major source of concern remains the large current account deficit of the United States, which rose to a record $149 billion (or 5.4 per cent of GDP) in the first quarter of 2004, up from $127 billion in the final quarter of 2003. A record monthly United States trade deficit in April suggests that there was a further deterioration in the external balance in the second quarter. For 2004 as a whole the current account deficit is expected to correspond to just under 5 per cent of GDP in 2004.

The domestic counterpart to this external imbalance is now the general government budget deficit, given that the private sector returned to its financial balance in 2003. This pattern will persist in 2004. The re-emergence of "twin deficits" in the United States, however, does not imply that a reduction in the fiscal deficits will lead to a proportionate reduction in the external imbalance. This will also depend on the private sector's spending and saving behaviour.

From a global perspective, the main counterparts to the United States external deficit are the considerable surpluses of Japan and other Asian economies. The euro area had only a small external surplus in 2003 corresponding to about half a percentage point of aggregate euro area GDP. This is expected to remain more or less unchanged in 2004. The recent upturn in the nominal effective exchange rate of the dollar has not been helpful for correcting the United States external imbalance. This will require not only greater exchange rate flexibility in Asia, but also a sustained growth of domestic demand in the rest of the world.

The financing of the United States current account deficit relies on the continued willingness of foreigners to buy dollar-denominated assets. In the face of waning FDI in the United States and reduced demand from foreign private investors for United States equities, an increasing role has been played by foreign central banks, especially in Asia, which have bought United States treasury bills, the major objective being to prevent a depreciation of the dollar against their currencies. But given the inherent difficulties of sterilization, the accumulation of large foreign reserves have at the same time led to a surge in domestic liquidity in these countries.

Japan: a sustained recovery at last?

In Japan, real GDP rose by 1.5 per cent in the first quarter of 2004 compared with the preceding quarter, equivalent to a seasonally adjusted annual rate of more than 6 per cent. Real GDP in the first quarter was 5 per cent above its level in the same quarter of 2003. This was the eighth consecutive quarterly increase in GDP, and there is now increasing optimism that the recovery will be sustained. Growth forecasts for 2004 have been raised amid expectations that the long period of deflation is coming to an end. The recovery is no longer driven solely by exports but also by a strengthening of private domestic demand, namely consumption and business investment, reflecting the improved economic outlook. Monetary conditions continue to be very relaxed. The Bank of Japan has kept money market rates close to zero since March 2001. The real effective exchange rate, moreover, is at a level that ensures strong price competitiveness of Japan's business sector, a reflection of the repeated official interventions in the foreign exchange markets to limit the appreciation of the yen against the dollar.[11] Yields on 10-year government bonds have edged upward in 2004, reaching 1.7 per cent in the first half of June, their highest level in more than three years. This reflects the improved economic outlook and expectations of a return to positive rates of inflation in the medium term, but there have also been portfolio shifts from bonds

---

[10] Statement of 24 April 2004. In Dubai on 20 September 2003, the G7 emphasized that "more flexibility in exchange rates is desirable for countries or economic areas that lack such flexibility". *Statement of G7 Finance Ministers and Central Bank Governors* (Washington, D.C.), 24 April 2004 [www.g7.utoronto.ca].

---

[11] It has been reported that for the first time in seven months the Japanese finance ministry did not intervene in the foreign exchange market in April 2004. *Financial Times* (London), 3 May 2004.

to equities in response to improved corporate profitability, and leading to lower bond prices. The stance of fiscal policy is slightly restrictive in 2004, although the budget deficit is nevertheless projected to correspond to some 8 per cent of GDP. Government debt has surged to 160 per cent of GDP. Accordingly, the consolidation of public finances is a major priority in the years ahead.

Strong growth in emerging market economies in Asia and Latin America

Asia will remain the world's most dynamic region in 2004. Real GDP is forecast to increase by some 6.5 per cent over 2003. Exports remain a major driving force, stimulated by the global recovery and the continuing boom in China, which has led to the growing importance of intraregional trade. In many countries, economic activity is supported by low interest rates and expansionary fiscal policies. To these factors can be added the official interventions in the foreign exchange markets to ensure stable – and widely regarded as significantly undervalued – exchange rates against the dollar.

In China, the growth of real GDP was more than 9 per cent in 2003 and only a moderate slowdown is expected for 2004. But there are increasing concerns about the risks of overinvestment in some sectors – facilitated by the rapid growth of bank credit – which have increased the vulnerability to a downturn in demand, domestic and foreign. There are also signs of upward pressures on the prices of raw materials and other inputs as well as for consumer goods. The authorities have taken measures designed to slow down the pace of investment and reduce the rate of credit expansion, but so far the central bank has refrained from raising interest rates. There are concerns that in view of the limited policy instruments available in China's mixed economic system, the slowdown in economic activity could be more sudden than intended. Given China's new position as a major growth pole in the world economy, a "hard landing" of its economy would have adverse implications not only for the rest of the Asian region but also for the world economy at large.

In Latin America and the Caribbean, the recovery of economic activity in 2003 is set to gain momentum in 2004. Real GDP is expected to increase by nearly 4 per cent compared with 1.5 per cent in 2003. This marked improvement largely reflects changes in international economic environment. Prices and export volumes of raw materials (especially of metals) have been boosted by strong demand from China and other Asian countries as well as the United States. But intraregional trade has also been strengthening driven by the pick-up in domestic demand and improved business and consumer confidence. Other major supportive factors are competitive real exchange rates and the marked reduction in sovereign risk ratings reflected in low yield spreads in the international bond markets. Favourable changes in the

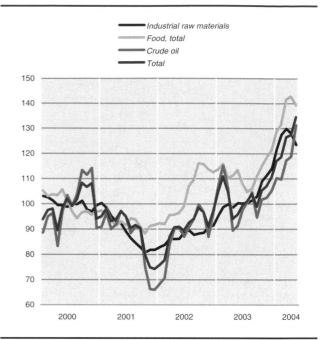

CHART 1.1.3

International commodity prices, January 2000-May 2004
(Indices, 2000=100)

Source: Hamburgisches Welt-Wirtschafts-Archiv (HWWA) (Hamburg) [www.hwwa.de].

Note: The HWWA index measures changes in the import cost of raw materials for the aggregate of OECD member countries. Indices are calculated on the basis of current dollar prices. Food including tropical beverages and sugar.

terms of trade combined with strong export growth led to a record trade surplus and the first current account surplus in more than three decades in 2003. The outlook for 2004, however, is vulnerable to changes in the international environment, and especially to interest rate developments given the region's considerable external financing requirements.

Strong upward pressure on international commodity prices

The nascent global recovery has been accompanied by substantial increases in international commodity prices, especially of oil, in the first five months of 2004. Crude oil prices rose well above the OPEC target range of $22-$28 per barrel. Non-energy commodity prices (in dollars) softened somewhat in May (chart 1.1.3), but on average they were still some 23 per cent higher than in the same month of 2003.

Crude oil prices peaked on 1 June 2004, at a record $42.2 p/b.[12] In May 2004, the average monthly spot price for Brent crude was $37.6 p/b, $11.7 or 45 per cent higher than in 12 months earlier. The average OECD import price of crude oil, in dollars, also rose by some 45 per cent over the same period.

_____

[12] Nymex crude futures (July delivery, Western Texas Intermediate).

BOX 1.1.1

The macroeconomic impact of higher oil prices

The recent sharp rise in the price of crude oil has brought back into focus the question of the macroeconomic effects of higher oil prices on economic activity. It is well known from similar episodes in the past that a pronounced and sustained rise in the oil price can have adverse effects on economic growth, inflation, trade balances and government financial balances in net oil importing countries.

The basic parameters that influence the order of magnitude of the impact of higher oil prices on the economy are the oil intensity of economic activity (i.e. oil consumption per unit of real GDP) as well as the degree to which countries depend on imported oil (i.e. the proportion of oil consumption that has to be covered by imports). For the group of industrialized countries combined, the oil intensity of their economies has been declining since the first oil shock in 1973. In 2002, it was some 50 per cent lower than in 1973. There has also been a decline in their dependence on net oil imports over the same period, although the import share is still around 55 per cent. As a result, a given rise in the oil price now has a proportionately much smaller impact on macroeconomic performance than in 1973 or in 1979. What also matters is the savings propensity in the oil exporting countries, which determines the extent to which their higher oil revenues lead to higher spending on the goods and services produced in the (net) oil importing countries in the short term.

The main "transmission mechanism" by which a surge in oil prices impacts the net oil importing countries is via a deterioration in their terms of trade. The resulting decline of real incomes dampens domestic demand for non-energy products with adverse effects on domestic economic activity. The higher oil price will be reflected in a general rise of the price level of the importing economy as a result of higher prices for final energy products and for goods that use oil and/or energy as a relatively important input. These are the direct (or first-round) effects of higher oil prices. Possible second-round effects include mainly demands for higher wages as workers resist the erosion of their real income, but this process will largely depend on the monetary policy stance and the credibility of the central bank.

A joint study by the IEA and the OECD suggests that a sustained increase in crude oil prices by $10 p/b, from $25 to $35, would reduce the aggregate real GDP of the OECD countries by 0.4 percentage points in the first and second years after the price increase.[1] The impact on the growth rate would be somewhat larger (0.5 percentage points) for the euro area on account of its greater dependence on oil imports. The impact would be somewhat below average (0.3 per cent) in the United States, because of the larger proportion of oil demand met by domestic production. The adverse effects on economic growth would be accompanied by an increase in consumer price inflation, which for the OECD area as a whole would amount to some 0.5 percentage points, with a somewhat larger increase (0.6 percentage points) in the euro area. The IMF has estimated that a permanent increase in oil prices by $5 p/b would lower real GDP in the industrial countries by 0.3 percentage points after one year.[2] The effects on the United States and the euro area would be similar with an aggregate output decline of 0.4 percentage points. Linear extrapolation to a $10 p/b oil price rise would lead to a doubling of these effects; but this may not be straightforward. For the CIS as a group the impact of higher oil prices can be assumed to be positive, given that the region includes a number oil exporting countries, notably Russia.

It is noteworthy that the impact of a $10 rise in oil prices on the growth of real GDP in the OECD area is now about half the magnitude of the estimated impact at the time of the oil price shock of 1989-1990.[3] This reflects the sharp fall in oil intensity over this period.

But these estimates depend on the specification of the economic model used for this purpose, which can differ in important respects. It has been argued that the IMF and OECD model simulations ignore, *inter alia*, important costs of intersectoral labour reallocation resulting from a rise in oil prices.[4] Alternative empirical estimates (based on advanced econometric techniques) point to an oil price-GDP elasticity of around -0.055 for the United States.[5] This would suggest that the recent increase in the oil price could have a larger impact on economic activity than currently assumed.

---

[1] International Energy Agency (IEA), *Analysis of the Impact of Higher Oil Prices on the Global Economy* (Paris), May 2004 [www.iea.org].

[2] IMF, *World Economic Outlook* (Washington, D.C.), April 2002, p. 52, table 1.12. The table has been reproduced in the IMF, *World Economic Outlook* (Washington, D.C.), April 2003, p. 55.

[3] *OECD Economic Outlook,* No. 48 (Paris), December 1990.

[4] D. Jones, P. Leiby and I. Paik, "Oil price shocks and the macroeconomy: what has been learned since 1996", *The Energy Journal*, Vol. 25, No. 2, 2004, pp. 1-34.

[5] Ibid.

TABLE 1.1.1

International commodity prices, 2002-2004

(Annual percentage changes)

Item	Weight	Prices in dollars			Prices in euros		
		2002	2003	May 2004	2002	2003	May 2004
Food	9.9	12.0	8.1	22.9	6.1	-9.4	18.5
Industrial raw materials	22.6	-1.6	17.3	23.1	-6.5	-2.1	18.7
Agricultural products	10.1	-0.6	21.6	11.0	-5.8	1.7	7.0
Non-ferrous metals	9.1	-4.2	11.9	35.5	-8.8	-6.8	30.7
Iron ore, scrap	3.4	2.7	17.9	29.7	-2.6	-1.4	25.0
Non-energy materials	32.6	2.7	14.2	23.1	-2.6	-4.5	18.7
Energy	67.4	-0.4	14.4	50.1	-5.9	-3.9	44.9
Crude oil	62.7	1.4	15.4	43.9	-4.1	-3.3	38.9
Coal	4.8	-18.0	5.1	127.6	-22.0	-12.8	119.3
Total above	100.0	0.6	14.4	40.5	-4.8	-4.2	35.5

Source: Hamburgisches Welt-Wirtschafts-Archiv (HWWA) (Hamburg) [www.hwwa.de].

Note: Weights correspond to the average shares of the various product categories in total OECD commodity imports in 1999-2001.

The increase in oil prices largely reflects the rise in global demand for oil, especially in the United States and Asia, in the presence of relatively tight supply conditions. Forecasts for world oil demand were steadily raised in the first half of 2004. Global demand is now expected to grow by 2.3 mb/d to 81.1 mb/d in 2004, the largest absolute increase since 1981.[13] In the United States, crude oil inventories have fallen below their medium-term average, and Indonesia and Venezuela have been struggling to meet their production quotas. But higher prices also incorporate a significant risk premium on account of the political instability in the Middle East and associated fears of major supply disruptions caused by terrorist attacks in the region. There was considerable buying by financial investors (hedge funds), building long speculative positions.[14] The dollar depreciation since 2002, moreover, led oil producers to raise prices in dollar terms to offset their terms of trade deterioration vis-à-vis other major currencies.[15]

Oil prices fell in the wake of the decision by OPEC on 3 June 2004 to raise the official production target from 23.5 mb/d to 25.5 mb/d from 1 July 2004. A further increase to 26 mb/d, from 1 August 2004, was agreed at the same time.[16] But there are indications that OPEC-10 (which excludes Iraq) had already raised production to 26 mb/d in May 2004 and that a further increase to 27.4 mb/d in June 2004 had been agreed.[17] The temporary interruption to supply from Iraq (which had produced some 2 mb/d in May 2004) due to terrorist attacks in mid-June 2004 had no noticeable impact on oil prices.

Against this backdrop, the spot price of Brent crude in mid-June was $34.7 p/b, down from $39.1 p/b at the beginning of the month. The average spot price of Brent crude was $33.5 p/b in the first half of 2004,[18] up from $28.9 p/b in the same period of 2003. The rise is expected to dampen economic growth in the net oil importing countries, but the adverse effects of a given increase in the price of oil has diminished due to the marked decline in the oil intensity of economic activity over the past decades (box 1.1.1). Although crude oil prices, in dollars, in the first half of 2004 were at their highest levels since 1980, in real terms (i.e. deflated by the United States CPI) they have fallen by a third over this period. Broadly the same holds for euro-denominated real oil prices (deflated by the average EU CPI).

In 2003, the appreciation of the euro against the dollar more than offset the rise in the dollar prices of commodities for the euro area economies, but this was no longer the case in 2004: nevertheless, commodity prices in euros still rose somewhat less than in dollars (table 1.1.1).

1.2 Recent economic developments in the ECE region

(i) Output and demand

With the global context increasingly positive, the ECE economies gained momentum in the second half of 2003 and in early 2004. Economic growth picked up in all the major subregions. The United States continued to lead the way, but the euro area narrowed the growth gap somewhat in the first quarter of 2004 (table 1.2.1). Economic growth in the new member countries of the European Union continued to exceed that in the old

---

[13] IEA, *Monthly Oil Market Report,* 10 June 2004 [www.iea.org].

[14] Investors are "long" when they buy assets in the hope of selling them later at higher prices.

[15] The dollar is the unit of account in commodity markets, and commodity exporters have traditionally attempted to offset a dollar depreciation by raising prices. This holds for raw material prices in general, not only for oil.

[16] However, this further increase in output quotas is subject to review in the light of market conditions in the second half of July 2004.

[17] Including Iraq, OPEC 2004 production rose to 28.2 mb/d in May 2004. *Financial Times* (London), issues of 5 June and 18 June 2004.

[18] Period up to 21 June 2004.

TABLE 1.2.1

Changes in quarterly real GDP in major economies, 2003-2004
(Percentage change over the previous period, seasonally adjusted)

	2003				2004
	QI	QII	QIII	QIV	QI
France	0.2	-0.3	0.6	0.6	0.8
Germany	-0.2	-0.2	0.2	0.3	0.4
Italy	-0.2	-0.1	0.4	0.0	0.4
United Kingdom	0.3	0.6	0.8	0.9	0.6
Canada	0.7	-0.2	0.3	0.8	0.6
United States	0.5	0.8	2.0	1.0	1.0
Japan	0.1	0.9	0.7	1.8	1.5
Total above	0.3	0.5	1.2	1.0	1.0
Memorandum items:					
Euro area	0.0	-0.1	0.4	0.4	0.6
EU-15	0.0	0.0	0.5	0.5	0.6
EU-25	0.1	0.0	0.5	0.5	0.6
Western Europe	0.0	0.0	0.5	0.5	0.6
WECEE	0.0	0.0	0.5	0.5	0.6
Western Europe and North America	0.3	0.4	1.2	0.8	0.8

Source: Eurostat; OECD national accounts; national statistics.

Note: Western, central and eastern Europe (WECEE) includes EU-25 plus Iceland, Norway and Switzerland.

TABLE 1.2.2

Changes in real GDP and main expenditure items in the United States, 2003-2004
(Percentage change over previous period, seasonally adjusted)

	2003				2004
	QI	QII	QIII	QIV	QI
Private consumption	0.6	0.8	1.7	0.8	0.9
Government consumption	0.2	1.7	0.0	0.2	0.5
Gross fixed investment	0.0	1.6	3.5	1.8	1.3
Stockbuilding[a]...............................	-0.2	-0.1	0.0	0.2	0.2
Total domestic demand	0.3	1.1	1.7	1.1	0.9
Exports	-0.5	-0.3	2.4	4.8	1.8
Imports	-1.7	2.2	0.2	3.9	2.5
Net exports[a]	0.2	-0.3	0.2	-0.1	-0.2
GDP...	0.5	0.8	2.0	1.0	1.0

Source: As for table 1.2.1.

[a] Percentage point contribution to GDP growth.

members by a significant margin, and became increasingly broad based. The same can be said of the economies of south-east Europe. In the CIS, GDP growth continued at a high rate but, driven to a large extent by the boom in energy prices, was less broadly based.

United States economy maintains strong momentum

The strong momentum of the United States economy in the last two quarters of 2003 carried over into the first quarter of 2004 (table 1.2.2). Real GDP rose by 1 per cent compared with the final quarter of 2003, raising its level to 5 per cent above the first quarter of 2003. The expansion appears to be well established as job creation has picked up. Economic growth continued to be driven mainly by buoyant domestic demand but it

CHART 1.2.1

Quarterly growth in real GDP and contribution of major expenditure items in the United States, 2000-2004
(Percentage change over previous quarter, seasonally adjusted at annual rates)

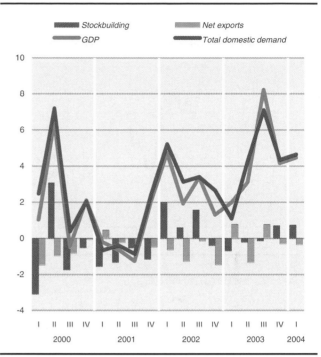

Source: United States Department of Commerce.

Note: Real net exports and changes in stockbuilding: percentage point contributions to real GDP growth.

was also supported by large gains in exports. Changes in real net exports, however, continued to subtract from overall economic growth (chart 1.2.1). Private consumption remained the mainstay of the recovery, boosted by strong growth in disposable incomes and by improved prospects for employment. The household savings ratio remained very low at slightly more than 2 per cent of personal disposable income in the first quarter. Consumer confidence strengthened in the second quarter of 2004 (chart 1.2.2).

Non-residential private fixed investment continued to expand. Within the total, continuing cutbacks of business expenditures on structures were more than offset by the strong growth of spending on equipment and software. The latter was stimulated by the improved corporate profits and rising capacity utilization. Capacity utilization in industry increased in May 2004 for the ninth consecutive month but the average rates are still significantly below their long-term average.[19] Business confidence in the first quarter of 2004 rose to its highest level in more than a decade (chart 1.2.2).

_____

[19] Survey data from the Institute for Supply Management, however, suggest that capacity utilization may be significantly higher than indicated by the official statistics. If so, this would suggest that the rate of obsolescence of the existing capital stock is higher than assumed. But in the absence of firmer evidence it is difficult to judge whether this is in fact the case.

CHART 1.2.2

Consumer confidence and quarterly business confidence in the United States, January 2000-May 2004

(Indices)

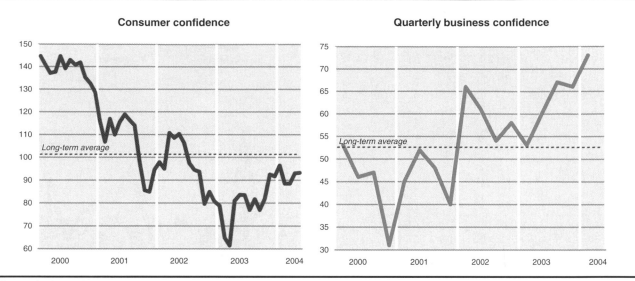

Consumer confidence

Quarterly business confidence

Source: Conference Board [www.conference-board.org/consumerconfidence.cfm].

Note: Long-term average for 1990-2002.

In Canada, economic activity strengthened after the third quarter of 2003, when the effects of the outbreak of SARS and the power cuts in Ontario had diminished. The recovery was driven by strong export growth to the United States, which accounts for almost 90 per cent of Canada's exports. Strong growth of private consumption and fixed investment also supported domestic economic activity in the first quarter of 2004.

Euro area recovery gains moderate momentum

In the euro area, the recovery gained some momentum in the first quarter of 2004, when real GDP rose by 0.6 per cent (table 1.2.3). The recovery continues to be led by strong export growth, which was buoyed by robust demand in overseas markets, offsetting the dampening effects of the earlier appreciation of the euro. Total domestic demand rose only 0.2 per cent in the first quarter. This partly reflected the unexpected weakness of fixed investment, which was largely due to a sharp fall in construction in Germany which, in turn, was due to special factors. Partial data show a relatively strong increase in fixed investment in several countries of the euro area. Investment continued to be supported by improved profit margins and favourable financing conditions, which also contributed to a significant improvement in business confidence (chart 1.2.3). The overall weakness of investment was accentuated by a fall in government consumption expenditures in the first quarter of 2004. This was partly offset by a moderate upturn of private consumption, which had been very weak in the three preceding quarters. But the sustainability of this upturn is by no means evident given the low level of consumer confidence (chart 1.2.3) and the modest outlook for the labour markets in the euro area. In addition, higher oil prices have started to erode household purchasing power.

TABLE 1.2.3

Changes in real GDP and main expenditure items in the euro area, 2003-2004

(Percentage change over the previous period, seasonally adjusted)

	2003				2004
	QI	QII	QIII	QIV	QI
Private consumption	0.5	0.0	0.1	0.0	0.6
Government consumption	0.5	0.6	0.7	0.4	-0.2
Gross fixed investment	-0.8	-0.3	-0.2	0.6	-0.1
Stockbuilding[a]	0.2	0.0	-0.3	0.6	-0.2
Total domestic demand	0.4	0.0	-0.1	0.9	0.2
Exports	-1.3	-0.8	2.2	0.2	1.7
Imports	-0.4	-0.5	1.1	1.6	0.8
Net exports[a]	-0.4	-0.1	0.4	-0.5	0.3
GDP	0.0	-0.1	0.4	0.4	0.6

Source: As for table 1.2.1.

[a] Percentage point contribution to GDP growth.

With overall domestic demand remaining weak, changes in real net exports accounted for the bulk of GDP growth in the first quarter of 2004 (chart 1.2.4). The available short-term indicators suggest that the recovery continued to be driven by strong export growth in the second quarter. New industrial orders rose significantly in the March-April period, but these were mostly due to foreign demand, domestic retail sales remaining weak.

Different growth patterns in the three major economies of the euro area...

Among the three major economies in the euro area, economic activity in France improved markedly in the first quarter. Real GDP rose by 0.8 per cent (table 1.2.2) and was supported by strong gains in private

CHART 1.2.3

Consumer confidence and industrial confidence in the euro area, January 2000-May 2004
(Balances)

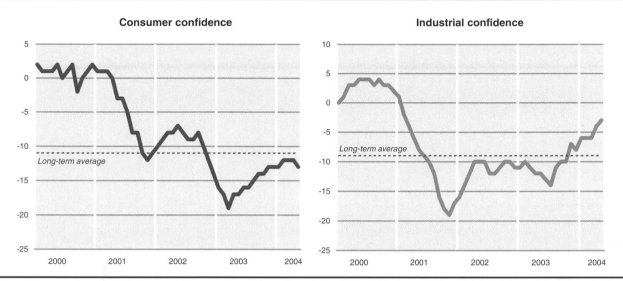

Source: European Commission, *Business and Consumer Survey Results* (Brussels), various issues [europa.eu.int/comm/economy_finance/indicators_en.htm].

Note: Balances are percentage point differences between positive and negative responses. Long-term average is for 1990-2002.

CHART 1.2.4

Quarterly growth in real GDP and contribution of major expenditure items in the euro area, 2000-2004
(Percentage change over previous quarter, seasonally adjusted at annual rates)

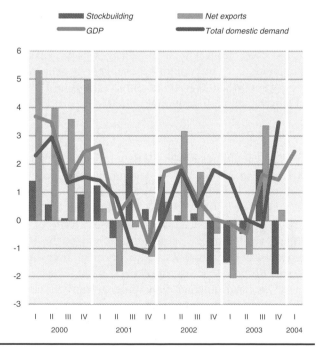

Source: Eurostat NewCronos Database.

Note: Real net exports and changes in stockbuilding: percentage point contributions to real GDP growth.

consumption. Fixed investment spending remained lacklustre and export growth slowed to virtual stagnation. In sum, changes in real net export slightly subtracted from economic growth. In contrast, domestic demand in

Germany remained the "weak spot" of the economy in the first quarter of 2004, when it fell by nearly half a percentage point. This reflected the pronounced fall in fixed investment and government consumption expenditures, and the stagnation of private consumption. But exports were buoyant, and the resulting changes in real net exports largely offset the weakness of domestic demand, leading to a quarterly increase in real GDP of 0.4 per cent. In Italy, real GDP also rose by 0.4 per cent in the first quarter of 2004, despite a further sharp fall in exports, which was largely a reflection of the deteriorating export competitiveness in manufacturing due to weak productivity growth and rising unit labour costs. The weakness of exports was more than offset by an upturn in domestic demand, reflecting both stronger private consumption and fixed investment. The upturn in fixed investment followed four consecutive quarters of contraction.

...and in the smaller euro area economies

The performance of the smaller economies in the euro area has also varied considerably, reflecting differences in the stimuli they received from their main trading partners and in the dynamics of internally generated demand. In Spain, the rate of economic growth has been resilient to the deteriorating international environment since mid-2000, largely because of the strong growth of domestic demand. Quarter-to-quarter real GDP growth has fluctuated narrowly around 0.6 per cent since the beginning of 2002. Among the other countries of the euro area, the recovery maintained its momentum in Belgium and the Netherlands on the back of favourable changes in real net exports. The growth of total domestic demand was weak in the first quarter of 2004, real GDP rising in both countries by 0.7 per cent

TABLE 1.2.4

Quarterly real GDP and industrial output in the new EU member countries, 2003-2004
(Percentage change over the same period of the preceding year, not seasonally adjusted)

	GDP					Industrial output				
	2003QI	2003QII	2003QIII	2003QIV	2004QI	2003QI	2003QII	2003QIII	2003QIV	2004QI
Cyprus [a]	2.1	1.2	1.8	2.9	3.4	4.5	-1.7	-0.3	1.2	1.0
Czech Republic	2.8	2.9	3.4	3.3	3.1	6.3	5.0	6.0	6.1	9.0
Estonia	5.8	3.5	5.2	6.2	6.8	12.8	7.4	10.1	9.5	7.5
Hungary	2.7	2.5	2.9	3.6	4.2	4.1	4.2	6.8	9.9	10.7
Latvia	8.8	6.2	7.3	7.5	8.8	8.7	5.9	7.8	4.2	9.2
Lithuania	9.6	6.8	8.8	10.6	7.7	20.9	4.3	20.0	19.3	9.8
Malta [b]	-3.9	-1.6	-0.3	-1.3	..	-0.8	-0.8	8.3	-0.1	..
Poland	2.3	3.9	4.0	4.7	6.9	4.4	9.3	9.1	11.8	18.9
Slovakia	4.1	3.8	4.2	4.7	5.5	10.7	4.7	2.3	4.2	6.6
Slovenia	2.2	2.1	2.3	2.5	3.7	0.8	-0.3	0.2	4.9	4.1
Total above	3.3	3.7	4.2	4.5	5.7	5.7	6.3	7.1	8.6	12.1
Memorandum items:										
Euro area [a]	1.0	-0.1	0.3	0.7	2.0	0.9	-0.8	-0.1	1.4	1.2
EU-15 [a]	1.2	0.3	0.6	0.9	2.3	0.6	-0.6	0.0	1.2	1.0
EU-25 [a]	1.2	0.4	0.7	1.0	2.4	0.8	-0.3	0.4	1.7	1.7

Source: National statistics; Eurostat; OECD; UNECE secretariat estimates.

[a] Industrial output adjusted for the number of working days.

[b] Value added in manufacturing for industrial output.

compared with the final quarter of 2003. In Finland the rate of growth accelerated to 0.7 per cent in the first quarter of 2004, up from 0.3 per cent in the preceding quarter. Economic activity was stimulated by exports and personal consumption expenditures. In Ireland, the quarterly pattern of economic growth remains very volatile,[20] but there has been a clear underlying improvement of domestic demand and exports since the beginning of 2003. Real GDP rose by 0.6 per cent in the first quarter of 2004 compared with the preceding quarter. In Portugal, real GDP also rose by 0.6 per cent in the first quarter of 2004, supported by domestic demand. The change in real net exports slightly dampened economic growth.

Solid growth in other west European economies

In the United Kingdom the recovery continued in the first quarter of 2004, but the rate of growth slowed down to 0.6 per cent compared with the final quarter of 2003 when there was an equivalent increase by 0.9 per cent. Strong growth of private consumption, which in turn was supported by further large gains in house prices and rapid job creation, remained the main driving force. Government spending also continued to support economic growth. In contrast, business fixed investment remained relatively weak, but with enterprise profitability rising and relatively little slack in the economy, expenditures on machinery and equipment are expected to pick up in the course of 2004. Real exports declined in the first quarter of

2004, reflecting the effects of the earlier appreciation of the pound.

In the other west European economies (Denmark, Norway, Sweden and Switzerland), economic activity continued to improve in the first quarter of 2004, supported by strong export growth, except in Norway, where exports fell compared with the preceding quarter. Total domestic demand fell in Sweden and Switzerland, because of unfavourable changes in inventory accumulation. In contrast, changes in inventories strongly supported overall economic activity in Denmark and Norway in the first quarter of 2004.

Strong growth prevails in the new EU member states

The economies of the 10 new member countries of the European Union (EU-10) continued to grow more rapidly than the other 15 members (EU-15) during the first quarter of 2004 (table 1.2.4). Since the first quarter of 2003, growth has accelerated in central Europe, which accounts for the bulk of economic activity in the 10 new member states. Growth has also become more broadly based, with private consumption and fixed investment as well as external demand expanding strongly. The three Baltic economies continued to grow rapidly but in Cyprus and Malta aggregate output was relatively subdued.

Output may well continue to grow rapidly this year and next with the expected strengthening of recovery in the European Union and the removal of the remaining trade barriers among the old and new member states. Both factors should boost demand for goods and services from the EU-10 countries. Further, the elimination of barriers to labour mobility among the new EU economies

---

[20] The seasonally adjusted time series for Ireland have to be interpreted cautiously because of the short period of seven years on which the seasonal adjustment factors are based.

CHART 1.2.5

Economic sentiment in the new EU economies, January 2000-May 2004
(Balances of positive and negative replies, seasonally adjusted)

Economic sentiment indicator

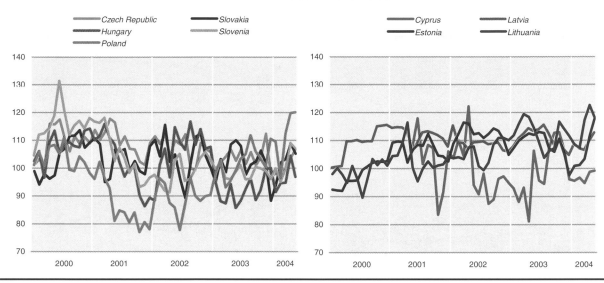

Source: Eurostat, NewCronos Database.

Note: The economic sentiment indicator is scaled to have the mean of 100 and standard deviation of 10 over the time period 1990-2003.

is likely to result in an improved allocation of resources and thus be conducive to stronger growth.[21] Economic confidence in the new EU economies points to continued economic dynamism and is generally higher than that shown by comparable indicators for the EU-15 (chart 1.2.5).[22] The improvement in sentiment was noticeable in the months preceding the accession and in the first month of EU membership, the economic confidence indicator in May remaining well above its long-term average in all the acceding countries except Cyprus and Hungary. This suggests that a positive one-off accession boost to growth may well materialize.

National accounts and industrial production data for the first quarter of 2004 indicate a brisk rate of economic expansion throughout central Europe. Growth was generally supported by accommodating monetary policy

and in the case of Poland by a considerable loosening of fiscal policy. It was also driven by the strengthening demand in western Europe. Strong export growth continued and all the central European economies continued to increase their shares of EU imports. The underlying factors have included the expanding capacities of export-oriented foreign firms and rapid productivity growth.

Final consumption made a significant contribution to GDP growth in 2003 except in Slovakia, where real wages and private consumption declined (chart 1.2.6). In the first months of 2004, the pace of consumer spending picked up in Poland, Slovakia and Slovenia (table 1.2.5). Part of the increase was based on expected post-accession price increases.[23] The persistently high levels of unemployment in Poland and Slovakia limit the scope for a lasting and stronger growth in consumer spending. In contrast, private consumption expenditure grew remarkably in 2003 in the Czech Republic and Hungary, reflecting very large but unsustainable increases in real wages and a rapid growth of consumer credit. A gradual implementation of budget consolidation and slower real wage growth in both countries suggest that final consumption is likely to grow more slowly in the short run. This slowdown can already be detected in the latest available quarterly national accounts (table 1.2.5).

---

[21] Labour mobility across the enlarged EU will be restricted by a series of protective measures by the old EU-15 members against the new entrants for up to seven years. Hungary and Poland imposed reciprocal restrictions. However, former restrictions on employment of labour among acceding countries disappeared. This means that, for example, the unemployed from southern Slovakia can now fill job vacancies in adjacent regions of Hungary, some of which have experienced labour bottlenecks. Until May 2004, binding and relatively low quotas restricted such cross-border employment.

[22] The improved confidence is visible in the harmonized Eurostat indicators as well as national measures. For instance, the business confidence indicator of a Polish private employers' association rose by 10 per cent in May, reaching its highest level ever. "Sharp rise in leading confidence indicator reflects strong economic recovery, but an all-out boom is still some time off", *Polish News Bulletin*, 4 June 2004.

[23] The sometimes irrational fears of price increases for consumer goods such as sugar or rice led to some panic-driven stockpiling in central Europe and the Baltic states in the run-up to accession. Similarly, expectations of higher car prices resulted in rapid automobile sales in the Czech Republic and Poland until April 2004.

CHART 1.2.6

Contribution of final demand components to annual change in real GDP in new EU economies, 2000-2003
(Percentage point contributions)

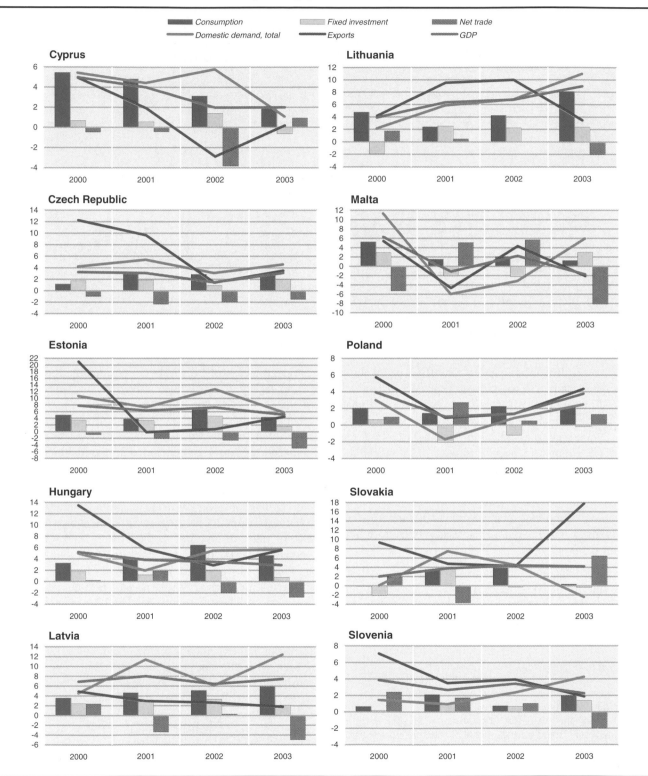

Source: UNECE calculations, based on national statistics.

Note: Growth contributions to annual percentage changes in real GDP.

TABLE 1.2.5

Components of real demand in the new EU member countries, 2002-2004
(Percentage change over the same period of the preceding year)

	Private consumption [a]			Government consumption [b]			Gross fixed capital formation			Exports of goods and services			Imports of goods and services		
	2002	2003	2004QI	2002	2003	2004QI	2002	2003	2004QI	2002	2003	2004QI	2002	2003	2004QI
Cyprus	2.5	2.4	4.8	8.5	1.7	0.2	8.0	-3.4	16.2	-5.1	0.3	4.9	1.5	-1.2	9.9
Czech Republic	4.0	4.9	3.9	5.7	2.2	-1.6	0.6	7.4	9.5	2.8	5.7	8.3	4.3	7.9	11.3
Estonia	10.3	5.7	5.6	5.9	5.8	3.6	17.2	5.4	-8.5	0.6	6.0	21.4	5.4	9.0	10.9
Hungary	9.3	6.5	3.0	4.8	1.9	1.3	8.0	3.0	18.9	3.7	7.2	17.4	6.2	10.3	16.6
Latvia	6.9	8.6	..	1.5	2.5	..	10.4	7.8	..	6.3	4.3	..	4.5	13.1	..
Lithuania	6.1	11.0	11.4	1.9	5.7	8.8	11.1	11.4	16.1	19.5	6.0	7.6	17.6	8.8	14.5
Malta	2.6	0.3	..	2.8	6.0	..	-13.3	21.1	..	3.0	-2.2	..	-2.0	6.4	..
Poland	3.4	3.1	4.0	0.4	0.4	1.0	-5.8	-0.9	3.5	4.8	13.0	10.4	2.6	7.9	6.5
Slovakia	5.3	-0.4	3.0	4.7	2.9	-2.3	-0.9	-1.2	0.9	5.5	22.6	15.8	5.2	13.8	12.0
Slovenia	0.4	2.9	3.7	2.5	1.9	0.6	2.6	5.4	8.0	6.8	3.1	8.8	4.8	6.4	10.4

Source: National statistics; Eurostat; OECD; UNECE secretariat estimates.

a Expenditures incurred by households and non-profit institutions serving households.

b Expenditures incurred by the general government on both individual consumption of goods and services and collective consumption of services.

Accelerating real investment generally contributed to output growth. In Hungary, business investment picked up noticeably in the first quarter of 2004, especially in the export-oriented and FDI-dominated manufacturing sector. Investment spending also accelerated in the Czech Republic, driven by improved corporate profitability. In Poland and Slovakia, following two years of decline, fixed capital formation was rising in the first quarter of 2004. Improved profitability in the non-financial corporate sector underpinned business investment in both countries.

Imports increased considerably throughout the region, a consequence of the rapid growth of both domestic demand and exports. Net trade continued to make a positive contribution to GDP growth in Poland and Slovakia in the first quarter of 2004 while remaining negative in the other three central European countries.

Real GDP continued to grow rapidly throughout the Baltic region in the first quarter of 2004, led by Latvia. Growth in Lithuania remained high, despite a slight deceleration from the previous quarter. Domestic demand was the main factor driving growth in Latvia and Lithuania. The expenditure of private households continued to be fuelled by strong wage growth and rapidly expanding consumer credit. Gross fixed capital formation appears to have remained strong in both countries. Exports of goods and services from the Baltic region grew rapidly, reflecting the improved competitiveness due to foreign controlled firms. Buoyant domestic demand and exports by FDI firms, however, also induced a rapid growth of imports such that real net exports had a negative impact on the growth of aggregate output. In contrast, the contribution of domestic demand to GDP growth became relatively subdued in Estonia; although investment expenditure declined in the first quarter of 2004, consumption remained buoyant and the contribution of net exports increased significantly.

Expansionary fiscal policies in Cyprus failed to invigorate output growth in 2002 and 2003. Following the liberalization of international financial transfers, monetary policy was tightened in 2004 and the government announced spending cuts. This and the lower than expected tourism revenues in the first quarter of 2004 suggest that GDP growth may remain subdued for the year as a whole despite a relatively buoyant first quarter, when it was driven by strong but probably unsustainable private consumption and investment growth. Malta is likely to experience positive GDP growth in 2004, after a weak expansion in 2002 and a decline in 2003. The preliminary balance of payments data for the first quarter of 2004 show a significant improvement in the merchandise trade balance and tourism receipts over the same period of the previous year.

Strong output growth continues in south-east Europe and the CIS

Both GDP and industrial output grew strongly in the first quarter of the year in south-east Europe, driven by growing domestic demand and exports. Output in the CIS region continued to grow vigorously in the first quarter of 2004 (table 1.2.6). Rising prices of energy and other commodities provided the principal stimulus to growth in resource-based economies and, indirectly, to other parts of the CIS region through increased demand for manufactured goods and market services. The acceleration of investment also made a large contribution to the growth of output.

The four EU candidate countries in the region – Bulgaria, Croatia, Romania and Turkey – achieved rapid output growth in 2003 and the early months of 2004. In Bulgaria, Romania and Turkey, the main impetus to growth on the demand side was provided by exports, private consumption and investment. In Croatia, investment and exports of goods and services were the principal sources of growth (chart 1.2.7). All four countries

TABLE 1.2.6

Quarterly real GDP and industrial output in south-east Europe and the CIS, 2003-2004

(Percentage change over the same period of the preceding year, not seasonally adjusted)

	GDP					Industrial output				
	2003QI	*2003QII*	*2003QIII*	*2003QIV*	*2004QI*	*2003QI*	*2003QII*	*2003QIII*	*2003QIV*	*2004QI*
South-east Europe	6.3	4.0	5.1	5.3	8.2	..	..	..	..	..
Albania	..	..	..	..	..	21.8	7.7	8.8	-3.2	10.3
Bosnia and Herzegovina	..	..	..	..	..	2.2	7.3	4.1	-0.8	19.8
Bulgaria	3.5	4.2	4.4	4.9	5.3	19.3	12.0	12.8	17.2	16.7
Croatia	4.9	5.0	3.9	3.3	4.2	4.6	7.1	3.5	1.3	5.6
Romania	4.4	4.3	5.5	4.8	6.1	1.1	4.3	4.4	2.8	5.9
Serbia and Montenegro	..	..	..	..	..	-3.1	-1.9	-4.3	-2.7	10.7
The former Yugoslav Republic of Macedonia	2.1	3.1	5.6	2.1	-3.6	3.5	3.6	15.0	-1.1	-26.1
Turkey	8.1	3.9	5.5	6.1	10.1	79.3	4.6	10.4	10.7	10.6
CIS	7.5	8.0	6.7	8.7	8.0	7.1	8.4	8.6	9.0	9.4
Armenia	11.4	16.9	15.6	11.6	7.5	10.6	26.1	24.0	0.2	2.8
Azerbaijan	7.9	12.2	11.3	13.2	10.6	5.9	6.5	5.1	6.9	4.2
Belarus	5.6	4.7	7.3	8.9	9.3	7.0	5.8	6.6	7.6	12.9
Georgia	6.5	12.3	8.4	8.5	9.5	2.8	14.8	13.1	11.4	17.3
Kazakhstan	10.5	9.6	7.7	9.2	9.0	10.4	8.8	4.4	11.3	9.3
Kyrgyzstan	4.6	0.8	7.8	10.8	5.7	7.5	-3.5	32.0	23.9	8.0
Republic of Moldova	5.4	7.3	5.9	8.4	6.1	12.8	22.6	21.1	3.9	16.7
Russian Federation	7.5	7.9	6.5	7.6	7.4	6.1	7.5	6.9	7.4	7.6
Tajikistan	12.1	5.2	6.6	16.8	9.1	14.1	9.2	1.8	15.8	9.7
Turkmenistan	..	..	..	..	..	..	..	..	..	..
Ukraine	7.9	9.3	6.6	13.4	10.8	10.7	14.0	20.5	17.4	18.8
Uzbekistan	2.2	5.4	4.4	5.9	4.8	4.0	7.0	6.9	6.8	8.8
Total above	7.1	6.8	6.2	7.6	8.1	..	..	..	..	..
Memorandum items:										
South-east Europe without Turkey	3.9	4.0	4.6	4.1	5.6	3.9	5.0	4.7	3.6	7.7
CIS without Russian Federation	7.5	8.3	7.3	10.8	9.2	9.3	10.5	12.3	12.5	13.3
Low-income CIS economies	5.4	7.9	7.6	9.8	7.0	6.5	9.2	11.2	8.7	8.2

Source: National statistics; Eurostat; OECD; UNECE secretariat estimates.

Note: Low-income CIS economies: Armenia, Azerbaijan, Georgia, Kyrgyzstan, Republic of Moldova, Tajikistan and Uzbekistan.

continued to enjoy rising revenues from tourism that helped to boost their export of services. In Croatia, after a deceleration in 2003, private consumer spending is set for a recovery in 2004. Real investment growth reached double-digit levels in Bulgaria and picked up in Croatia and Romania. The double-digit expansion of gross fixed capital formation in Turkey resulted from a combination of cutbacks in the public sector that were more than offset by considerable increases in spending on machinery and equipment in the private sector, reflecting improved profitability and successful macroeconomic stabilization.[24] This dynamism reflected to some extent rising inflows of FDI, especially in the three low-wage countries (Bulgaria, Romania and Turkey) that have become increasingly attractive locations for foreign investment. The rapid growth of domestic demand stimulated import growth, resulting in an increasingly negative contribution of net exports to GDP growth in all four countries.

Recent developments in the other economies of south-east Europe indicate positive growth of real

industrial output in Albania, Bosnia and Herzegovina, and Serbia and Montenegro. Although growth accelerated in Serbia and Montenegro, the relatively poor export performance and rapidly rising imports suggest a potential risk of macroeconomic imbalance. To improve the weak responsiveness of supply, the new government has decided to continue the structural reforms started by its predecessor and has secured new official external financing on preferential terms to support economic activity. In Albania and Bosnia and Herzegovina, industrial growth picked up sharply in the first quarter of 2004, following declines in the last quarter of 2003. In contrast, industrial output started to slide in the early months of 2004 in The former Yugoslav Republic of Macedonia despite merchandise exports continuing to grow (for details see section (iv) below, footnote 62).

Driven by strong external demand for crude oil and natural gas, and by a rapid expansion of consumption and investment, output growth in the CIS remained among the most dynamic in the world in the first quarter of 2004. In the key Russian economy, real output continued to grow at a brisk pace in 2004, apparently unaffected by capital market fluctuations. The stock market swung from a rapid expansion in the first quarter to an even more rapid reversal that reduced market capitalization by about one

---

[24] For a discussion of the composition and trends in investment, see Central Bank of the Republic of Turkey, *Monetary Policy Report*, 2004-I [www.tcmb.gov.tr/yeni/eng/index.html].

CHART 1.2.7

Contribution of final demand components to annual changes in real GDP in selected south-east and CIS economies, 2000-2003
(Percentage point contributions)

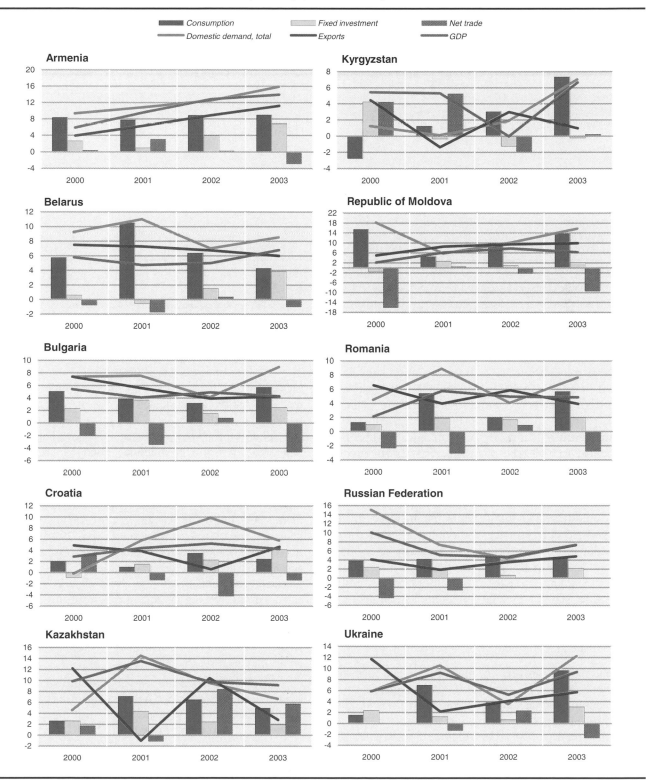

TABLE 1.2.7

Components of real demand in selected south-east European and CIS economies, 2002-2004
(Percentage change over the same period of the preceding year)

	Private consumption [a]			Government consumption [b]			Gross fixed capital formation			Exports of goods and services			Imports of goods and services		
	2002	2003	2004QI	2002	2003	2004QI	2002	2003	2004QI	2002	2003	2004QI	2002	2003	2004QI
Bulgaria	3.5	6.4	4.9	4.1	7.2	6.9	8.5	13.8	21.4	7.0	8.0	8.0	4.9	14.8	17.7
Croatia	6.5	4.1	3.9	-1.8	-0.3	-1.6	10.1	16.8	8.9	1.2	10.1	6.4	8.8	10.9	5.9
Romania	4.8	7.1	9.3	-8.9	6.1	1.9	8.2	9.2	7.3	17.6	11.1	10.2	12.0	16.3	12.4
The former Yugoslav Republic of Macedonia	12.5	..	..	-11.1	..	..	17.6	..	..	-5.5	..	..	10.3	..	..
Turkey	2.1	6.6	10.6	5.4	-2.4	2.4	-1.1	10.0	52.6	11.1	16.0	10.3	15.8	27.1	31.2
Armenia	9.1	8.4	..	3.2	14.0	..	22.2	35.1	..	34.9	..	..	18.8	..	..
Azerbaijan	8.0	9.7	..	14.5	22.1	..	84.0	61.5	..	-6.3	19.6	..	16.4	57.6	..
Belarus	10.9	7.0	..	0.4	0.6	..	6.7	17.7	..	10.1	9.4	..	9.1	10.4	..
Kazakhstan	12.2	7.3	..	-4.3	5.8	..	10.2	7.9	..	22.6	5.9	..	4.3	-6.3	..
Kyrgyzstan	4.7	11.2	..	-0.2	-1.2	..	-7.4	-1.4	..	8.1	2.5	..	13.1	1.8	..
Republic of Moldova	6.3	16.7	..	30.3	-0.5	..	5.7	13.3	..	19.0	18.9	..	15.7	25.0	..
Russian Federation	8.7	7.8	..	2.6	2.2	..	3.5	12.2	..	9.6	13.7	..	14.6	19.5	..
Ukraine	9.0	12.1	..	-6.7	14.8	..	3.4	15.8	..	7.4	10.3	..	3.3	16.4	..

Source: National statistics; Eurostat; OECD; UNECE secretariat estimates.

[a] Expenditures incurred by households and non-profit institutions serving households.

[b] Expenditures incurred by the general government on both individual consumption of goods and services and collective consumption of services.

third between April and the mid-June. The correction appears to have eliminated a speculative bubble but alternative explanations have been advanced, including renewed capital flight.[25] Although the external environment remains favourable, the still fragile nature of private property rights poses the principal threat to economic growth in the longer term. In neighbouring Ukraine, the central bank raised interest rates in June in response to the danger of overheating: economic activity was expanding at record rates and fuel prices were rising rapidly. Activity was driven by industrial output and rising domestic expenditure, while the increase in fuel prices was partly a response to shortages associated with the shutdown of refining capacity for maintenance work. A remarkable expansion of credit supported output growth in Ukraine; however, the share of non-performing loans has remained very high, implying a significant risk to the sustainability of growth in the longer term. Both GDP and industrial production continued to grow steadily in Kazakhstan, the third largest CIS economy.

The strong growth of real wages and pensions throughout the CIS supported large increases in consumption. Private consumption grew more rapidly than government consumption in a number of CIS economies (table 1.2.7). The volume of retail sales also grew strongly in most CIS countries up to and including the first quarter of 2004 (table 1.2.8). Poverty rates have probably continued to diminish throughout the region as growth in the seven low-income countries (CIS-7) appears to have been sustained and to have exceeded the CIS average in three of them (Azerbaijan, Georgia and Tajikistan).[26] Consumption growth in the CIS-7 countries was supported by large inflows of workers' remittances. They have led to personal consumption rising faster than GDP in recent years in the Republic of Moldova, a trend that can hardly be sustained, given the suspension of preferential lending a year ago in response to stalled structural reforms. In contrast, Georgia launched an ambitious reform programme intended to support restructuring and boost output growth.

Capital spending has accelerated since 2003 in a number of CIS countries and remains strong in most of them (table 1.2.9). In Russia, real investment, seasonally adjusted, has been increasing since April 2003, driven by improved profitability. In Ukraine, real investment outlays accelerated sharply in the first quarter of 2004 across the business, government and household sectors. During the same period, a considerable increase of investment in Azerbaijan and Georgia was due to the construction of new oil and gas pipelines from the Caspian Sea to Turkey. Capital formation in the non-energy sector also started to recover across the CIS region.

Exports of goods and services have grown strongly in a number of CIS countries in recent years. The available data indicate that in 2003 they made a remarkable contribution to output growth in the four largest CIS economies as well as in Armenia and the Republic of Moldova. The contribution was smaller in Kyrgyzstan but it exceeded that of final consumption in Armenia, Belarus and Russia (chart 1.2.7).

---

[25] Troika Dialog Research, *Economic Monthly* (Moscow), June 2004, pp. 8-11.

[26] The other low-income CIS countries are Armenia, Kyrgyzstan, the Republic of Moldova and Uzbekistan. For a comparison of economic reforms and poverty trends in this region, see IMF and World Bank, *Recent Performance of the Low-income CIS Countries*, 23 April 2004.

TABLE 1.2.8

Volume of retail trade in south-east Europe and the CIS, 2002-2004
(Percentage change over the same period of the preceding year)

	2002	2003	2004 Jan.-Mar.
South-east Europe			
Albania	-1.4	..	..
Bosnia and Herzegovina	..	..	..
Bulgaria	2.6	4.7	12.2
Croatia	13.5	3.7	2.8
Romania	0.8	5.7	16.4
Serbia and Montenegro	17.4	..	..
The former Yugoslav Republic of Macedonia	6.0	13.0	20.9
Turkey	..	..	..
CIS			
Armenia	15.6	14.5	9.5
Azerbaijan	9.6	10.9	11.4
Belarus	12.9	9.9	15.8
Georgia	3.7	8.8	5.1
Kazakhstan	8.2	10.0	5.2
Kyrgyzstan	8.2	13.5	15.3
Republic of Moldova	22.3	18.2	20.8
Russian Federation	9.2	8.0	10.3
Tajikistan	17.5	24.5	16.4
Turkmenistan	40.0	..	..
Ukraine	16.2	19.5	20.1
Uzbekistan	1.7	5.1	5.1

Source: National statistics, CIS Statistical Committee and direct communications from national statistical offices to UNECE secretariat.

Note: Retail trade covers goods. Recent statistics for The former Yugoslav Republic of Macedonia are subject to regular and large revisions.

TABLE 1.2.9

Real investment outlays in selected CIS economies, 2002-2004
(Percentage change over the same period of the preceding year)

	2002	2003	2004QI
Armenia	45.0	41.0	11.0
Azerbaijan	84.2	71.2	71.3
Belarus	6.0	17.7	24.6
Georgia	18.0	68.0	69.0
Kazakhstan	10.6	10.6	16.4
Kyrgyzstan	-9.6	-8.6	4.8
Republic of Moldova	11.0	16.0	14.0
Russian Federation	2.6	12.5	13.1
Tajikistan	..	..	..
Turkmenistan	..	..	..
Ukraine	8.9	31.3	52.1
Uzbekistan	3.8	4.5	..

Source: National and CIS Statistical Committee data; direct communications from national statistical offices to UNECE secretariat.

Note: "Investment outlays" (also called "capital investment" in some transition economies) mainly refers to expenditure on construction and installation works, machinery and equipment. Gross fixed capital formation is usually estimated by adding the following components to "capital investment": net charges in productive livestock, computer software, art originals, the cost of mineral exploration and the value of major renovations and enlargements of buildings and machinery and equipment (which increase the productive capacity or extend the service life of existing fixed assets).

The strong growth of exports and domestic demand led to large increases in imports of goods and services. In 2003, the contributions of net trade to overall economic growth were broadly neutral in Kyrgyzstan and Russia

and negative in a number of CIS economies, particularly in the Republic of Moldova (chart 1.2.7). In Kazakhstan, however, the net export contribution to GDP growth was positive. In the first four months of 2004, merchandise imports grew more than exports in Russia, but nevertheless, the large merchandise trade surplus continued to increase. The continued strong appreciation of the real exchange rate suggests that import growth in Russia is likely to keep outpacing that of exports and that the external balance could deteriorate rapidly if the export prices of oil and gas were to decline significantly.

On the supply side, industrial diversification appears to have started in a number of CIS countries. The contribution of different producing sectors to growth has changed in Russia, with that of fuels and energy sector falling, while that of non-resource industries has increased. Nevertheless, according to some estimates the major resource industries (oil, gas and basic metals) still account for about one quarter of GDP growth, and their relative slowdown is mainly a result of inadequate oil pipeline capacity.[27] As in Russia, activity in the key machine-building industry picked up strongly in Kazakhstan, Kyrgyzstan and Ukraine between January and April 2004.[28]

(ii) Costs and prices

The large increases in crude oil and natural gas prices have fed through to prices of final energy products, and this started to put some upward pressure on consumer prices in the first half of 2004. Inflation rates and trends across the ECE region, however, continue to differ significantly. In western Europe and North America, the underlying inflationary pressures have generally remained moderate, although core inflation rates have started to edge up somewhat. There has also been a slight increase in medium-term inflationary expectations against the background of a continuing recovery and falling margins of spare capacity.[29] Rapid rates of disinflation have come to a halt in the new EU members partly due to an accelerated pace of price deregulation and increases in indirect taxes and excise duties and partly to demand pressures. Nevertheless, in spite of the sharp recovery in household consumption, disinflation

---

[27] *The World Bank Russian Economic Report*, No. 7, February 2004, and *BOFIT Russia Review*, No. 6, 11 June 2004. Such estimates are based on an assessment of growth with the aid of sector weights estimated by World Bank economists using input-output accounts to adjust the official value-added statistics. In the national accounts of Goskomstat, the slowdown in the growth of the energy sector appears as weaker growth of the trade sector that includes the trading subsidiaries of the oil and gas companies, which do not report profits on a consolidated basis.

[28] Detailed data for other CIS countries were not available at the time of writing this *Survey*.

[29] In Switzerland and the United Kingdom, concerns about missing their inflation targets led central banks to tighten monetary policy.

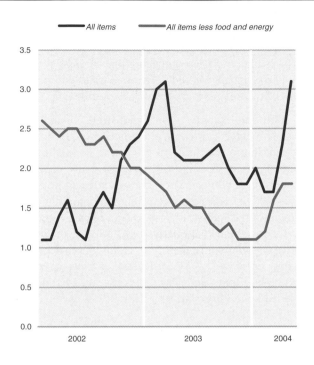

CHART 1.2.8

**Consumer prices in the United States,
January 2002-May 2004**

(Percentage change over same month of the previous year)

Source: United States Department of Labour [www.bls.gov/data/home.htm].
Note: Consumer price index for all urban consumers.

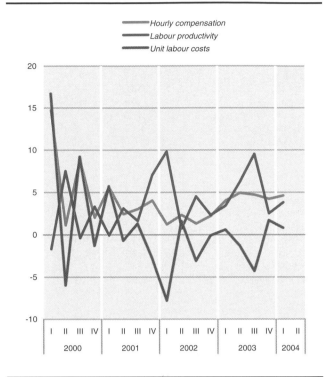

CHART 1.2.9

**Unit labour costs and main components in the United States,
2000-2004**

(Percentage change over previous period)

Source: United States Department of Labour [www.bls.gov/data/home.htm].
Note: Percentage changes expressed at seasonally adjusted annual rates. Non-farm business sector. Labour productivity is defined as output per hour worked.

continued strongly in most of the south-east European economies, reflecting both restrictive policy stances and increases in labour productivity. A sharp slowdown in the rate of increase in food prices, a continuing recovery in industrial labour productivity and the extension of price controls have led to a deceleration of inflation rates in the CIS economies.

Rising but still moderate inflation in North America and western Europe

In the United States, consumer price inflation tended to increase throughout the first five months of 2004 (chart 1.2.8), reaching a 3.1 per cent annual rate in May. While the rise in energy prices clearly explains much of the overall trend, the acceleration was broadly based and involved other major categories such as food and transport services. Core inflation also rose steadily, albeit much less markedly, from 1.1 per cent in January to 1.8 per cent in May.[30] At the same time, the year-on-year growth rates of producer and import prices accelerated in April.

Only a moderate degree of inflationary pressure was due to domestic factors. The growth of labour costs remained modest in the first quarter of 2004, although a

slowdown in productivity growth since the final quarter of 2003 led to an increase in unit labour costs after a prolonged decline (chart 1.2.9). Nevertheless, margins of spare capacity are still relatively large and intense competition continues to keep the pricing power of firms in check. Overall, therefore, expectations are for only a marginal increase in rates of inflation in the short run. Forecasts of the average annual inflation rate in 2004 have been raised slightly from 2 per cent at the beginning of the year to 2.25 per cent in June 2004.

In Canada, the headline rate of consumer price inflation rose to 2.5 per cent year-on-year in May 2004, almost 1 percentage point higher than in April; this largely reflected the surge in oil prices. Core inflation remained well below 2 per cent during the first five months of 2004, and was only 1.5 per cent in May. Given relatively large margins of spare capacity and some upward pressure on the Canadian dollar in early 2004, the short-run inflation outlook remains favourable. Current forecasts are for consumer price inflation to remain close to the mid-point of the central bank's target range of 1 to 3 per cent for the remainder of 2004.

In the euro area, the surge in energy prices also affected the headline inflation rate. The harmonized consumer price index (HICP) rose year-on-year by 2.5 per cent in May (chart 1.2.10). (The increase is influenced

---

[30] Core inflation excludes food and energy prices (and some other minor products characterized by high volatility) and is thus used to measure the underlying trend of inflation.

CHART 1.2.10

Consumer prices in the euro area, January 2002-May 2004
(Percentage change over same month of the previous year)

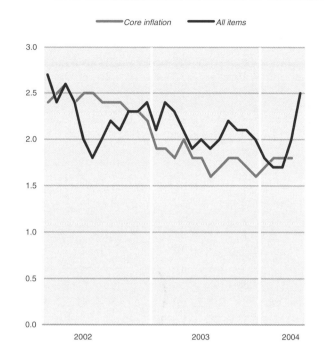

Source: Eurostat, NewCronos Database.

Note: Harmonized index of consumer prices. Core inflation is defined as consumer price inflation excluding energy, food, alcohol and tobacco prices.

by a significant statistical base effect, reflecting the marked decline of energy prices a year ago.) Higher prices for services (especially administered prices such as those for healthcare) and processed food also contributed to the higher rate of inflation. Core inflation, however, remained some 1¾ per cent in the first four months of the year. The average euro area inflation data mask some significant variations across countries, ranging from price stability in Finland to inflation of more than 3 per cent in Greece, Luxembourg and Spain in May 2004 (table 1.2.10).

The short-term outlook for inflation remains closely linked to developments in the oil markets. Although oil prices have stabilized and may even fall in the second half of 2004, the average euro area inflation rate is expected to overshoot slightly the ECB's target ceiling of 2 per cent for some months to come. Most recent forecasts put average annual inflation at between 1.9 per cent and 2.3 per cent in 2004.[31] This modest rate of inflation reflects the fact that domestic cost pressures are expected to remain weak given the moderate pace of the recovery expected for 2004 and 2005. The growth rate of unit labour costs in the total economy decelerated in the second half of 2003, as a result of wage moderation and an acceleration in the growth of labour productivity (chart 1.2.11). The medium-term inflation outlook is thus quite

---

[31]   ECB, *Monthly Bulletin*, June 2004.

favourable, with the average annual rate forecast to return below the 2 per cent ceiling in 2005.

In the United Kingdom, the inflationary impact of higher fuel prices has been rather moderate, with a headline inflation rate of only 1.5 per cent in May 2004. But there are concerns that the pick-up in growth, tighter labour market conditions, with unemployment at its lowest level since 1984, and pressures on supply capacity may drive inflation up in the medium term.

Disinflation comes to a halt in the new EU members...

After falling rapidly in 2003, consumer price inflation picked up or remained high in the first half of 2004 in most of the new members of the European Union (table 1.2.10). This reversal of the downward trend was partly expected due to the deregulation of a broad range of prices, increases in direct taxes and excise duties, and other changes related to their formal entry into the EU in May.[32] However, other factors also contributed to the upturn in inflation: food and domestic fuel price increases accelerated, accommodating monetary policies (and also in the case of Poland a relatively loose fiscal policy) and rising real household incomes all intensified demand pressures (except in the Czech Republic and Hungary).

Rapidly rising world commodity prices also led to an increase in import prices, but in some of the new EU members, particularly in Lithuania and Slovakia, the effect of these external pressures on domestic prices was partly offset by the appreciation of nominal effective exchange rates. In contrast, in Poland and, to a lesser extent, Hungary and Latvia, imported inflation increased due to the depreciation of their currencies.[33] However, in Poland this effect was mitigated by a double-digit decline in unit labour costs.

The major upside risk to price levels in the second half of 2004 is the possibility of further increases in world commodity prices, particularly of oil and natural gas. Such a development would affect not only producer and consumer prices but also the rates of growth of industrial output and productivity which were instrumental in dampening the impact of accelerated wage inflation on unit labour costs in the first half of 2004.

...but continues in south-east Europe

Disinflation continued strongly in most of the south-east European economies in the first half of 2004 (table 1.2.11). One of the main factors behind this development was a reduction in imported inflation underpinned in some countries by an appreciation of the nominal effective exchange rate (most of the currencies in the region being

---

[32]   UNECE, *Economic Survey of Europe, 2004 No. 1*, chap. 3.3.

[33]   The nominal effective exchange rate of the zloty depreciated some 9 per cent between the first quarter of 2003 and 2004.

TABLE 1.2.10

Consumer price indices in Europe, North America and Japan, 2002-2004

(Percentage change over the same period of the preceding year)

	2002 annual average	2003 annual average	2003QIII	2003QIV	2004QI	April 2004	May 2004
France	1.9	2.2	2.1	2.4	2.0	2.4	2.8
Germany	1.3	1.1	1.0	1.2	1.0	1.7	2.1
Italy	2.6	2.8	2.9	2.7	2.3	2.3	2.3
Austria	1.8	1.3	1.1	1.2	1.4	1.5	2.1
Belgium	1.6	1.4	1.6	1.6	1.2	1.7	2.4
Finland	2.0	1.3	1.1	1.1	0.2	-0.4	-0.1
Greece	3.9	3.4	3.4	3.2	2.9	3.1	3.1
Ireland	4.7	3.9	3.9	3.2	2.1	1.7	2.1
Luxembourg	2.0	2.6	2.3	2.0	2.2	2.7	3.4
Netherlands	3.9	2.2	2.1	1.8	1.4	1.5	1.7
Portugal	3.7	3.3	3.0	2.5	2.2	2.4	2.4
Spain	3.6	3.2	3.0	2.7	2.2	2.8	3.4
Euro area	2.3	2.1	2.0	2.0	1.7	2.0	2.5
Denmark	2.4	1.9	1.6	1.3	0.7	0.5	1.1
Sweden	1.9	2.4	2.3	1.9	0.7	1.1	1.5
United Kingdom	1.3	1.4	1.4	1.3	1.3	1.2	1.5
EU-15	2.0	2.0	1.9	1.9	1.6	1.8	2.3
Cyprus	2.8	4.1	3.3	3.5	1.4	0.5	1.5
Czech Republic	1.8	0.2	–	0.9	2.4	2.3	2.7
Estonia	3.5	1.1	0.9	1.1	0.7	1.5	3.9
Hungary	5.4	4.9	4.9	5.6	6.9	7.0	7.6
Latvia	1.9	3.0	3.5	3.5	4.4	5.2	6.4
Lithuania	0.4	-1.2	-1.0	-1.3	-1.3	-0.7	1.0
Malta	2.2	0.7	0.1	1.9	2.7	2.9	2.4
Poland	1.9	0.7	0.8	1.5	1.7	2.3	3.3
Slovakia	3.3	8.5	9.1	9.5	8.4	8.0	8.3
Slovenia	7.6	5.7	5.6	4.9	3.8	3.6	3.9
New EU members-10	2.7	2.0	2.0	2.6	2.9	3.2	4.1
EU-25	2.1	2.0	1.9	2.0	1.7	1.9	2.5
Iceland	5.3	1.4	1.0	1.5	1.3	1.5	2.4
Israel	5.7	0.7	-1.6	-2.1	-2.5	-1.5	-0.6
Norway	0.8	2.0	1.5	0.8	-1.1	0.4	1.0
Switzerland	0.6	0.6	0.5	0.5	0.1	0.5	0.9
WECEE	2.1	2.0	1.9	2.0	1.7	1.9	2.4
Canada	2.3	2.8	2.1	1.7	0.9	1.6	2.5
United States	1.7	2.2	2.2	1.9	1.8	2.3	3.1
Japan	-0.9	-0.3	-0.2	-0.5	-0.1	-0.4	-0.5
Memorandum items:							
CEBS-8	2.7	2.0	2.0	2.6	2.9	3.2	4.1
Western Europe	2.0	2.0	2.0	1.9	1.7	1.9	2.2
Western Europe and North America	1.8	2.2	2.1	1.9	1.7	2.2	2.7

Source: UNECE Statistical Database, Eurostat NewCronos Database.

Note: International harmonized consumer price indices (HICP) for EU-15, Cyprus, Iceland, Malta and Norway. Western, central and eastern Europe (WECEE) includes EU-25 plus Iceland, Norway and Switzerland. Central Europe and Baltic states (CEBS-8) includes the new EU members less Cyprus and Malta. Western Europe includes EU-15 plus Iceland, Norway and Switzerland. For the euro area, EU-15 and EU-25 regional averages are computed using the HICP. For the other regional aggregates, national definitions of the consumer price index are used. For data on south-east Europe and European CIS countries, see table 1.2.11.

pegged to the euro). Another major factor was the strong growth of industrial labour productivity, which outstripped wage growth in most of these economies. Rising incomes and in some cases an expansion of consumer credit provided a boost to household consumption. Nevertheless, the macroeconomic policy stance in most of these countries remained rather restrictive, contributing to the decline in inflationary pressures.

In the first half of 2004, year-on-year rates of inflation accelerated only in Bulgaria and Serbia and

Montenegro. In Serbia and Montenegro, the recent disinflationary trend was largely reversed by rising excise duties and soaring fuel prices. In Bulgaria, the surge in inflation from mid-2003 partly reflects stronger consumer demand supported by both increasing real wages and a rapid expansion of bank lending. Consumer prices were also affected by a rise in excise duties at the start of 2004 and a continued upward trend in food prices. In contrast, in Bosnia and Herzegovina, and in The former Yugoslav Republic of Macedonia, consumer prices actually fell

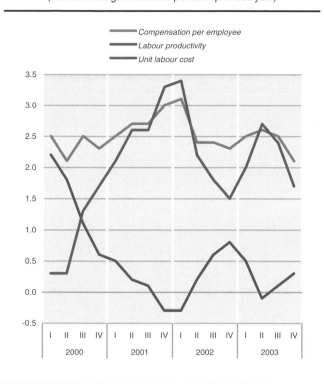

CHART 1.2.11

Unit labour costs and main components in the euro area, 2000-2003
(Per cent change over same period of previous year)

Compensation per employee
Labour productivity
Unit labour cost

Source: European Central Bank, *Monthly Bulletin* (various issues).
Note: Labour productivity is defined as output per person employed.

during the first half of 2004; this was partly due to soaring unemployment, which hit real household incomes in spite of rising real wages. In Albania, a tight fiscal policy and subdued domestic demand kept the year-on-year monthly inflation rates low and, on a cumulative basis, there was virtual price stability in the first half of 2004. In Croatia, a tightening of the macroeconomic policy stance and an appreciating exchange rate allowed gradual disinflation to continue in the first half of 2004.

In Turkey, inflation fell to 18.4 per cent at the end of 2003, below the IMF-agreed target of 20 per cent and well below the rate of nearly 30 per cent in December 2002. In May 2004, the year-on-year rate of change was 8.9 per cent, again well below the year-end target of 12 per cent. This spectacular rate of disinflation (after three decades of chronically high inflation) was mainly due to the impact of a prolonged appreciation of the lira, particularly against the dollar, but also against the euro since April 2003, which has reduced imported inflation significantly.[34] In 2003, public sector wage increases have also been modest, in line with the IMF-agreed

targets. One of the achievements of the macroeconomic stabilization process of the last two years is that the ambitious inflation targets were met together with high rates of output growth, which allowed significant improvement in productivity and hence a sharp decline in unit labour costs. However, further progress towards price stability will require maintaining fiscal discipline and a cautious incomes policy.[35]

Disinflation in Romania continued in 2004, the cumulative rate of change in January-May amounting to some 3 per cent. Thus, the year-end target of 9 per cent does not seem overambitious, even though the year-on-year rate of over 12 per cent in May remained by far the highest in the region. However, in the run up to the forthcoming general and presidential elections in November there may be mounting pressure on the government to increase social spending and public sector wages, which could have an inflationary impact. Planned increases in energy prices may also add to such pressures. Nevertheless, given the strong growth of exports and fixed investment, productivity may be expected to improve further and alleviate the cost pressure on prices.

Inflation slowed down in the CIS but contrary pressures are mounting

Disinflation prevailed in most CIS countries in the first half of 2004 (after a widespread upturn of inflation in 2003) as the effects of internal and external cost pressures as well as strong consumer demand were largely offset by countervailing factors (table 1.2.11). Wage inflation continued to accelerate, rising at double-digit rates in many countries and well above the rates of change in producer prices. However, the continued surge in labour productivity reined in the growth of industrial unit labour costs. More importantly, in the first half of 2004 food prices, which have a large weight in the consumer basket of the CIS economies, rose less rapidly than in 2003, when the prices of many staple goods, in particular in the second quarter, surged in the wake of poor harvests. In addition, in early 2004, a number of CIS countries extended existing price controls and postponed planned increases in regulated tariffs, as they also did in the last quarter of 2003. Thus, reported inflation rates in 2004 may not fully reflect the mounting inflationary pressures in many of the region's economies. In fact, recently there has been increasing concern about overheating, particularly in the commodity exporting CIS economies, which are also receiving large capital inflows. As discussed in section (v) below, this presents the governments and monetary authorities with certain dilemmas in choosing the right policy mix to contain the rise in inflation without hampering output growth.

---

[34] In 2003, Turkey enjoyed large net financial inflows. Net inflows of portfolio investment reached $2.3 billion, reflecting increased confidence in the Turkish economy and strong international demand for "emerging market" assets in general. For similar reasons and in parallel with economic growth, Turkey received net inflows of "other investments" amounting to $3.3 billion.

[35] In early 2004, the government announced substantial increases for pensions and minimum wages. However, under pressure from the IMF, it then raised taxes and cut spending to cover the costs.

TABLE 1.2.11

Inflation in south-east Europe and the CIS, 2002-2004

(Percentage change over the same period of the preceding year)

														Industrial producer prices
				Consumer prices										
			Total				Food		Non-food		Services			
			2003		2004		2004		2004		2004		2004	
	2002	2003	QIII	QIV	QI	QII	QI	QII[a]	QI	QII[a]	QI	QII[a]	QI	QII
South-east Europe														
Albania	5.3	2.5	3.1	3.2	3.9	2.8	2.7	-0.5	..	..	..	..	4.1	..
Bosnia and Herzegovina	0.9	0.2	0.8	0.9	0.9	-0.4	2.6	-0.8	1.1	-0.5	0.3	0.3	0.5	3.0
Bulgaria	5.8	2.3	3.1	4.7	6.4	6.4	8.9	7.4	2.4	4.3	7.3	7.9	1.9	7.5
Croatia	1.8	2.2	3.0	2.7	2.7	2.2	5.8	1.5	-1.0	1.4	2.7	3.1	0.1	2.9
Romania	22.5	15.4	15.1	14.9	13.6	12.4	11.6	9.6	14.7	14.1	16.4	16.1	19.0	18.8
Serbia and Montenegro	19.3	9.6	7.9	7.6	8.2	9.4	4.6	7.8	7.4	9.1	15.1	12.5	6.3	8.6
The former Yugoslav Republic of Macedonia	2.3	1.1	2.1	2.0	1.9	-0.7	0.1	-2.8	0.5	-0.5	5.3	2.4	-1.6	-0.4
Turkey	45.0	25.3	25.1	19.4	14.1	9.5	14.5	7.4	..	..	..	..	9.3	9.2
CIS														
Armenia	1.0	4.7	5.1	7.5	7.8	7.9	11.8	11.3	0.3	0.3	1.9	2.8	24.9	15.0
Azerbaijan	2.8	2.1	1.6	2.8	5.5	6.7	8.8	10.8	0.8	0.8	-0.1	0.0	5.1	2.3
Belarus	42.8	28.5	28.3	27.0	22.4	20.3	24.2	21.4	15.3	13.3	24.5	28.5	27.3	26.3
Georgia	5.7	4.9	5.2	6.8	5.9	5.4	..	..	..	..	..	..	4.1	4.7
Kazakhstan	6.0	6.6	5.8	7.1	6.7	6.8	7.0	7.3	6.5	6.5	5.8	5.5	4.0	12.9
Kyrgyzstan	2.1	3.1	1.1	5.1	5.3	2.4	5.1	-0.5	1.3	2.5	17.7	17.3	8.5	13.1
Republic of Moldova	5.3	11.7	15.3	16.8	14.6	13.3	16.8	14.0	11.8	11.6	13.3	13.7	..	..
Russian Federation	16.0	13.6	13.5	12.5	10.8	10.3	9.2	8.9	8.1	7.8	19.5	17.8	19.0	23.0
Tajikistan	12.2	16.3	14.3	15.5	8.5	5.4	5.6	1.7	7.4	7.1	29.9	24.5	14.5	16.9
Turkmenistan	..	..	..	..	..	..	..	..	..	..	..	..	..	..
Ukraine	0.8	5.2	6.5	7.8	7.4	7.0	9.1	8.6	1.8	2.9	7.0	6.3	14.1	19.5
Uzbekistan	..	..	..	..	..	..	..	..	..	..	..	..	..	..

Source: UNECE secretariat estimates, based on national statistics.

[a] April-May except for Armenia, Azerbaijan, Belarus, Georgia, Republic of Moldova and Tajikistan, for which only the year-on-year change in April is shown.

In Russia, the cumulative inflation rate in January-May was 5.4 per cent, which compares with the government's end-year target for 2004 of 8-10 per cent. However, it may be difficult to meet this as the underlying inflationary pressures remain strong due to booming consumer demand, an acceleration of industrial producer prices and a rapid expansion of the money supply. In addition, the effect of one-off disinflationary factors, such as the 2 percentage point cut in VAT and the abolition of the regional sales tax, which lowered inflation at the start of the year, will also fade in the coming months.

In Ukraine, after a significant acceleration in the fourth quarter of 2003 (following a disastrous grain harvest), the rate of consumer price inflation fell considerably in the first half of 2004. However, the wide and growing gap between the trends in producer and consumer prices increases the risk of a post-election surge of inflation, as price controls on various consumer goods may be lifted and producer price increases allowed to be finally passed on to consumers. Nevertheless, the risk of a return to double-digit inflation rates is likely to remain low as long as fiscal and monetary policies are not loosened further in advance of the October elections.

Despite a further strengthening of domestic demand and large public sector wage rises, the rate of consumer price inflation also fell in Kazakhstan in the first half of 2004. However, industrial price inflation accelerated sharply in the second quarter and this may feed into consumer prices in the second half of the year, halting or even reversing the slow downward trend in consumer price inflation. In view of the inflationary risks of a possible overheating of the economy and the ongoing surge in capital inflows, the authorities may need to tighten macroeconomic policy in the coming months.

Increased wage pressures were mitigated by surging productivity

The moderate deceleration of industrial wage increases in 2003 in the central European economies came to a halt in the first quarter of 2004 (table 1.2.12), and on average gross wages rose faster than industrial producer prices. Real product wages continued to increase at a particularly fast pace in the Czech Republic, Hungary and Slovakia, reaching 11 per cent in the latter where there was also a slight producer price deflation. Nevertheless, measured labour productivity in industry continued to improve significantly in the first quarter of 2004 as a result of the sharp acceleration in the growth of industrial output and of enterprise restructuring. Rates of

TABLE 1.2.12

Wages and unit labour costs in industry ^a in the new EU member countries, 2003-2004
(Percentage change over the same period of the preceding year)

	Nominal gross wages		Real product wages [b]		Labour productivity [c]		Unit labour costs [d]		Real unit labour costs [e]	
	2003	2004 [f]	2003	2004 [f]	2003	2004 [f]	2003	2004 [f]	2003	2004 [f]
Cyprus	..	..	..	..	..	..	..	..	..	..
Czech Republic	5.9	9.0	7.6	7.1	8.5	15.5	-2.4	-5.6	-0.9	-7.3
Estonia	9.8	6.1	9.6	5.4	5.8	7.8	3.8	-1.6	3.6	-2.3
Hungary	9.4	11.8	6.7	6.6	10.3	11.8	-0.8	0.0	-3.3	-4.7
Latvia	8.5	11.9	5.1	6.3	5.3	15.3	3.0	-2.9	-0.2	-7.8
Lithuania	4.4	1.8	4.7	3.6	14.5	9.8	-8.8	-7.2	-8.6	-5.6
Malta	..	..	..	..	..	..	..	..	..	..
Poland	3.0	6.6	0.3	2.1	12.0	19.6	-8.0	-10.9	-10.4	-14.7
Slovakia	7.3	10.8	3.8	11.1	4.8	7.2	2.4	3.4	-1.0	3.7
Slovenia	7.6	6.0	4.9	2.7	3.2	5.8	4.2	0.2	1.6	-2.9

Source: UNECE secretariat estimates, based on national statistics and direct communications from national statistical offices.

^a Industry = mining + manufacturing + utilities.

^b Nominal wages deflated by producer price index.

^c Gross industrial output deflated by industrial employment.

^d Nominal wages deflated by productivity.

^e Real product wages deflated by productivity.

^f First quarter.

productivity growth reached nearly 20 per cent in Poland and exceeded 15 per cent in the Czech Republic.[36] As a result, unit labour costs generally declined or stabilized.

These favourable developments in unit labour costs, combined with a more rapid increase in producer prices, led to a further fall in labour's share of industrial value added in the first quarter of 2004. Real unit labour costs increased only in Slovakia (reflecting a combination of relatively slower output growth and double-digit wage inflation), while the rate of decline reached nearly 15 per cent in Poland.[37]

The decline in real unit labour costs suggests, *ceteris paribus*, that unit operating surpluses continued to rise in early 2004 in tandem with the acceleration of wage inflation. Appreciating nominal effective exchange rates in Hungary, Slovakia and Slovenia are likely to have added to the increase in profit margins in these countries.

In the three Baltic states, the changes in industrial unit labour costs in the first quarter of 2004 were similar to those in central Europe. Underpinned by large gains in measured labour productivity (particularly in Latvia), combined with lower rates of wage growth in Estonia and Lithuania, unit labour costs declined in both nominal and real terms. Hence, unit operating profits were given a

strong boost, particularly in Lithuania where the nominal effective exchange rate of the litas appreciated by more than 7 per cent over the year to the first quarter of 2004.

The development of wages varied greatly among the south-east European economies in the first quarter of 2004 (table 1.2.13). According to the available data, wage growth continued to decelerate in Bosnia and Herzegovina, The former Yugoslav Republic of Macedonia, Serbia and Montenegro and Turkey and maintained its pace in Croatia. In contrast, in Bulgaria and especially in Romania, average gross wages in industry rose faster than in 2003 as a whole. On the other hand, the marked acceleration in measured labour productivity alleviated or more than offset (in the case of Bosnia and Herzegovina, Bulgaria and Croatia) the effect of higher wages on unit labour costs. As a result, real unit labour costs were generally on the decline with the exception of The former Yugoslav Republic of Macedonia where industrial output reportedly collapsed in the first quarter.[38]

In the CIS, rapid wage growth in industry accelerated further in the first quarter of 2004: wages rose much faster than producer prices in all the CIS economies (table 1.2.13). However, the rapid growth of industrial

---

[36] In the Czech Republic more than one third of the gain reflects the large reduction in manufacturing employment.

[37] It has to be borne in mind that gross wages have been used as a proxy for the total compensation of employees, which implies that the rates of change in employers' contributions (i.e. obligatory social security charges and other mandatory payments) are assumed to be equal to that of gross wages.

[38] The absence of employment data for the first quarter of 2004 prevents any accurate assessment of the changes in labour productivity in Serbia and Montenegro and in Turkey. However, given the double-digit growth rates of industrial production and the incomes policies in place, increased labour productivity growth probably offset much of the growth in wages, particularly in Turkey where wage growth was much lower than in Serbia and Montenegro in the first quarter of 2004.

TABLE 1.2.13

Wages and unit labour costs in industry [a] in south-east Europe and the CIS, 2003-2004

(Percentage change over the same period of the preceding year)

	Nominal gross wages [b]		Real product wages [c]		Labour productivity [d]		Unit labour costs [e]		Real unit labour costs [f]	
	2003	2004 [g]	2003	2004 [g]	2003	2004 [g]	2003	2004 [g]	2003	2004 [g]
South-east Europe										
Albania	..	..	..	..	..	..	..	..	..	..
Bosnia and Herzegovina	8.2	2.6	5.4	2.1	10.2	26.1	-1.9	-18.7	-4.3	-19.1
Bulgaria	5.2	6.0	0.2	4.0	12.4	15.4	-6.4	-8.1	-10.8	-9.9
Croatia [g]	5.2	5.2	3.2	5.0	5.7	6.9	-0.5	-1.6	-2.4	-1.7
Romania	19.5	24.0	-1.3	4.2	2.6	5.9	16.5	17.1	-3.8	-1.6
Serbia and Montenegro	25.5	20.0	18.5	12.9	..	..	..	..	..	..
The former Yugoslav Republic of Macedonia	4.8	4.1	4.8	5.8	8.7	-22.0	-3.5	33.5	-3.5	35.6
Turkey	25.0	15.0	-0.2	0.8	9.0	..	14.5	..	-8.5	..
CIS										
Armenia	23.7	31.2	19.3	5.1	..	..	..	..	..	..
Azerbaijan	21.5	19.6	2.5	13.7	5.4	..	15.3	..	-2.7	..
Belarus	32.2	35.1	-3.8	6.2	11.5	..	18.6	..	-13.7	..
Georgia	..	..	..	..	..	..	..	..	..	..
Kazakhstan	14.5	21.3	4.6	16.6	5.8	..	8.2	..	-1.2	..
Kyrgyzstan	17.8	16.6	9.7	7.4	16.2	..	1.4	..	-5.6	..
Republic of Moldova	31.8	25.8	21.6	..	16.1	..	13.5	..	4.7	..
Russian Federation	24.8	28.6	8.0	8.1	10.1	9.6	13.3	17.4	-1.9	-1.3
Tajikistan	40.3	43.3	21.7	25.1	10.4	..	27.0	..	10.2	..
Turkmenistan	..	..	..	..	..	..	..	..	..	..
Ukraine	23.0	28.8	14.2	12.9	20.8	..	1.8	..	-5.5	..
Uzbekistan	..	..	..	..	..	..	..	..	..	..

Source: UNECE secretariat estimates, based on national statistics and direct communications from national statistical offices.

[a] Industry = mining + manufacturing + utilities.

[b] Net wages in total economy for Bosnia and Herzegovina, Serbia and Montenegro, and The former Yugoslav Republic of Macedonia.

[c] Nominal wages deflated by producer price index.

[d] Gross industrial output deflated by industrial employment.

[e] Nominal wages deflated by productivity.

[f] Real product wages deflated by productivity.

[g] First quarter.

production accompanied by stable or falling employment in most of these economies led to significant gains in measured labour productivity in 2003 and probably also in early 2004.[39] In 2003, the rate of productivity growth in Ukraine exceeded 20 per cent and was in double digits in most of the other CIS economies.[40] Rates were relatively lower but still high in Azerbaijan and Kazakhstan.

This generally favourable productivity performance allowed a slowdown in the growth of unit labour costs in 2003 although the rates of change remained in double digits, except in Kyrgyzstan and Ukraine. Furthermore, given the continued acceleration of producer prices during the same period, real unit labour costs (in other words, labour's share of industrial value added) fell or increased at a much slower rate than in 2002.

_____

[39] At the time of writing this *Survey*, employment data for the first quarter of 2004 were only available for Russia.

[40] In Ukraine, labour productivity in 2003 was nearly double its level in 1998.

(iii) Labour markets

Labour market developments typically lag behind movements in the business cycle. During downturns firms tend to hoard labour, and thus at the beginning of the cyclical upturn output can be increased without hiring new staff. This is reflected in the procyclical behaviour of labour productivity. The recovery therefore needs to consolidate and business prospects to be firmly placed on an upward sloping trend before firms are induced to raise their effective demand for new labour. Yet, in many countries, a sustained improvement in labour market performance will also require the implementation of additional structural reforms designed to further enhance labour market flexibility.

Against this backdrop, changes in labour market conditions in the first half of 2004 reflected not only the differential strength of economic growth in the various countries, but also differences in the importance of structural factors. In the United States, new job creation has started to underpin the recovery. In contrast, in the euro area, the hiring of labour has remained sluggish in the face of prospects for an only moderate recovery of output. In the United Kingdom, the continuing strength of output growth has been associated with further improvements in labour market performance.

Among the new EU member states, there has been new job creation in some countries but some labour market rigidities need to be softened in order to increase the rate of labour utilization, particularly in the central European economies. Despite some recent improvements, unemployment remains high on average in the south-east European region. In the CIS, recovery has so far failed to significantly raise levels of employment, even if the underlying labour market dynamics are obscured by the poor quality of the available statistics.

The United States labour market shows signs of improvement

In the United States the recovery in 2003 was associated with a weak demand for labour, giving rise to fears of a "jobless recovery". However, towards the end of the first quarter of 2004, indications of a changing trend emerged. In fact, between March and May 2004 more than 900,000 new jobs were created in several key sectors of the economy, including services, which had been sluggish since the 2001 recession. But the rise in employment has been offset by an increase in the labour force with the result that the unemployment rate has remained virtually flat at 5.6 per cent since December 2003 (table 1.2.14). Labour market conditions are expected to improve in the second half of 2004, but this will require the recovery to be sustained at a sufficiently high rate. The slowdown in productivity growth (chart 1.2.9) also suggests that firms may now be operating at high levels of utilization of their existing labour resources pointing to a more favourable trade-off between output and productivity growth for labour markets.

Persistently high average unemployment in the euro area

In the euro area the average unemployment rate edged up to 9 per cent in April 2004. Given that the recovery is still rather weak, employment growth has yet to pick up. It should be recalled that employment levels in the whole economy stagnated in 2003. This suggests that the "excess labour" retained by firms during the cyclical downturn is now being more fully utilized. The increase in labour productivity towards the end of 2003 (chart 1.2.11) also suggests that the creation of new jobs might be further delayed, if firms can produce more output with their existing workforces. Indeed, the average annual rate of employment growth is currently forecast at only 0.3 per cent in 2004 with some gain in momentum only later in 2005.

Labour market data for the euro area as a whole hide significant differences among countries (tables 1.2.14 and

TABLE 1.2.14

Unemployment in Europe, North America and Japan, 2002-2004
(Per cent of labour force)

	2002	2003	2003 QIV	2004 QI	2004[a]
France	8.9	9.4	9.5	9.5	9.7
Germany	8.7	9.6	9.7	9.7	9.1
Italy	9.0	8.6	8.5	..	8.6
Austria	4.2	4.1	4.5	4.5	4.5
Belgium	7.3	8.1	8.3	8.5	8.3
Finland	9.1	9.0	8.9	9.0	8.9
Greece	10.0	9.3	9.3	..	8.4
Ireland	4.3	4.6	4.6	4.5	5.0
Luxembourg	2.8	3.7	3.9	4.0	4.7
Netherlands	2.7	3.8	4.2	4.6	5.3
Portugal	5.0	6.3	6.6	6.8	6.8
Spain	11.3	11.3	11.2	11.2	10.9
Euro area	8.4	8.8	8.9	8.9	8.8
Denmark	4.6	5.6	5.9	5.9	5.8
Sweden	4.9	5.6	6.0	6.3	6.1
United Kingdom	5.1	5.0	4.9	4.7	5.0
EU-15	7.7	8.1	8.1	8.1	8.1
Cyprus	3.9	4.4	4.6	4.7	4.1
Czech Republic	7.3	7.8	8.1	8.2	8.2
Estonia	9.5	10.1	9.7	9.4	9.7
Hungary	5.6	5.8	5.8	5.9	5.7
Latvia	12.6	10.5	10.5	10.6	10.3
Lithuania	13.6	12.7	12.1	11.7	11.5
Malta	7.5	8.2	8.6	8.9	8.6
Poland	19.8	19.2	19.1	19.1	19.6
Slovakia	18.7	17.1	16.6	16.6	16.5
Slovenia	6.1	6.5	6.5	6.4	6.4
New EU members-10	14.7	14.3	14.2	14.1	14.1
EU-25	8.8	9.1	9.1	9.1	9.1
Iceland	3.2	3.4	3.4	3.0	3.1
Israel	10.3	10.7	10.9	..	10.7
Norway	3.9	4.5	4.6	4.3	4.4
Switzerland	3.2	4.1	4.2	4.1	3.8
WECEE	8.6	8.9	8.9	8.9	8.8
Canada	7.7	7.6	7.5	7.4	7.4
United States	5.8	6.0	5.9	5.6	5.5
Japan	5.4	5.3	5.1	4.9	5.0
Europe, North America and Japan	7.2	7.4	7.3	7.2	7.1
Memorandum items:					
CEBS-8	15.0	14.4	14.3	14.3	14.5
Western Europe	7.6	7.9	8.0	8.0	7.9
Western Europe and North America	6.9	7.1	7.1	6.9	6.8

Source: UNECE Statistical Database; Eurostat NewCronos Database; *OECD Economic Outlook,* No. 75; IMF, *World Economic Outlook,* April 2004; European Commission, *European Economy Forecasts,* Spring 2004; *Consensus Forecasts,* May 2004.

Note: Unemployment is measured by the standardized unemployment rate as defined by Eurostat. Quarterly data are seasonally adjusted. Western, central and eastern Europe (WECEE) includes EU-25 plus Iceland, Norway and Switzerland. Central Europe and Baltic states (CEBS-8) includes the new EU members less Cyprus and Malta. Western Europe includes EU-15 plus Iceland, Norway and Switzerland.

[a] Forecasts.

1.2.15). In spite of the free movement of labour, members of the euro area – and indeed of the EU as a whole – still have rather independent labour markets. At the same time, aggregates are mostly reflecting developments in the four largest economies (France, Germany, Italy and Spain).[41] In these countries, high levels of unemployment have tended to persist, despite some improvements in recent years. Among the major problems are high rates of youth unemployment, a large share of long-term unemployment in the total, relatively low activity rates among older workers and limited rates of female participation. These stylized facts suggest that, in addition to sluggish economic growth, labour market problems also arise from structural deficiencies. Indeed, all of the four largest economies of the euro area have initiated labour market reforms to remove entry and re-entry barriers, to facilitate and stimulate job search, to increase participation rates and to soften rigidities (including the reduction of high non-wage labour costs and the reform of job protection legislation).

Positive labour market performance in the United Kingdom

Against a background of strong economic growth, the labour market statistics show a rather positive picture for the United Kingdom. Employment continued to grow in the first quarter of 2004, albeit at a more moderate rate than in previous quarters. At the same time, the unemployment rate fell to 4.7 per cent, its lowest level since 1984. This low figure suggests that the bulk of unemployment is now mainly frictional and that medium- and long-term unemployment has been largely eliminated. This positive overall picture, however, masks sectoral differences, with the number of jobs in manufacturing having fallen to its lowest level since 1978, as well as regional disparities.

Structural rigidities in some of the new EU members

In the new EU member states, the average rate of unemployment fell from 14.5 per cent in the first quarter of 2003 to 14.1 per cent in the first quarter of 2004, still well above the average of the EU-15 (table 1.2.14). The share of long-term unemployment and the youth unemployment rate were also on average above those in the rest of the union (charts 1.2.12 and 1.2.13). At the same time, rapid rates of economic growth on average have so far failed to generate notable increases in employment.

Yet, cross-country differences are also important within this group. In Hungary, employment has increased, but so has long-term unemployment, suggesting that new jobs have been taken up by the short-term unemployed and by part of the previously inactive population. In Slovakia, employment grew considerably in 2003, but there was a slowdown in the first quarter of 2004 following a rapid increase in unit labour costs. There has also been

---

[41] Also see S. Nickell, *A Picture of European Unemployment: Success and Failure*, Centre for Economic Performance (CEP) Discussion Paper, No. 577 (London), July 2003.

TABLE 1.2.15

Employment in Europe, North America and Japan, 2002-2004
(Total economy, per cent change over the same period previous year)

	2002	2003	2004 [a]
France	0.7	0.0	0.1
Germany	-0.6	-1.0	-0.1
Italy	1.8	1.2	0.3
Austria	-0.2	0.4	0.4
Belgium	-0.3	0.6	0.3
Finland	0.9	-0.4	0.1
Greece	0.1	0.8	1.7
Ireland	1.3	1.4	0.8
Luxembourg	3.2	1.0	0.9
Netherlands	0.9	-0.5	-1.3
Portugal	0.7	0.2	0.2
Spain	1.5	1.9	2.1
Euro area	0.6	0.2	0.3
Denmark	-0.6	-0.6	0.1
Sweden	0.2	-0.3	-0.4
United Kingdom	0.2	0.7	0.4
EU-15	0.5	0.2	0.3
Cyprus	1.4	0.5	0.7
Czech Republic	0.8	-0.6	-0.4
Estonia	1.3	1.5	0.6
Hungary	0.3	3.0	0.6
Latvia	1.6	1.7	0.5
Lithuania	-7.4	2.4	1.3
Malta	-0.7	-1.4	-0.2
Poland	-3.0	-1.2	0.4
Slovakia	-1.1	2.3	0.6
Slovenia	-0.4	-0.3	0.1
New EU members-10	-1.7	0.0	0.3
EU-25	0.1	0.2	0.3
Iceland	-0.7	1.4	2.1
Israel	0.9	2.0	..
Norway	0.4	-0.6	0.5
Switzerland	0.6	-0.1	0.7
WECEE	0.2	0.2	0.4
Canada	2.2	2.2	1.6
United States	-0.5	0.8	1.0
Japan	-1.3	-0.2	0.0
Europe, North America and Japan	-0.3	0.5	0.6
Memorandum items:			
CEBS-8	-1.7	0.1	0.6
Western Europe	0.3	0.3	0.5
Western Europe and North America	0.0	0.8	0.9

Source: UNECE Statistical Database; Eurostat NewCronos Database; *OECD Economic Outlook*, No. 75; IMF, *World Economic Outlook*, April 2004; European Commission, *European Economy Forecasts*, Spring 2004; *Consensus Forecasts*, May 2004.

Note: Western, central and eastern Europe (WECEE) includes EU-25 plus Iceland, Norway and Switzerland. Central Europe and Baltic states (CEBS-8) includes the new EU members less Cyprus and Malta. Western Europe includes EU-15 plus Iceland, Norway and Switzerland.

[a] Forecasts.

employment growth in the Baltic countries, with unemployment falling in Estonia and Lithuania. In contrast, total employment fell in Poland, where labour productivity growth allowed firms to expand output without recruiting new staff. In the Czech Republic, employment fell mostly

CHART 1.2.12

Youth unemployment in the new EU member countries, 2002 and 2003

(Percentage of workforce aged between 15 and 24)

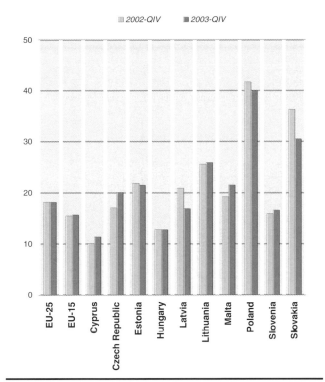

CHART 1.2.13

Long-term unemployment in the new EU member countries, 2002 and 2003

(Percentage share of total unemployment)

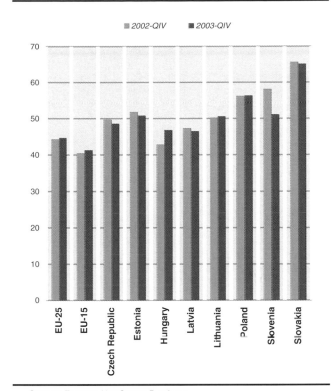

Source: Eurostat, NewCronos Database.

Source: Eurostat, NewCronos Database.

Note: Data for Cyprus and Malta are not available.

as a consequence of rationalization measures and redundancies in industry.

Weak employment growth in the presence of strong economic growth is to some extent the consequence of structural rigidities that affect the functioning of labour markets in some countries, particularly in central Europe (the Czech Republic, Hungary, Poland and Slovakia). On the demand side, the sustained growth in labour costs and relatively strict employment protection rules tend to reduce firms' willingness to hire new staff. On the supply side, generous out-of-work benefits (particularly in the Czech Republic and Poland) distort job search incentives and favour employment in the grey economy. Moreover, low labour mobility implies a significant variation of unemployment rates across regions (as observed in Hungary, for example). Since increasing labour utilization is critical for sustaining the growth of real GDP per head, such rigidities need to be reduced in order to increase the efficiency of labour markets.[42] To this end, structural reforms have already been started but they need to be taken further to make labour legislation more flexible (for example, by reducing the period of advance notice of dismissals, by increasing the flexibility

of labour contracts and by differentiating the minimum wage between regions and different categories of labour), to reduce the non-wage components of labour costs, eliminate skill mismatches and to support the acquisition of skills required by the fast-growing sectors and firms.

Despite some improvement unemployment remains high in south-east Europe

In 2003, there were improvements in the labour markets of a number of south-east European countries for the first time since 1998. The available data suggest a further reduction in rates of unemployment in the early months of 2004. In April, the average unemployment rate in south-east Europe was 15.5 per cent, more than 1 percentage point lower than a year earlier (table 1.2.16). In the 12 months to April 2004, the rate of unemployment fell in Albania, Romania and most noticeably (by nearly 2 percentage points) in Bulgaria and Croatia. These positive trends were the result of a relatively strong economic recovery in the region supported in some cases by state sponsored employment programmes that include incentives for investment in regions with high unemployment, and the launching of public works programmes.

Despite these improvements, however, the situation in the labour markets remains rather tense, posing major challenges to economic policy. Moreover, there is a wide

---

[42] The experiences of Ireland and Spain show that real income convergence with the more advanced EU members requires, in addition to strong productivity growth, high rates of labour utilization.

TABLE 1.2.16

Registered and labour force survey unemployment in south-east Europe and the CIS, 2003-2004

(Per cent of labour force)

	Registered unemployment[a]						Labour force survey unemployment				
	2003				2004		2003				2004
	April	June	Sept.	Dec.	Mar.	April	QI	QII	QIII	QIV	QI
South-east Europe	16.8	16.1	15.5	15.8	16.3	15.5	..	..	..	..	..
Albania	15.5[b]	15.2	15.0	15.0	14. 9[b]	..	..	..	..	..	..
Bosnia and Herzegovina	43.1	43.1	43.8	44.0	44.9	44.6	..	..	..	..	..
Bulgaria	14.9	13.7	12.8	13.5	13.7	13.2	15.6	13.7	12.7	12.7	13.3
Croatia	20.4	18.9	18.3	19.1	19.1	18.6	..	14.1[c]	..	14.4[c]	..
Romania	8.1	7.3	6.7	7.2	7.7	7.3	7.1	6.9	6.2	6.7	..
Serbia and Montenegro[d]	27.6	27.7	27.6	27.4	..	..	..	..	..	15.2[e]	..
Turkey	..	..	..	..	..	..	12.3	10.0	9.4	10.3	..
The former Yugoslav Republic of Macedonia	44.6	44.4	44.6	45.3	45.9	45.9	..	36.7[f]	..	..	..
CIS	2.7	2.5	2.4	2.6	2.7	2.6	..	..	..	..	..
Armenia	10.2	10.0	9.8	9.8	9.8	9.7	..	..	..	..	..
Azerbaijan	1.4	1.4	1.4	1.4	1.4	1.4	..	..	..	..	..
Belarus	3.3	3.2	3.2	3.1	3.0	2.8	..	..	..	..	..
Georgia	..	..	..	..	..	..	..	12.4[g]	..	..	..
Kazakhstan	2.6	2.4	2.0	1.8	1.9	1.9	9.3	8.3	7.9	9.1	8.6
Kyrgyzstan	3.1	3.1	3.0	3.0	3.0	3.0	13.0[h]	..	..	..	..
Republic of Moldova	2.1	1.8	1.5	1.2	2.0	1.8	9.8	6.9	6.6	8.7	11.3
Russian Federation	2.1	2.1	2.1	2.3	2.3	2.3	8.9	8.0	7.9	8.2	8.7
Tajikistan	2.5	2.4	2.5	2.4	2.3	2.2	..	..	..	..	..
Ukraine	4.0	3.7	3.5	3.6	3.9	3.8	9.4	8.8	9.2	9.0	9.0

Source: National statistics and direct communications from national statistical offices to UNECE secretariat; for Bosnia and Herzegovina: The Economist Intelligence Unit (these figures cover only the Bosnian-Croat Federation, data for Republika Srpska are not available).

a Registered unemployment rates in Serbia and Montenegro and The former Yugoslav Republic of Macedonia are UNECE secretariat estimates. Both National Statistical Offices report only the number of registered unemployed. The rates are the officially reported number of registered unemployed as a percentage of the labour force as reported in the labour force surveys.

b March.

c Average for the first and the second half of 2003.

d Data exclude Kosovo and Metohia.

e October.

f April.

g First half of the year.

h February-April, preliminary estimates.

variation across countries in terms of the incidence of unemployment and rates of employment growth, which reflects the diversity of macroeconomic situations and the various patterns of labour market adjustment. In Romania, the rate of unemployment (7.3 per cent in April) was comparable to the EU-15 average (8.1 per cent in the first quarter of 2004) but it stood at some 13 and 15 per cent in Bulgaria and Albania, respectively, and was nearly 19 per cent in Croatia.[43]

It is difficult to accurately assess developments in Bosnia and Herzegovina, Serbia and Montenegro and The former Yugoslav Republic of Macedonia due to the

lack of reliable and timely data.[44] In December 2003, the total number of people registered as unemployed in these countries amounted to 1.7 million people. In Serbia and Montenegro alone, the number of unemployed exceeded 1 million people. Partial data suggest that, in contrast to other countries of the region, the already very high unemployment rates in these three economies probably increased further in the early months of 2004. Unemployment in these countries is not expected to fall in the short run as privatization and structural reforms are

_____

[43] In Croatia, as well as in some neighbouring countries, however, the registered statistics tend to overestimate the incidence of unemployment, often by a considerable margin. See table 1.2.16 and, for a more detailed comment, UNECE, *Economic Survey of Europe, 2004 No. 1*, pp. 70-71, box 3.4.1.

_____

[44] Both Bosnia and Herzegovina and The former Yugoslav Republic of Macedonia report only the number of unemployed persons; unemployment rates are not given in the official statistics. The National Statistical Office of Serbia and Montenegro has stopped reporting monthly labour market indicators since mid-2002 due to difficulties in assessing the current situation. According to UNECE secretariat estimates, the registered unemployment rate in 2003 was around 28 per cent.

likely to result in further increases in joblessness. The combination of high unemployment and widespread poverty, which is a chronic problem in these countries, requires renewed efforts both by local policy makers and by the international community in order to reduce this potential threat to economic and social stability in the region.

Recovery remains "jobless" in the CIS

Despite the ongoing recovery in the CIS economies, which continued in the first quarter of 2004, the available statistics indicate little improvement in their labour markets. In 2003, employment in most countries (with the exception of Kazakhstan) was broadly flat or even declined, and there was little change in unemployment rates; registered unemployment still shows little change in the 12 months to April 2004 (table 1.2.16). The registered unemployment rates are very low, varying mostly between 1.4 per cent (Azerbaijan) and 3.8 per cent (Ukraine), the main outlier being Armenia (9.7 per cent).

However, these data do not provide reliable information as to the actual levels and changes in unemployment. The available labour force survey (LFS) data for some CIS countries portray a different and probably more realistic picture of labour market developments in the region. First of all the LFS data indicate much higher rates of unemployment. In the first quarter of 2004, in the countries conducting a regular quarterly LFS, the unemployment rate varied between some 9 per cent in Kazakhstan, Russia and Ukraine and more than 11 per cent in the Republic of Moldova. Less frequently reported LFS data indicate unemployment rates in Georgia and Kyrgyzstan above 12 per cent of the labour force (table 1.2.16). In all the countries for which both measures are available, the LFS unemployment rates are three to five times higher than the registered ones.

The LFS data also suggest little improvement in the first quarter of 2004. The unemployment rate continued to decline slightly in Kazakhstan (where, in the first quarter of 2004, it stood at 8.6 per cent, 0.4 percentage points lower than a year earlier) and, possibly, Ukraine.[45] In Russia, the rate was broadly unchanged from a year earlier but it increased considerably in the Republic of Moldova.[46]

However, the apparent jobless recovery in the CIS may be largely the result of the poor quality of labour market statistics in these economies, which fail to reflect the ongoing adjustment in their labour markets. Current labour market data for the CIS countries remain generally unreliable and this limits the possibilities for a comprehensive analysis of recent developments. Quarterly data on employment are incomplete and in some cases are only reported with long delays. Official statistics probably fail to capture the full extent of employment growth in these countries particularly if it is concentrated in small firms and in service sectors that are less well monitored than industry. Registered unemployment, which is the only available series on joblessness for many of these countries, is very unreliable and sometimes even misleading[47] since a large proportion of the jobless, although willing to work, do not register as unemployed.[48] In addition, past statistics probably understated the unemployment rates during the recession period when various forms of hidden unemployment (such as unpaid leave) were widespread in the CIS countries. With the recovery, the return of such workers from their "unpaid leave" is also not reflected in the statistics.

(iv) Merchandise trade, current accounts and capital flows in eastern Europe and the CIS

Exports and imports rush ahead before accession to the EU

The upturn in the global economy since the second half of 2003 and the approach of accession to the EU provided a strong impetus for trade in the central European and Baltic countries. For the year as a whole the volumes of merchandise exports and imports increased by 11 per cent and 10 per cent, respectively. This was much more than the 4.5 per cent growth in world trade in 2003, and places this group of economies among the most dynamic trading regions in the world.[49] Preliminary estimates indicate that in the first quarter of 2004 their exports increased by close to 12 per cent (year-on-year) in volume, while imports rose by 13 per cent.

---

[45] In Ukraine, the data for the first quarter of 2004 are not fully comparable with previous data as, starting in 2004, the National Statistical Office calculates the unemployment rate using new labour force numbers obtained from the 2002 census. The 2003 unemployment rates have not yet been revised.

[46] Current labour statistics in the Republic of Moldova should be treated with some caution, as the National Statistical Office recently reported difficulties in properly assessing performance in the labour markets. The main problem may be related to unreliable population/labour force statistics, which do not take into account mass emigration from the country, the scale of which is variously estimated at between one quarter and one fifth of the labour force. The last census was held in 1989, before independence, and the

government had to postpone the 2003 census for cost reasons. A new census might clarify the real scale of emigration and so allow a better assessment of labour market developments.

[47] Thus, in the Republic of Moldova, according to registration data, unemployment fell in the 12 months to March 2004 (from 2.2 to 2 per cent of the labour force). But according to the most recent labour force survey, it rose by 1.5 percentage points to 11.3 per cent in the first quarter, compared with 9.8 per cent a year earlier.

[48] Among the main reasons for this are the low unemployment benefits (often paid in arrears), and the inefficiency of local labour offices. For a more detailed discussion see UNECE, *Economic Survey of Europe, 2003 No. 1,* pp. 197-198.

[49] WTO, *Recent Trends in International Trade and Policy Developments,* Press/378, 11 June 2004 and UNECE secretariat estimates.

Led by a surge in Polish and Slovak exports, the year-on-year export growth of the new EU member countries combined was particularly strong in the last quarter of 2003, but it weakened slightly in the first three months of 2004.[50] Export revenues soared in dollar terms in 2003, due in part to the considerable depreciation of the dollar, whereas in euros they were much more in line with the growth of export volume (table 1.2.17 and chart 1.2.14).[51] Shipments from central Europe and the Baltic countries to all major markets rose strongly (table 1.2.18). Their share of extra-Community imports into the EU-15 exceeded 12 per cent in the first months of 2004.[52] An increased presence on non-EU markets was also evident: the largest increase was of central European exports to developed economies other than the EU, a reflection of the stronger economic recovery in those markets. A perceptible improvement in cost competitiveness over the last year in a number of central European and Baltic countries, as suggested by changes in their real effective exchange rates based on unit labour costs (chart 1.2.15), also supported their export performance. Much of the export growth in the new EU member countries is associated with foreign direct investment: firms with foreign participation accounted for the bulk of the increase in exports from the Czech Republic, Hungary and Slovakia and played an important role in Estonia and Poland.[53]

The acceleration of the growth in import volumes in the first quarter of 2004 was prompted by the generally robust growth of domestic demand in the central European and Baltic countries, but it was also partly driven by the exporting sectors' needs for raw materials, and for intermediate and capital goods. In addition, there was a one-off effect of stockpiling in anticipation of changes in administrative rules and customs duties upon accession to the EU on 1 May 2004.[54] These increases are clearly reflected in a surge in the volumes of imports of consumer and capital goods coming from non-EU markets.[55] The lower prices of manufactured goods from these markets, mainly due to the depreciation of the dollar since the beginning of 2003, also stimulated demand.[56] The impact of the recent rise in world commodity prices on import expenditures was still subdued in the first quarter of 2004; the value of total imports in fact increased somewhat less than exports (except in Latvia, Lithuania and Poland, table 1.2.17 and chart 1.2.14). Although this was not sufficient to reduce the trade deficits of the new EU members in dollar terms, in euros and in relation to GDP, the outcome was more positive.

The merchandise trade of the new EU member countries is expected to continue to grow rapidly in 2004. Trading under the internal EU market rules offers new opportunities and challenges, in particular for small- and medium-size exporters and those trading in agricultural goods.[57] According to the European Commission, the new members could increase their sales on the internal EU market by about one third, and quite rapidly.[58] Strong import demand from outside the EU should also support their exports. Imports, too, are likely to expand if exports rise and domestic demand remains strong. But, if oil and other commodity prices on the world markets remain high until the end of 2004, the negative impact on the merchandise trade balance of

---

[50] The exceptions were Cyprus and Malta, where exports declined or stagnated in real terms.

[51] Average export prices expressed in euros in fact declined in the majority of these countries in 2003 and in early 2004, although exporters from the three Baltic countries, Slovakia and Slovenia were able to command on average slightly higher export prices in the first quarter of 2004. These price developments were in part an outcome of changes in world commodity prices (table 1.1.1) and exchange rate movements, which in some cases also exerted downward pressure on export prices for manufactured goods.

[52] From 1 May 2004, these exports came under the internal market regulations of the enlarged EU, which led to a further reduction in trade barriers within the EU-25. According to Eurostat, the changeover from 15 to 25 member states was supposed to increase intra-Community trade by about 16 per cent, increasing the intra/extra trade ratios up to 206 per cent for exports and 184 per cent for imports. The figures for EU-15 were 161 per cent and 151 per cent, respectively, in 2002. In trade with the rest of the world the EU-25 remains the leading exporter and second biggest importer, although the absolute levels of these trade flows are lower than those for the EU-15. Eurostat, "Trade in a 25-member European Union", *Statistics in Focus*, Theme 6, No. 4, 2003 and Eurostat, Comext, *Intra- and Extra-EU Trade*, CD-ROM No. 6, 2004.

[53] However, in some instances the concentration of multinational companies in one or two industrial sectors of a country makes its export revenues dependent on a narrow range of goods, thus increasing its vulnerability to the risk of global demand shocks in one of these sectors (the automotive sector in Slovakia, for example).

[54] Large increases in imports from east Asian countries are a good indicator. In some cases, the EU import regime is less favourable than that secured by central European and Baltic countries under bilateral trade agreements, which were cancelled upon accession to the EU.

[55] Machinery and equipment imports were among the fastest growing segments in general: the business sector of the new EU member countries was investing in machines not only to meet growing foreign demand but also to meet the strict conditions set by the EU for the equipment of production facilities, particularly in the agricultural products and food sectors.

[56] In 2003, export dollar unit values for manufactured goods were on average 13 per cent higher than in the previous year in the EU and remained unchanged in the United States. Expressed in euros, they were lower by 6 and 17 per cent, respectively. United Nations, *Monthly Bulletin of Statistics*, May 2004.

[57] According to EBRD estimates, the new EU members from central Europe and the Baltic countries faced relatively high rates of EU-15 protection prior to accession, the agricultural sector being the most significant. EBRD, *Transition Report 2003* (London), p. 81.

[58] Commission of the European Communities, *Report on the Implementation of the Internal Market Strategy (2003-2006)*, COM(2004) 22 final (Brussels), 21 January 2004, p. 8.

TABLE 1.2.17

International trade and external balances of the east European and CIS economies, 2002-2004

(Rates of change and ratio, per cent)

	Merchandise exports in dollars (growth rates)			Merchandise imports in dollars (growth rates)			Trade balance (per cent of GDP)			Current account (million dollars)			Current account (per cent of GDP)		
	2002	2003	2004[a] Jan.-Mar.	2002	2003	2004[a] Jan.-Mar.	2002	2003	2004[a] Jan.-Mar.	2002	2003	2004 Jan.-Mar.	2002	2003	2004[a] Jan.-Mar.
New EU members	13.5	29.1	27.5	11.1	26.1	26.8	-7.5	-7.1	-6.7	-18 133	-21 202	-5 014*	-4.3	-4.3	-3.8*
Cyprus	-13.8	9.3	14.4	3.2	9.8	24.5	-32.0	-27.8	-26.9	-517	-282	..	-5.1	-2.2	..
Czech Republic	15.2	26.6	25.6	11.7	25.9	24.4	-3.0	-2.9	-0.2	-4 166	-5 570	-637	-5.6	-6.2	-2.6
Estonia	3.6	31.6	39.5	11.3	35.4	28.3	-19.2	-21.6	-18.8	-716	-1 199	-276	-10.2	-13.2	-10.9
Hungary	12.6	23.7	30.3	11.7	26.4	28.8	-5.0	-6.1	-4.9	-4 675	-7 357	-2 128	-7.2	-8.9	-9.3
Latvia	13.9	26.2	34.3	15.2	28.9	35.6	-19.1	-21.2	-20.9	-647	-956	-252	-7.0	-8.7	-8.4
Lithuania	20.4	30.7	26.5	22.3	26.1	29.8	-16.0	-14.2	-13.2	-734	-1 218	-429	-5.2	-6.7	-9.0
Malta	13.2	11.1	22.0	4.0	19.8	16.7	-14.8	-18.3	-18.7	-4.6	-271	-172	-1.2	-6.0	-14.6*
Poland	13.6	30.6	22.7	9.6	23.4	25.5	-7.4	-6.9	-8.4	-5 007	-4 085	-864	-2.6	-2.0	-1.6
Slovakia	14.0	51.7	37.6	13.2	35.9	33.4	-8.9	-2.0	-0.1	-1 939	-280	135	-8.0	-0.9	1.4
Slovenia	11.6	23.3	26.0	7.4	26.7	23.5	-2.6	-3.9	-3.4	314	15	60	1.4	0.1	0.8
South-east Europe	14.4	28.5	27.0	19.7	31.9	37.1	-12.0	-12.9	-13.9	-10 049	-18 533	-9 030*	-3.4	-4.9	-9.3*
Albania	8.2	35.2	..	13.1	24.1	..	-23.9	-23.1	..	-407	-407	..	-8.4	-6.7	..
Bosnia and Herzegovina	-2.5	42.5	46.7	12.0	20.6	25.5	-37.4	-34.0	-26.4	-1 750	-2 096	..	-32.0	-31.0	..
Bulgaria	11.3	30.7	25.6	8.9	35.9	38.2	-14.2	-16.6	-17.0	-827	-1 666	-617	-5.3	-8.4	-12.0
Croatia	5.1	25.7	23.6	17.2	32.4	23.2	-26.0	-23.8	-23.9	-1 916	-2 039	-1 464	-8.5	-7.2	-18.9
Romania	21.8	27.0	33.6	14.8	34.4	37.1	-8.7	-11.2	-10.2	-1 535	-3 254	-337	-3.4	-5.7	-2.7
Serbia and Montenegro [b]	19.5	11.5	18.0	30.7	18.8	40.8	-25.8	-25.5	-27.0	-1 731	-1 943	-869	-11.0	-10.0	-14.7
The former Yugoslav Republic of Macedonia	-15.7	22.2	22.1	-4.7	15.3	13.8	-23.4	-20.1	-18.7	-362	-278	-139	-9.6	-6.0	-10.5
Turkey	15.1	30.0	25.5	24.5	33.3	40.7	-8.5	-9.2	-11.8	-1 522	-6 850	-5 204	-0.8	-2.9	-8.5
CIS	6.0	23.8	23.0	9.8	23.9	32.7	10.6	10.7	15.2	30 279*	36 993*	13 948*	6.5*	6.5*	8.8*
Armenia	47.8	34.2	14.3	12.5	28.6	9.5	-20.4	-21.1	-33.9	-148	-187	-63	-6.3	-6.7	-16.6
Azerbaijan	-6.3	19.6	2.9	16.4	57.7	48.4	8.0	-0.5	0.8	-768	-2 021	-738	-12.3	-28.3	-42.2
Belarus	7.7	24.2	26.7	11.2	26.5	21.5	-7.3	-8.8	-3.5	-337	-505	..	-2.3	-2.9	..
Georgia	8.7	27.7	34.1	6.8	44.6	45.5	-11.3	-15.5	-22.4	-231	-392	..	-6.8	-9.8	..
Kazakhstan	11.9	33.4	27.0	2.1	26.5	58.0	12.5	15.4	20.2	-866	-69	..	-3.5	-0.2	..
Kyrgyzstan	2.0	19.8	30.8	25.6	22.1	56.2	-6.3	-7.0	-11.2	-35	-31	..	-2.2	-1.6	..
Republic of Moldova	13.3	22.7	36.1	16.3	35.1	35.3	-23.7	-31.3	-24.6	-93	-149	..	-5.6	-7.6	..
Russian Federation	5.2	25.7	19.2	13.5	24.1	28.5	13.4	13.7	17.4	29 116	35 905	12 094	8.4	8.3	9.6
Tajikistan	13.1	8.3	34.5	4.8	22.3	43.6	1.4	-5.4	-6.1	-15	..	..	-1.2	..	..
Turkmenistan	-0.2	20.8	13.4	-21.0	20.8	26.9	6.2	6.1	14.2	..	..	..	..	..	..
Ukraine	10.4	28.5	45.2	7.6	35.6	39.2	2.3	0.1	7.5	3 173	2 891	..	7.5	5.8	..
Uzbekistan	-5.7	..	..	-13.5	..	..	2.8	..	..	..	..	..	..	..	..
Memorandum items:															
EU-25 (extra-EU trade)	6.2	17.4	22.6	0.9	17.9	16.5	-0.1	-0.1	-0.1	..	..	..	..	..	..
Baltic states	13.5	30.0	31.9	17.2	29.5	30.7	-17.7	-18.0	-16.8	-2 097	-3 373	-957	-6.9	-8.8	-9.2
Central Europe	13.7	29.5	27.3	10.8	26.2	26.7	-5.9	-5.4	-5.0	-15 473	-17 276	-3 045	-4.1	-3.9	-2.6
South-east Europe-7	13.6	26.6	29.0	14.9	30.3	33.0	-17.7	-19.2	-17.4	-8 527	-11 683	-3 661	-7.5	-8.2	-10.0
CIS without Russian Federation	7.8	19.2	31.9	5.0	23.5	37.2	2.7	1.4	6.8	1 163*	1 088*	..	1.0*	0.8*	..
Caucasian CIS	1.5	23.0	7.3	13.1	46.4	37.1	-3.0	-8.9	-10.9	-1 147	-2 599	..	-9.6	-18.7	..
Central Asian CIS	6.1	5.7	24.4	-4.8	-2.4	50.4	8.2	9.3	14.5	-434*	1 450*	..	-0.9*	2.5*	..
Three European CIS	9.6	27.1	39.4	9.1	32.5	33.1	-0.8	-3.0	3.7	2 744	2 237	..	4.7	3.2	..

Source: UNECE secretariat calculations, based on national statistics and direct communications from national statistical offices.

Note: Foreign trade growth is measured in current dollar values. Trade balances are related to GDP at current prices, converted from national currencies at current dollar exchange rates. GDP values in some cases are estimated from reported real growth rates and consumer price indices. For country groups see tables 1.2.18 and 1.3.2.

[a] Aggregates are weighted averages for countries listed below. Growth rates over the same period of the previous year.

[b] Merchandise trade data for January-March 2004 and current account figures starting from 2002 refer to Serbia only.

some of these countries could be substantial. Maintaining and strengthening the competitiveness of the export sector (rising productivity, low unit labour costs) and containing the booming import demand for consumer goods are therefore important challenges for policy makers (see section (v) below).

Services contribute to a narrowing of their current account deficits in euros

The general widening of merchandise trade deficits in 2003 led to a general increase in the current account deficits of the EU acceding countries in 2003. In the first quarter of 2004, however, the increased surplus on

CHART 1.2.14

Merchandise trade flows and balances in the new EU member countries and south-east Europe, January 2001-April 2004
(Trade balance to GDP ratios and year-on-year indices of exports and imports in per cent)

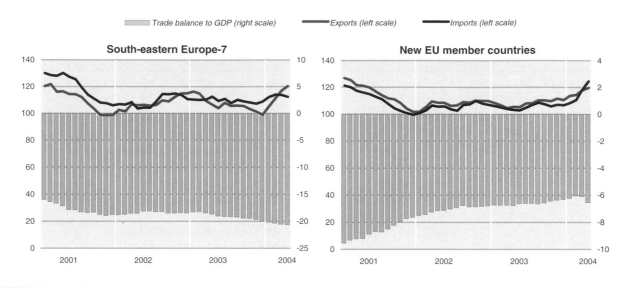

Source: UNECE secretariat calculations, based on national statistics.
Note: Merchandise trade balances cumulated over 12 months. Indices based on three-month moving averages for values of exports and imports expressed in euros.

services in most new EU member countries helped to improve their current accounts in both absolute terms and relative to GDP (table 1.2.17). Their aggregate surplus from trade in services increased by a third compared with the same period of 2003, mainly because of a surge in exports of services other than travel and transport. The balances on investment income worsened in a number of countries due to increases in reinvested earnings, among other factors. The balances of transfers also deteriorated owing mainly to lower workers' remittances and the ending of foreign assistance funds, particularly those related to the relief of flood damage experienced in central Europe in 2002.

There was a shift towards a more balanced structure of the financing of current account deficits in the first quarter of 2004 compared with the previous year: net inflows of FDI started to recover after a slump in the second half of 2003 while portfolio investment increased considerably, particularly in the Czech Republic, Hungary and Poland. FDI had been the leading source of external financing in the region for most of the pre-accession period, but in 2003 its role in financing the current account deficit diminished, particularly in Hungary. This decline was largely offset by increased borrowing abroad (Estonia and Hungary) and larger inflows of portfolio investments and other short-term capital.

The growth of south-east European imports again outstrips exports...

South-east European export growth generally accelerated (in euro terms) in the first quarter of 2004, after a dip during the second half of 2003 in some of these countries (chart 1.2.14). The exceptions were

Bulgaria and Turkey, where exports grew strongly but on a decelerating path in the first months of 2004 compared with the same period of 2003. Foreign direct investment and the outsourcing of activities by companies in the EU and other developed countries increased exports from the four EU candidate countries (Bulgaria, Croatia, Romania and Turkey). Increased productivity, lower labour costs, cheaper trade financing and, in some instances, notably Turkey, improved export prices also helped. In Croatia, however, the steady appreciation of the currency in real effective terms since 2002 reduced the profit margins of exporters. A gradual improvement in regional cooperation, and improved access to the EU market under the EU sponsored Stabilization and Association Process, supported exports in the rest of the region.[59] Intraregional trade flows in south-east Europe have increased considerably in the past few years (table 1.2.18). However, the export capacities of these countries remain limited, due in part to insufficient restructuring, poor infrastructure, restricted access to financing and ongoing ethnic conflicts in some of them.[60]

_____

[59] Since signing a Memorandum of Understanding on Trade Liberalization and Facilitation in June 2001, Albania, Bosnia and Herzegovina, Bulgaria, Croatia, the Republic of Moldova, Romania, Serbia and Montenegro and The former Yugoslav Republic of Macedonia have developed a network of bilateral free trade agreements covering about 90 per cent of their mutual trade. However, the implementation of these agreements remains unsatisfactory and has been disrupted by frequent disputes and holdups.

[60] In fact, the merchandise trade (exports + imports) to GDP ratio in these small economies is very low: in 2003 it was below 40 per cent in Albania, some 52 per cent in Serbia and Montenegro (where it

TABLE 1.2.18

International trade of eastern Europe and the Russian Federation by direction, 2002-2004

(Value in billion dollars, growth rates in per cent)[a]

	Exports				Imports			
	Value	Growth rates			Value	Growth rates		
	2003	2002	2003	2004[b]	2002	2001	2002	2004[b]
Baltic states, *to and from:*								
World	14.6	13.5	30.0	31.9	21.5	17.2	29.5	30.7
European Union-25	10.4	10.6	25.4	33.0	13.7	19.8	27.4	31.8
Extra-European Union	4.2	22.4	43.4	29.3	7.8	12.7	33.2	29.1
CIS	1.8	15.2	20.8	25.8	4.2	6.7	37.8	22.4
South-east Europe	0.2	44.8	42.3	95.5	0.2	35.9	30.2	57.1
Developed market economies	1.9	41.5	104.8	28.6	1.7	21.6	31.3	25.7
Developing countries (residual)	0.4	9.0	-12.3	25.2	1.7	16.9	25.2	47.9
Central Europe, *to and from:*								
World	179.5	13.7	29.5	27.3	203.3	10.8	26.2	26.7
European Union-25	146.5	13.2	29.6	26.0	140.8	9.5	25.8	26.7
Extra-European Union	33.0	15.8	28.9	32.0	62.5	13.9	27.4	26.5
CIS	7.7	9.7	29.7	29.4	17.2	3.1	23.3	9.4
South-east Europe	8.2	29.5	30.9	29.8	4.3	24.3	39.2	26.6
Developed market economies	10.9	15.1	31.4	44.4	16.8	6.9	21.8	33.0
Developing countries (residual)	6.2	9.6	21.3	28.9	24.2	28.8	32.7	31.9
South-east Europe, *to and from:*								
World	83.5	14.4	28.5	27.0	132.7	19.6	32.0	37.1
European Union-25	50.2	13.3	31.0	28.9	74.3	18.8	33.1	39.1
Extra-European Union	33.3	16.1	24.9	24.2	58.4	20.5	30.5	34.8
CIS	3.5	0.2	27.9	33.5	14.0	8.9	31.3	44.3
South-east Europe	7.4	15.6	39.0	47.8	6.8	19.1	39.0	45.6
Developed market economies	7.8	12.0	9.3	8.1	13.7	8.8	19.4	34.7
Developing countries (residual)	14.7	23.5	27.4	20.3	23.9	37.4	34.8	26.6
Russian Federation, *to and from:*								
World	133.5	6.2	25.7	19.2	57.3	10.2	24.1	28.5
Intra-CIS	20.4	6.8	31.0	31.9	13.2	-8.7	28.6	31.0
Non-CIS countries	113.0	6.1	24.8	17.2	44.1	17.1	22.8	27.8
European Union-25	67.9	0.4	28.4	..	26.5	19.2	22.3	..
South cast Europe	7.5	5.3	34.7	..	1.4	19.5	24.8	..
Developed market economies	13.2	24.0	4.2	..	6.5	-0.9	22.5	..
Developing countries (residual)	24.4	13.1	25.7	..	9.8	25.9	24.2	..

Source: National statistics and direct communications from national statistical offices to UNECE secretariat; State Customs Committee data for the Russian Federation.

Note: Country groups shown are: Baltic states – Estonia, Latvia and Lithuania; central Europe – the Czech Republic, Hungary, Poland, Slovakia and Slovenia; south-east Europe – Albania, Bosnia and Herzegovina, Bulgaria, Croatia, Romania, Serbia and Montenegro, The former Yugoslav Republic of Macedonia and Turkey.

a Growth rates are calculated on values expressed in dollars.

b January-March 2004 over same period of 2003.

The import boom in south-east Europe in the first quarter of 2004 was generated by the generally robust growth of domestic demand and by export sector purchases of intermediate and capital goods, particularly in the four EU candidate countries. In the latter, imports of capital goods accelerated sharply, reflecting improved market confidence and favourable expectations. The appreciation of the real exchange rate in these countries also supported the rise in imports (for exchange rate developments in Bulgaria, Croatia and Romania, see chart 1.2.15). In the remaining four south-east European economies, imports of oil and oil derivatives, road

vehicles, textile products and machinery (in order of importance) predominated, indicating an upturn of private consumption and probably some recovery of industrial activity in Albania and Bosnia and Herzegovina.[61] In The former Yugoslav Republic of Macedonia, in contrast, the current slump in industrial activity was clearly reflected in the decline of real imports in the first quarter of 2004.[62] Merchandise trade deficits, in dollars, compared with the

---

had shrunk by 3 percentage points from the 2002 level), 65 per cent in Bosnia and Herzegovina and 78 per cent in The former Yugoslav Republic of Macedonia (where it had also declined by 4 percentage points from 2002).

---

[61] For Albania, this assessment is based on UNECE secretariat estimates, as the first quarter foreign trade data were not available at the time of writing this *Survey*.

[62] Since the beginning of 2004, there have been major disruptions in the operations of two important Macedonian companies (the lead and zinc smelter in Veles and the Balkan Steel company; in the latter it was due to difficulties in raising credit to finance working capital). *South East European Newswire*, 3 June 2004.

CHART 1.2.15

Real effective exchange rates in selected east European economies, 2000-2004

(Indices, first quarter 2000=100)

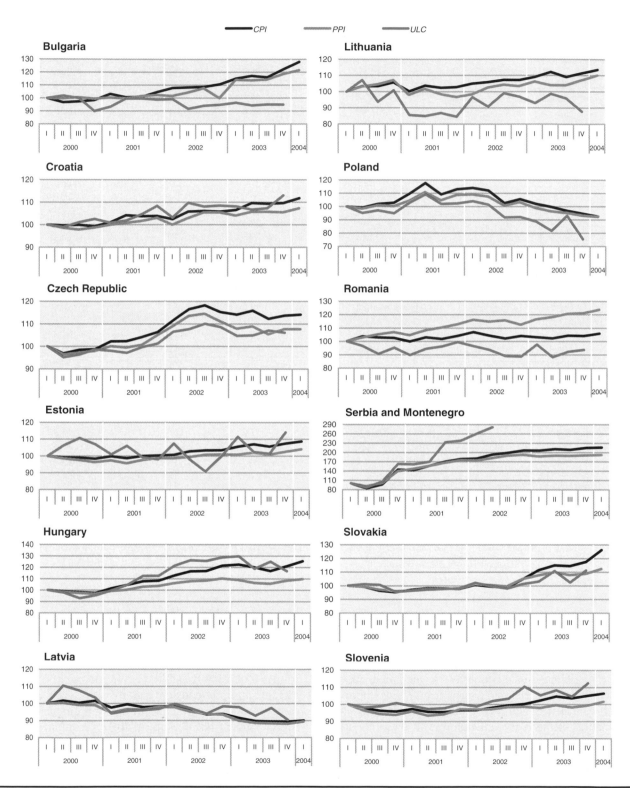

Source: National statistics; UNECE Common Database.

Note: The real effective exchange rates were computed from the nominal exchange rates against the euro and the dollar, deflated respectively by the domestic and European Union or United States consumer and producer price indices, and by indices of estimated unit labour costs in industry, while the shares of the EU and the rest of the world in total exports of individual transition economies were used to determine the euro and the dollar trade weights, respectively. An increase in the index denotes a real appreciation and vice versa.

first quarter of 2003, increased in all the south-east European economies, but in relation to GDP the deficit was noticeably higher only in Serbia and Montenegro (table 1.2.17).

...and their current account deficits are set to widen further

In aggregate, the south-east European region's current account deficit rose by $3.7 billion in the first quarter of 2004, year-on-year, to $9 billion. The gap also increased perceptibly in relation to GDP (table 1.2.17). Only in Romania and Turkey are current-account-to-GDP ratios in the range of 3 to 8 per cent; for all the others the ratios are in double digits, and in many cases present a major concern for policy makers. The recent developments in world commodity prices may drive up their import bills still further – in general, energy and food account for more than a quarter of their imports – and so enlarge their current account deficits.

In general, increased surpluses of services – net receipts on both the travel and transport accounts increased noticeably – have offset part of the deficit in merchandise trade. (The largest increase in net income from tourism was in Turkey, although this partly reflects a recovery from a low base-year income due to the Iraq war.) Net transfers (largely workers' remittances and financial assistance) also increased rapidly, particularly in Turkey and Romania, where they helped to offset a large part of the increase in the trade deficit.

The financing of current account deficits has not posed major problems for the four EU candidate countries, where there were increased inflows of net FDI and portfolio investments in the first quarter of 2004. FDI inflows (mainly privatization related) also increased considerably in the other south-east European economies, but at some 3 to 6 per cent of GDP they were too small to offset the rise in the overall deficits. These countries therefore had to raise additional loans, mostly from international financial organizations, which in turn may exacerbate the current account financing problems in the future.[63]

Attracting investors from abroad and improving the capacity to absorb foreign capital constitutes a major challenge for policy makers in the south-east European countries. Structural and institutional impediments, as well as inconsistent policies, still block progress in this respect; hence the urgent need for adequate medium- to long-term economic reform programmes. The prospect of EU membership and improved intraregional cooperation are of great importance as well, not least because they may help to support such programmes.

In the CIS commodities contribute to increased exports

In the first three months of 2004, the dollar value of total merchandise exports from the CIS increased by about a quarter, year-on-year, largely reflecting higher commodity prices (table 1.2.17).[64] The continuing economic recovery in the CIS countries and the strong demand for consumer and investment goods, together with exchange rate appreciations in real terms against the dollar throughout the region, led to greater imports from non-CIS countries.[65] Increased intra-CIS trade – up by a third in value – also contributed to the higher dollar value of total imports (table 1.2.19).

In the four largest CIS economies, Belarus, Kazakhstan, Russia and Ukraine, commodity price increases were accompanied by increased export volumes in the first quarter of 2004. Russian oil producers boosted their export revenues by increasing the volume of crude oil and oil products shipped, while the volume of natural gas exports was roughly flat. The value of machinery and equipment exports surged by more than a quarter supported by rapid economic growth in the region. In Ukraine, the very large increase in the dollar value of its exports reflected foreign demand for steel products and chemicals. The steel and chemicals sectors, accounting for almost half of Ukraine's export earnings, in the first quarter of 2004 exported 40 and 50 per cent more, respectively, in value compared with the first three months of 2003. Exports of machinery and equipment from Ukraine almost doubled in value on the strength of Russia's surging import demand. Similarly in Kazakhstan, crude oil and steel producers increased production and export volumes. The volume of oil exports rose by 16 per cent and that of various steel products by up to 15 per cent. In Belarus, the value of exports increased by a quarter and was broadly based on a range of major export items such as machinery and equipment, transport equipment, food and ferrous metals. As in the past, the increase was driven by greater import demand in Russia, Belarus' dominant trade partner, accounting for about half of its total exports.

In the Republic of Moldova, the rapid growth of exports was driven by sales of food and beverages to its traditional markets within the CIS. A good harvest in 2003 facilitated a 26 per cent increase in sales of food and wine as well as a 61 per cent increase in exports of fruit and vegetable products. These sectors account for over half of Moldova's exports. Exports of textiles – the second largest commodity group, largely going to the EU – also continued to expand.

_____

[63] For a more detailed account of external financing and FDI issues in south-east Europe see UNECE, *Economic Survey of Europe, 2004 No. 1.*

_____

[64] In comparison with the first quarter of 2003, prices of key natural resource exportables such as crude oil and natural gas were higher by 2 and 8 per cent, respectively, while prices for aluminium, copper and nickel increased by 18, 64 and 49 per cent, respectively. Gold and cotton prices also registered significant increases (16 and 26 per cent, respectively).

[65] In many countries, however, domestic currencies depreciated in real terms against the euro except in Kazakhstan, the Republic of Moldova and Russia. This may have dampened their demand for goods traded in euros. The values of aggregate CIS exports and imports in euros increased by 6 and 14 per cent, respectively.

TABLE 1.2.19

International trade of the CIS, 2002-2004

(Value in million dollars, growth rates in per cent)

	Export growth		Import growth		Trade balances		
	2003	2004ª	2003	2004ª	2002	2003	2004ª
Armenia	34.2	14.3	28.6	9.5	-482.0	-591.4	-129.4
CIS	31.6	5.0	2.6	-32.1	-205.5	-183.0	-25.8
Non-CIS	34.8	16.6	40.0	27.9	-276.5	-408.4	-103.6
Azerbaijan	19.6	2.9	57.7	48.4	501.9	-34.2	14.1
CIS	37.0	50.4	30.8	42.2	-406.9	-516.8	-172.6
Non-CIS	17.4	-1.5	74.9	52.5	908.8	482.6	186.7
Belarus	24.2	26.7	26.5	21.5	-1 071.4	-1 540.6	-148.4
CIS	24.4	35.8	27.2	21.0	-1 910.9	-2 552.7	-686.2
Non-CIS	24.0	18.1	25.1	22.7	839.5	1 012.1	537.8
Georgia	27.7	34.1	44.6	45.5	-383.6	-613.7	-229.9
CIS	27.0	43.6	23.5	51.8	-121.0	-143.4	-85.4
Non-CIS	28.3	28.8	58.5	41.9	-262.6	-470.3	-144.5
Kazakhstan	33.4	27.0	26.5	58.0	3 086.3	4 573.5	1 568.8
CIS	34.6	50.4	28.8	60.9	-848.8	-965.6	-313.0
Non-CIS	33.0	21.6	24.5	55.3	3 935.1	5 539.1	1 881.8
Kyrgyzstan	19.8	30.8	22.1	56.2	-101.2	-134.8	-39.8
CIS	19.4	37.9	27.1	78.9	-153.8	-208.6	-65.1
Non-CIS	20.0	27.3	16.0	30.3	52.6	73.8	25.3
Republic of Moldova	22.7	36.1	35.1	35.3	-394.7	-612.4	-106.9
CIS	20.9	38.6	45.1	36.3	-58.5	-169.8	-35.7
Non-CIS	25.0	33.6	28.5	34.6	-336.2	-442.6	-71.2
Tajikistan	8.3	34.5	22.3	43.6	16.5	-83.4	-29.5
CIS	-26.3	10.1	9.5	42.1	-359.1	-460.6	-152.8
Non-CIS	20.1	40.1	62.9	47.4	375.6	377.2	123.3
Turkmenistan	20.8	13.4	20.8	26.9	759.1	917.9	492.0
CIS	0.8	3.6	-0.5	3.5	684.4	700.0	250.2
Non-CIS	45.2	22.8	35.3	48.9	74.7	217.9	241.8
Ukraine	28.5	45.2	35.6	39.2	980.3	59.2	857.2
CIS	38.2	49.9	28.3	35.4	-4 590.8	-5 460.1	-1 845.5
Non-CIS	25.4	43.9	43.8	44.3	5 571.1	5 519.3	2 702.7
Uzbekistan	..	..	..	..	..	..	..
CIS	..	..	..	..	..	..	..
Non-CIS	..	..	..	..	..	..	..
Total above	27.4	31.9	31.8	37.2	2 911.2	1 940.2	2 248.2
CIS	27.4	38.2	26.5	33.2	-7 970.9	-9 960.6	-3 131.9
Non-CIS	27.4	29.5	38.0	42.6	10 882.1	11 900.7	5 380.1
Russian Federation	25.7	19.2	24.1	28.5	60 001.3	76 186.9	21 835.1
CIS	31.0	31.9	28.6	31.0	5 376.3	7 293.2	2 353.7
Non-CIS	24.8	17.2	22.8	27.8	54 625.0	68 893.7	19 481.4
CIS total	26.2	23.0	27.7	32.7	62 912.5	78 127.1	24 083.3
CIS	29.3	34.7	27.2	32.5	-2 594.6	2 667.4	-778.2
Non-CIS	25.4	20.3	28.0	32.8	65 507.1	80 794.4	24 861.5

Source: CIS Statistical Committee (Moscow), except for Turkmenistan – Dow Jones Reuters Business Interactive (Factiva).

ª January-March.

In the Caucasian region, Armenian exports of processed precious stones and metals to Belgium and Israel have continued to underpin the overall increase in exports. These two countries take about a third of all Armenian exports. Georgia's exports rose by a third mainly owing to higher prices for its shipments of metals such as copper and steel to Turkey and wine and beverages to Russia. The value of Azerbaijan's exports – over 80 per cent dependent on oil – was slightly up on

unchanged shipments of crude oil and refined products. A good agricultural harvest in 2003, however, boosted exports of processed foods (most of which went to Russia).

In central Asia, exports from Kyrgyzstan shifted towards traditional CIS markets: this reflected lower gold sales to non-CIS markets and much increased exports of agricultural products to CIS markets. In Tajikistan, higher prices for its two key exports – aluminium and textiles (including cotton fibre), which account for the bulk of its exports – boosted the total value of exports by a third. Exports of electricity, the third most important export, also increased substantially. In Turkmenistan, where the official data remain scant and their reliability questionable, the total value of exports is reported to have increased by 13 per cent due to an increase in the volume of natural gas exports.

High economic growth in the CIS region stimulates imports

The dollar value of total CIS merchandise imports increased by a third in the first quarter of 2004, year-on-year, on the strength of the continuing output growth in the region. The increases ranged from 22 per cent in Belarus to 58 per cent in Kazakhstan. Russian imports continued to be driven by domestic investment and consumption. In the first three months of 2004, year-on-year, imports of machinery and equipment rose by almost a half and capital goods are expected to continue to be the most important component of Russian imports. In other countries, the modernization of the existing capital stock and investment in new productive capacity have also contributed to increased imports. In Azerbaijan imports increased by almost a half as a consequence of the expansion of the pipeline infrastructure and further exploration and development of the country's oil and natural gas fields. Similarly, in Georgia, increased purchases of pipe and other capital imports for the construction of a pipeline contributed to a 50 per cent rise in the value of imports. In Kazakhstan imports of machinery, equipment and transportation vehicles increased by about 40 per cent and represented almost a quarter of total imports. In other countries, the increased dollar value of imports reflected more the higher prices for crude oil and natural gas. For example, the rise in Belarusian imports partly reflects a sharp increase in contract prices for imports of energy resources. Similarly, Tajikistan imported 30 per cent more mineral products (mostly crude oil) in value terms. Rising prices for mineral products also had a significant impact on the value of imports into Kyrgyzstan, the Republic of Moldova and Ukraine.

WTO membership continues to present a major challenge for the majority of the CIS countries. Of the eight remaining non-WTO members from the CIS, only Turkmenistan has not applied for membership.[66] The

_____

[66] The current WTO members from the CIS region are Armenia, Georgia, Kyrgyzstan and the Republic of Moldova.

others are at various stages of the accession process. Azerbaijan and Uzbekistan are at the early stages of document submissions, while others are negotiating goods and services schedules and market access issues.[67]

Most commodity exporting CIS countries increase their current account surpluses

In the first three months of 2004, the combined current account surplus of the CIS countries continued to rise reaching more than $14 billion (table 1.2.17). According to the preliminary balance of payments statistics, Belarus, Kazakhstan, the Republic of Moldova, Russia, Turkmenistan, Ukraine and Uzbekistan all had surpluses in the first three months of 2004. While the 6 per cent increase in the combined current account surplus represents a much lower rate of increase than that between the first quarters of 2002 and 2003, when it almost doubled, the continued strength of commodity prices ensured solid, and in many cases rising, surpluses in the natural resource exporting CIS countries. Only in Kazakhstan, despite rising volumes and prices of commodities, did the current account surplus, while still substantial, decline relative to the first quarter of 2003.

In those CIS countries with current account deficits (namely, those that are either not endowed with natural resources or are heavily engaged in upgrading their capital base with imported capital goods), there was no problem in financing them. In particular, FDI has remained a major source of finance for many CIS countries. Thus, in Azerbaijan, with the largest current account deficit in the region (42 per cent of GDP for the January-March 2004 period) FDI inflows amounted to 57 per cent of GDP and investment outlays increased by 71 per cent, year-on-year. The CIS region, in aggregate, attracted FDI inflows of almost $5 billion during the first three months of 2004 with Russia and Azerbaijan accounting for 80 per cent of the total.

Russia accounted for over half of the aggregate current account surplus of the CIS in the first quarter of 2004. The country's surplus was equivalent to some 10 per cent of GDP and largely reflects the rising revenue from crude oil and natural gas exports, which more than offset the steady growth in imports of goods and services. In general imports have been boosted by the rapid growth of domestic demand for investment and consumer goods and the real effective appreciation of the rouble.

(v) Macroeconomic policy

Monetary policy remains very accommodative in the United States...

In the United States, the stance of monetary policy remained very accommodative in the first half of 2004. The target for the federal funds rate had been fixed at 1

per cent since late June 2003, when it was reduced by a quarter of a percentage point. Short-term economic prospects at that time were rather uncertain and there was still concern at the lingering risks of (moderate) deflation. Against that background, the Federal Reserve wanted to provide additional support to economic activity and to seek greater "insurance against a further substantial drop in inflation, however unlikely".[68] The setting for monetary policy started to change in the second half of 2003, when the recovery was gaining strong momentum. But against persistent labour market weakness in early 2004, the FOMC reassured financial markets that it would be "patient in removing its policy accommodation".[69] In May 2004, with more evidence confirming sustained strong output growth, a pick-up in hiring and a moderate rise in inflation, the FOMC started to prepare markets for a reversal of the sharp fall in interest rates since mid-2001 by noting that "policy accommodation can be removed at a pace that is likely to be measured".[70] Expectations in financial markets were for the FOMC to start raising interest rates at the end of June 2004. Against this background, short-term interest rates in money markets were already rising somewhat in May 2004, a trend that continued into June (chart 1.2.16). In fact the Federal Reserve did raise its target for the Federal Funds Rate by one quarter of a percentage point, to 1.25 per cent, on 30 June. This is a key turning point for monetary policy in the United States and, indeed, the global economy. But real short-term interest rates have remained negative. The rise in energy prices and the risk of rising inflationary expectations associated with higher levels of resource utilization have led the monetary authorities to signal that they are prepared to raise interest rates at a more rapid pace than currently expected should inflationary pressures endanger the goal of price stability.[71]

The monetary policy stimulus was amplified in 2003 by a substantial real effective depreciation of the dollar, which began in early 2002. In the first half of 2004, however, the depreciation of the real exchange rate (which is a traditional measure of price competitiveness) was partly reversed. In May 2004, the dollar had appreciated in real effective terms by some 4 per cent compared with January, but it was still nearly 10 per cent below its peak of February 2002 (chart 1.2.17). Overall monetary conditions, as measured by a weighted average

---

[67] In May 2004, the EU and Russia agreed terms for Russia's accession to the WTO. This agreement brings the largest CIS economy a step closer to WTO membership, but Russia has yet to reach similar deals with its other key trade partners.

[68] The Federal Reserve Board, *Monetary Policy Report to the Congress*, February 2004, p. 3, sect. 1 [www.federalreserve.gov/boarddddocs].

[69] FRB Press Release, FOMC statement, 16 March 2004 [www.federalreserve.gov/FOMC].

[70] Ibid., 4 May 2004.

[71] The Federal Reserve Board, *Remarks by Chairman Alan Greenspan at the International Monetary Conference* (London), 8 June 2004 [www.federalreserve.gov/BoardDocs] (accessed on 9 June 2004).

CHART 1.2.16

Nominal short-term and long-term interest rates, January 2000-June 2004
(Per cent per annum)

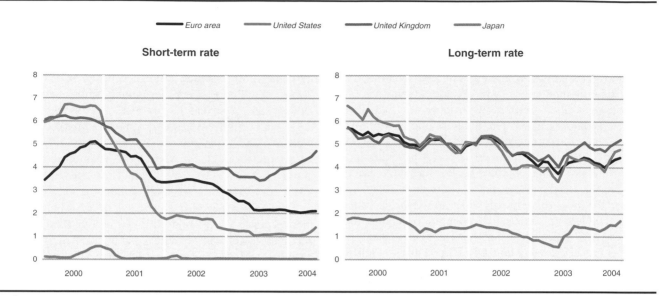

Euro area ■■■ United States ■■■ United Kingdom ■■■ Japan

Short-term rate   **Long-term rate**

Source: European Central Bank [www.ecb.int]; OECD, *Main Economic Indicators* (Paris).

Note: Average monthly rates. June 2004: average of daily rates for 1-15 June. Short-term interest rates refer to three-month interbank rates; long-term interest rates are measured by yields on 10-year (central) government bonds.

of changes in real short-term interest rates and the real effective exchange rate, have remained very supportive of economic activity in the first half of 2004, given the proportionately much smaller effect that changes in the real exchange rates have on economic activity compared with interest rates (chart 1.2.18).

...and in the euro area

In the euro area, monetary policy has also remained very accommodative in 2004. The minimum bid rate for the ECB's main refinancing operations has been 2 per cent since June 2003, when it was lowered by half a percentage point. In line with this, three-month money market rates (EURIBOR) were hovering within a narrow margin around 2.1 per cent until mid-June 2004 (chart 1.2.16). Given the prospects for only a moderate strengthening of the recovery in 2004 and 2005, the cyclical downside risks associated with the surge in oil prices, and favourable medium-term inflation prospects,[72] the ECB has adopted a wait-and-see policy, emphasizing that currently it has no bias towards either tightening or a further easing of monetary policy,[73] despite the fact that rising energy and food prices pushed the headline inflation rate above the 2 per cent ceiling in May 2004. Overall monetary conditions had tightened somewhat during 2003 as a result of the real appreciation of the euro, which offset the lowering of

official interest rates in June 2003. The moderate real depreciation of the euro combined with a fall in real short-term interest rates, however, has led to a slight improvement of monetary conditions during the first half of 2004 (charts 1.2.17 and 1.2.18).

Inflationary risks prompt a monetary tightening in the United Kingdom

In the United Kingdom, monetary policy was further tightened in the first half of 2004, the base rate being progressively lifted in four steps (by increments of 25 basis points) from 3.5 per cent in November 2003 to 4.5 per cent in June 2004. These decisions reflect the concerns of the Monetary Policy Committee of the Bank of England about the risks of failing to meet the government's medium-term inflation target in view of projected output growth above trend and the associated pressures on productive capacity and prices. A major concern of monetary policy remains the continuing rise in house prices, which is generally seen to have turned into a speculative bubble. Higher house prices have had a strong impact on household spending via equity withdrawal and increased consumer borrowing. Household debt has risen to high levels (some 100 per cent of GDP or 120 per cent of disposable incomes) and there are concerns that a progressive increase in interest rates could trigger an abrupt correction of prices in the housing market with concomitant adverse effects on consumer spending and the overall economy.

Long-term interest rates have started to rise

In the international bond markets, the improvement in short-term economic prospects have led to a rise in

---

[72] The ECB forecasts headline inflation (HICP) within a range of 1.1 to 2.3 per cent in 2005. ECB, *Monthly Bulletin*, June 2004, p. 63.

[73] ECB, *Introductory Statement (by Jean-Claude Trichet, President of the ECB) to the Press Conference*, 3 June 2004 [www.ecb.int/key].

CHART 1.2.17

**Real effective exchange rates of major currencies,
January 1999-May 2004**

(Indices, January 1999=100)

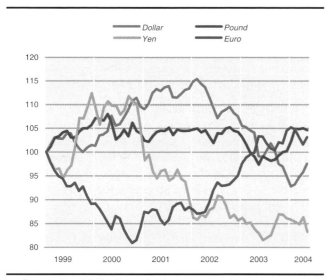

Source: Eurostat, NewCronos Database.

Note: Deflated by consumer prices indices.

CHART 1.2.18

**Monetary conditions index for the euro area,
January 2000-May 2004**

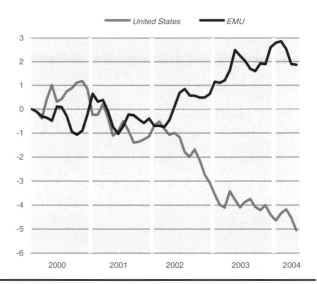

Source: UNECE secretariat calculations.

Note: The monetary conditions index is computed as $MCI = \theta_R(R_t - R_0) + \theta_e(e_t - e_0)$, where R is the three-month real short term interest rate, e is the real effective interest rate (in logs), θ_R and θ_e are weights and t is a time index. A fall in the index denotes a loosening of monetary conditions. The base period ($t = 0$) is January 2000. Weights are set to $\theta_R = 0.1$ and $\theta_e = 0.9$ for the United States and to $\theta_R = 0.2$ and $\theta_e = 0.8$ for the euro area. These are the weights commonly used in the literature and reflect empirically estimated output elasticities.

yields on long-term government bonds since April 2004 (chart 1.2.16). This reflects the combined effect of the anticipated monetary tightening (and associated higher short-term interest rates) and a rise, albeit moderate, in longer-term inflationary expectations, which, in turn, is probably mainly related to the better economic outlook and the deterioration of government financial positions. The average monthly yields on 10-year government bonds in the United States rose from 3.8 per cent in March 2004 to 4.8 per cent in June 2004.[74] The average yield on long-term bonds in the euro area rose over the same period by some 40 basis points to 4.4 per cent, leading to a widening yield spread in favour of dollar-denominated bonds. In the United Kingdom, long-term bond yields increased by 50 basis points to 5.2 per cent between March and June 2004.

Fiscal policy continues to support economic activity in the United States...

In the United States, fiscal policy also strongly supported economic activity in 2003 via higher expenditures on defence and homeland security, tax cuts and the working of automatic stabilizers. Consequently, there was a significant deterioration of the government's finances. The general government budget deficit rose to 4.8 per cent of GDP in 2003, up from 3.3 per cent in 2002. Most of this deficit is estimated to be structural, i.e. it will only be partly reversed in a cyclical recovery. Fiscal policy in the United States is expected to remain accommodative through 2004 although the stimulus to economic activity will be much less than 2003. Household incomes will receive another boost from tax

refunds which, however, will fade in the second half of the year. Only a small reduction in the budget deficit is currently projected for 2004.

...but has shifted to a neutral stance in the euro area

Fiscal developments in the euro area in 2003 were influenced by the impact of the automatic stabilizers on government net revenues during the cyclical downturn. The average budget deficit rose to 2.7 per cent of GDP, up from 2.3 per cent in 2002.[75] The cyclically adjusted budget deficit, however, actually fell by 0.3 percentage points to 2.2 per cent of (potential) GDP in 2003, a pointer to the slightly restrictive stance of fiscal policy.[76] The European Commission has forecast that the average actual budget deficit in the euro area in 2004 will remain unchanged (as a per cent of GDP) from 2003. The impact of fiscal policy is likely to be neutral in 2004, as indicated in the projection of an unchanged cyclically adjusted budget balance. The stability of the average budget deficit, however, masks the fact that six countries

---

[74] Average value for the first half of June 2004.

[75] European Commission, *Economic Forecasts* (Brussels), Spring 2004.

[76] This is also reflected in the surplus on the cyclically adjusted primary balance (which excludes interest payments), which rose slightly by 0.1 percentage points of (potential) GDP between 2002 and 2003.

(France, Germany, Greece, Italy, the Netherlands and Portugal) will have excessive deficits in 2004, i.e. deficits that exceed the 3 per cent threshold of the Stability and Growth Pact (SGP). Italy avoided an excessive deficit in 2003 only with the help of one-off fiscal measures. France and Germany will breach the 3 per cent budget deficit ceiling for the third consecutive year in 2004. Gross government debt in the euro area will increase to 70.9 per cent of GDP in 2004, half a percentage point more than in 2003.

Strong growth in government spending supports economic activity in the United Kingdom

In the United Kingdom, there was a significant deterioration in the government's finances in 2003, the result of a large increase in government spending, which supported economic activity and thereby helped to offset the cyclical downturn of 2002. The cyclically adjusted budget deficit rose by 1.5 percentage points to 2.9 per cent of potential output in 2003. The actual budget deficit amounted to 3.2 per cent of GDP, twice the level of 2002. Fiscal policy is forecast to be neutral in 2004, and the actual budget deficit should fall back below the EU's 3 per cent limit. Gross government debt is relatively low and projected to rise slightly above 40 per cent of GDP in 2004.

The new EU members set convergence targets...

After accession, the new EU members automatically assumed the obligations of the EU's Stability and Growth Pact, including the rules and norms of the EU's fiscal policy framework; consequently, they are subject to the regular budgetary surveillance by the European Commission. They are also required to submit to the European Commission stability and convergence programmes, which set out the course of action they intend to take in order to meet the SGP targets. Most of the new EU member countries submitted their convergence programmes in May, immediately upon their accession. Table 1.2.20 summarizes some of the main medium-term policy targets that these countries have set for themselves.[77]

One of the most challenging policy targets for some of these economies will be the required fiscal consolidation. In 2003 the general government deficits of four central European countries – the Czech Republic, Hungary, Poland and Slovakia – exceeded the EU's reference value of 3 per cent of GDP.[78] According to the medium-term policy programmes, Poland will seek to reduce its general government deficit below 3 per cent of GDP by 2006; Slovakia by 2007 and Hungary by 2008.

The Czech stability and convergence programme targets the elimination of the "excessive" budget deficit by 2008. In all these cases, the consolidation will require some painful adjustment efforts which – with the exception of Poland – are already underway.[79] In this regard, the current strengthening of economic growth in central Europe and the Baltic region presents the governments of these countries with an opportunity to push ahead with some of the needed measures as the cyclical upturn provides them with an additional financial cushion.

Given the fact that many of the new EU members are still undergoing major structural adjustments, the European Commission seems to have taken a more flexible position with respect to their current fiscal deficits noting that "it could be appropriate, from an economic point of view, to allow for a multi-annual adjustment period in some cases when correcting a deficit of more than 3 per cent".[80] It therefore appears likely that the new EU members that are considered to be facing serious structural challenges may be granted (albeit informally) a certain grace period for meeting the stringent rules of the SGP.[81] Although the European Commission may be demonstrating on this occasion a pragmatic approach, such a tacit deviation from the general EU fiscal rules highlights once again the difficulties of enforcing these rules, which, at least partly, arise from their excessive rigidity. A more appropriate solution – as reflected in recent public debates – would be to modify the SGP rules to allow greater flexibility to national policy makers in dealing with both cyclical and long-term structural adjustment.[82]

...and prepare for EMU entry

EU enlargement has also brought to the policy forefront the different standing of the new EU members with respect to the possible date of their accession to the EMU. Three countries – Estonia, Lithuania and Slovenia – joined the EU's exchange rate mechanism ERM-2 already in June 2004, immediately after their accession to the EU.[83] The agreement on participation of the three currencies in ERM-2 stipulates the application of the standard fluctuation band

---

[77] The candidate countries Bulgaria and Romania have also made further progress towards EU membership: in June, Bulgaria closed successfully all the negotiation chapters while Romania is expected to do the same by the end of the year. This may pave the way for the signing of the accession treaty already in 2005 so that the two countries could join the EU in January 2007, as planned.

[78] The same holds for Cyprus and Malta.

[79] In Poland, the 2004 budget contains a further fiscal stimulus to revitalize the economy. The fiscal adjustment has been postponed to 2005, in the context of a broader reform of public spending.

[80] European Commission, "Commission recommendations on the 2004 update of the broad guidelines of the economic policy of the member states and the Community (for the 2003-2005 period)", COM (2004) 238, 7 April 2004, p. 7 [europa.eu.int/comm/economy_finance/publications/european_economy/2004/comm2004_238en.pdf].

[81] According to the EU's fiscal rules, a deficit in excess of the 3 per cent reference value is only allowed in a severe recession; a country that violates this reference value in normal times can be subject to sanctions under the "excessive deficit procedure". For a discussion see UNECE, *Economic Survey of Europe, 2004 No. 1*, pp. 10-15.

[82] Ibid.

[83] Cyprus has also signalled its intention to join ERM-2 in 2004.

TABLE 1.2.20

Convergence targets in selected new EU member countries, 2003-2008

(Per cent)

	2003	2004	2005	2006	2007	2008
Czech Republic...						
Consumer prices, average annual percentage change	0.1	3.1	2.8	2.5	2.5	..
General government balance, per cent of GDP	-13.6	-5.6	-4.9	-4.0	-3.5	..
General government debt, per cent of GDP	39.7	40.5	41.8	43.2	44.0	..
Estonia						
Consumer prices, average annual percentage change	1.3	3.1	3.0	2.8	2.8	2.8
Long-term interest rates, annual average	4.1	4.3	4.5	4.6	4.9	4.9
General government balance, per cent of GDP	2.6	0.7	0.0	0.0	0.0	0.0
General government debt, per cent of GDP	5.8	5.4	5.1	4.7	3.4	3.2
Hungary						
Consumer prices, average annual percentage change	4.7	6.5	4.5	4.0	3.5	3.0
Long-term interest rates, annual average	6.82	7.50	6.50	6.25	6.25	6.25
General government balance, per cent of GDP	-5.9	-4.6	-4.1	-3.6	-3.1	-2.7
General government debt, per cent of GDP	59.1	59.4	57.9	56.8	55.6	53.7
Latvia						
Consumer prices, average annual percentage change	2.9	4.5	3.7	3.0	3.0	..
General government balance, per cent of GDP	-1.8	-2.1	-2.2	-2.0	-2.0	..
General government debt, per cent of GDP	15.3	16.2	16.8	17.3	17.7	..
Lithuania						
Consumer prices, average annual percentage change	-1.2	0.9	2.0	2.1	2.5	..
Long-term interest rates, annual average	5.3	5.0	5.3	5.7	6.1	..
General government balance, per cent of GDP	-1.7	-2.7	-2.5	-1.8	-1.5	..
General government debt, per cent of GDP	21.5	22.4	22.2	21.4	21.0	..
Poland [a]						
Consumer prices, average annual percentage change	0.7	2.0	2.8	2.9	2.9	..
General government balance, per cent of GDP	-4.2	-5.7	-3.9	-2.8	..	..
General government debt, per cent of GDP	44.8	47.6	51.4	51.3	..	..
Slovenia						
Consumer prices, average annual percentage change	5.6	3.3	3.0	2.5	2.4	..
General government balance, per cent of GDP	-1.8	-1.9	-1.8	-1.5	-0.9	..
General government debt, per cent of GDP	28.6	29.1	29.5	29.4	28.4	..
Slovakia						
Consumer prices, average annual percentage change	8.5	8.1	4.0	2.9	2.5	..
General government balance, per cent of GDP	-3.6	-4.0	-3.9	-3.9	-3.0	..
General government debt, per cent of GDP	42.8	45.1	46.4	46.1	45.5	..

Source: Czech Republic, Estonia, Hungary, Latvia, Lithuania, Slovakia and Slovenia: national convergence programmes adopted in early 2004; Poland: medium-term public finances strategy (Warsaw), 2004.

[a] Ceiling values of the medium-term public finances strategy.

of ±15 per cent around their central parity rates (which were also part of the agreement). In principle the application of the standard band is more appropriate for these economies than the narrow ±2.25 per cent band; however, the width of the band at present has little practical importance for Estonia and Lithuania, which joined ERM-2 with a unilateral commitment to preserve their existing currency board arrangements. While these three economies might be ready to adopt the euro in late 2006 or early 2007, the other new EU members appear to have abandoned their earlier ambitious timetables for EMU accession.[84] Thus, according to recent statements by government officials, the Czech Republic and Hungary now seem to be contemplating joining ERM-2 only in 2008 and adopting the euro by 2010; however, no firm plans to this effect have yet been announced. The National Bank of Poland has also reformulated its official target

date for euro zone entry from "2007" to "as soon as possible after 2007"; the government is taking an even more cautious view on the possible accession date. Latvia and Slovakia seem to be targeting EMU accession in 2008 but in both cases the goal is still not supported by an explicit timetable. Obviously, the policy debate regarding the adoption of the single currency by the new members will continue for some time to come.

Despite country-specific differences, monetary policy in all the new EU members is now directly targeting nominal convergence – although at varying speeds – on the euro zone economies. The smooth completion of EU enlargement has had a positive impact on risk premia in the acceding countries and this, in turn, has allowed the central banks in Slovenia and Slovakia to lower interest rates in the first half of 2004.[85] The lowering of the basic interest rate

---

[84] The Maastricht criterion for exchange rate stability requires participation without severe tensions in ERM-2 for at least two years prior to EMU entry.

[85] The central banks cut their key rates by 2.25 percentage points to 5 per cent in Slovenia and by one and a half percentage points to 4.5 per cent in Slovakia.

in Slovakia was also prompted by a rapid appreciation of the koruna (triggered by a massive inflow of short-term capital) that was considered a threat to competitiveness. The National Bank of Hungary also reduced its key rate by 1 percentage point; despite this move, however, nominal interest rates in Hungary generally remain rather high following the turmoil on the foreign exchange market in 2003.[86] Elsewhere in eastern Europe, progress with disinflation in Albania and Romania has allowed the central banks to reduce their refinancing rates.

However, there are indications that rising inflationary expectations – partly reflecting the effect of high-energy prices – may prompt changes in the central banks' policy stance. Thus, the central bank of Latvia raised its refinancing rate in March by half a percentage point in an attempt to check the inflationary pressures arising from the rapidly growing economy. In June both the Czech National Bank and the National Bank of Poland also raised their key interest rates.[87]

The CIS: coping with risks of overheating...

The strong economic growth in the CIS region has been highly beneficial for these economies, contributing to rising incomes and living standards of the population. At the same time, the current economic boom in the region, which is largely associated with the general surge in world commodity prices, is posing some new policy challenges. Rapid growth in some cases has been accompanied by growing inflationary pressures and thus increasing concerns about overheating. In Ukraine these prompted the central bank in June to raise its discount rate by half a percentage point to 7.5 per cent (the first change in the central bank's intervention rate since December 2002). At the same time, however, Ukraine's parliament adopted in June a controversial amendment to the 2004 budget, which implies a substantial loosening of the fiscal policy in 2004.[88] Such a fiscal relaxation is not consistent with the current monetary policy objectives (and the macroeconomic situation in general) and may compromise the central bank's effort to prevent a surge in inflation, especially as regards the prices of services.

Kazakhstan's rapidly growing economy is also exposed to inflationary risks associated with overheating;

moreover, in this case the risks are compounded by an ongoing surge in capital inflows (mostly related to oil revenue). Raising interest rates in such circumstances could lead to even larger capital inflows thus aggravating the macroeconomic situation. But the policy response to the combined risk of overheating and exchange rate appreciation so far has been more coherent in Kazakhstan than in the case of Ukraine: the government has announced plans to tighten its fiscal policy while the central bank maintains a neutral stance.

...and risks of "Dutch Disease" in Russia

While Russia's economy as a whole undoubtedly benefits from the windfall revenue gains related to the rise in oil prices, its central bank is faced with some serious macroeconomic policy dilemmas. Thus, with an ever-expanding inflow of foreign exchange (reflecting not only the swelling current account surplus but also growing short-term capital inflows), the symptoms of the "Dutch Disease" are becoming quite visible in Russia.[89] The trend towards real exchange rate appreciation (which emerged after the 1998 rouble collapse) has intensified since the beginning of 2003 and accelerated further in the first months of 2004 (chart 1.2.19). As a result, the real exchange rate of the rouble is already approaching the levels it had reached during the bubble years prior to the 1998 financial crisis. Although the macroeconomic situation in Russia is now completely different from what it was in 1998 and there is no immediate danger of a repetition of such a crisis, the appreciation of the rouble has now reached the point where it can seriously damage the competitiveness of local manufacturers and is obviously becoming a burden for the economy as a whole.[90]

---

[86] For details see "The forint under attack", in UNECE, *Economic Survey of Europe, 2004 No. 1*, p. 51, box 3.1.1.

[87] In Poland the central bank rates were raised by half a percentage point and in the Czech Republic by a quarter of a percentage point. Even after this change the central bank rates in the Czech Republic remained the lowest in eastern Europe with the key two-week report rate standing at 2.25 per cent.

[88] The amendment envisages a major increase in public spending in 2004, which was formally based on the stream of privatization revenue that was not initially included in the budget. However, when such revenues are used to finance current spending this is de facto equivalent to an increase in the general government deficit. Concerns have been voiced that the planned increase in budgetary spending in 2004 may be associated with the forthcoming presidential elections.

---

[89] It is well known that a resource windfall causes a shift in the current account position, which, in turn, is associated with a shift in the equilibrium real exchange rate towards appreciation (the core symptoms of the "Dutch Disease"). If this is a one-off shift (such as that generated by a natural resource discovery and its exploitation at a constant rate), then the shift in the equilibrium exchange rate to a higher level will also be a one-off equilibrium phenomenon. What is peculiar in the Russian situation is that during the last several years there have been a series of shifts in the current account position driven by increasing shipments of oil and rising oil prices. In turn, the persistent rise in the current account surplus has translated into a considerable cumulative real appreciation of the ruble. The recent surge in short-term capital inflows has added to the pressure on the current account. Given the nature of these driving forces, however, the current account position is rather volatile; for example, a fall in oil prices would move it in the opposite direction and might reverse the real appreciation of the rouble. Moreover, it is very likely that at present both the current account position and the real exchange rate have overshot their equilibrium levels.

[90] While all manufacturing firms are negatively affected by the real exchange rate appreciation with respect to the price competitiveness of their output, various factors may mitigate the impact. Thus, firms using imported inputs can partly offset this negative effect; firms importing investment equipment for restructuring may also benefit from the stronger rouble.

CHART 1.2.19

The rouble's real exchange rate against the dollar, January 1995-April 2004
(Indices, January 1995=100, per cent)

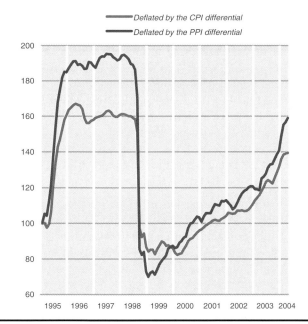

Source: UNECE secretariat calculations, based on national statistics.

Russia's recent attempts to address this problem highlight the complexity of the policy issues, especially in an environment of immature and relatively shallow financial markets. In the first half of 2004, Russia's central bank continued its massive purchases of foreign exchange in an attempt to prevent an even faster rate of appreciation of the real exchange rate, a policy to which it adhered throughout 2003.[91] However, the large injection of liquidity into the domestic money market has had detrimental side effects not only in terms of its pro-inflationary impact but also with respect to the efficiency of macroeconomic management per se. In particular, it has crippled the ability of the monetary authorities to intervene on the money market through another key instrument of monetary management, the central bank's interest rate. The problem is that as a result of the central bank's massive intervention on the foreign exchange market, Russia's banking system has become satiated with excess rouble liquidity and this has sharply reduced domestic interbank interest rates, especially during the first three months of 2004.[92] In April-May interbank rates

started to rise again; this was not the result of a policy correction, however, but rather the reflection of shaken confidence in the banking system following the collapse of two smaller banks which triggered massive withdrawals of bank deposits.[93] Subsequently, the central bank was forced to supply the markets with even more liquidity by lowering the minimum reserve requirement (from 9 per cent to 7 per cent) in June and cutting its discount rate again. For the time being the monetary authorities have managed to prevent an escalation of turbulence, but this episode highlights once again the fragility of Russia's financial system.

There is no easy fix for a real exchange rate appreciation driven by a persistent current account surplus based on exports of natural resources. Dealing with these problems generally requires a coherent policy approach. One of the macroeconomic policy targets should be to prevent a possible overshooting of the real exchange rate, since an excessively high rate may destroy jobs and firms that would otherwise be viable at the equilibrium rate.[94] The long-term solution requires reducing the dependence of the economy on exports of natural resources. Economic diversification has long been on the declared agenda of Russia's policy makers but, so far, very little has been achieved. The diversification of Russia's economy can only come about as a result of considerable private investment in sectors other than those related to oil and natural gas, but until now this has not materialized to any significant degree.[95] Investors' hesitance in this regard most likely reflects the still prevailing perception of high levels of business risk due to the uncertainties surrounding the protection of property rights and the rule of law.

In the short run, however, Russia's real exchange rate is likely to continue to appreciate as long as its

_____

[91] During the first five months of 2004 Russia's official foreign exchange reserves increased by $8.5 billion, reaching $85.6 on 4 June. While purchases of foreign exchange have not been sterilized by the central bank, their pro-inflationary impact has been partly sterilized through the operations of the newly established Stabilization Fund, which, during the same period, accumulated additional funds amounting to rouble 92 billion ($3.2 billion).

[92] In the first quarter of 2004, the average interbank market rate fell below 2 per cent per annum, while the central bank's intervention rate, after its reduction by 200 basis points in

January, was still 14 per cent per annum. As long as market interest rates remain so far below the central bank intervention rate, the latter can hardly have any effect on transactions in the money markets (and hence on money demand in general) as the banks can refinance one another through the interbank market.

[93] Initially, the financial supervisory authority cancelled the licence of Sodbiznesbank, a medium-sized bank, on the basis of a rule penalizing money-laundering operations. Subsequently, a run on Credit Trust, a relatively small bank related to Sodbiznesbank, forced it to close down.

[94] This also implies an accurate assessment of the equilibrium real exchange rate, which is not a trivial task. R. MacDonald and J. Stein (eds.), *Equilibrium Exchange Rates* (Boston, Dordrecht and London, Kluwer Academic, 1999); P. Clark, "Concepts of equilibrium exchange rates", *Economic Systems*, Vol. 20, No. 2-3, 1996, pp. 133-140; L. Halpern and C. Wyplosz, "Equilibrium exchange rates in transition economies", *IMF Staff Papers*, Vol. 44, No. 4 (Washington, D.C.), 1997, pp. 430-461.

[95] While fixed investment in Russia continues to grow (by 13 per cent year-on-year during the first quarter of 2004), the major part is absorbed by the energy-related sectors of the economy. Also, the aggregate level of fixed investment as a share of GDP (a little over 18 per cent in 2003) is considered to be rather low for sustaining high rates of long-term economic growth.

current account surplus continues to grow (which, in turn, is driven by the combination of a growing volume of oil exports, high world market prices for oil and inflows of financial capital), with negative effects on the competitiveness of local manufacturers. To remain competitive local firms must restructure and adjust in order to raise their productive efficiency and profit margins. But this requires the establishment of a market environment that will make firms responsive to market signals. In particular, it implies reducing the barriers to competition in, and increasing the flexibility of, the domestic product, labour and capital markets.

Addressing all these issues should thus be given high priority in Russia's policy agenda. A broader, stronger and competitive manufacturing base would reduce not only the Russian economy's reliance on the oil and gas sectors but also its vulnerability to fluctuations in the international prices of natural resources. To varying degrees, these issues (and the related policy implications) are also relevant for other CIS countries – such as Azerbaijan, Kazakhstan, Tajikistan, Turkmenistan and, to some extent, Ukraine – seeking ways to reduce their dependence on commodity exports.

1.3 The short-term outlook

A strong but uneven rebound of the global economy

The broad consensus of forecasters at mid-year is for the global economic upswing to continue at a brisk rate in the second half of 2004 and in 2005. The average annual growth rate of world output in 2004 should be broadly the same as at the peak of the previous cycle in 2000, namely, 4.7 per cent.[96] Among the G7 economies, the recovery is mainly driven by the United States, Japan and the United Kingdom. In contrast, the weak cyclical momentum in France, Germany and Italy is dampening the average growth rate of the euro area, which is lagging behind in the international growth cycle. The emerging markets in Asia, the CIS and eastern Europe continue to be important dynamos of global economic activity.

A further gradual tightening in the stance of United States monetary policy is expected in the second half of 2004, but global financing conditions should remain favourable and hence further stimulate private fixed investment. Oil prices have retreated from their peak in early June 2004 to some $35 p/b (spot price of Brent crude) at the end of June 2004. Assuming prices remain at that level for the rest of the year, the average price for the year would be some $34 p/b, an increase by some $5 p/b compared with the average in 2003. Accordingly, the impact on global economic growth would be relatively small and swamped by the strong underlying cyclical momentum. Against this background, inflation rates in the global economy are forecast to remain low in 2004

and 2005, supported by continued moderate growth of unit labour costs.

In the United States, the recovery is expected to be increasingly self-sustained, with output growth forecast to remain above trend. This should lead to further improvements in the labour markets, and the closing of the output gap in 2005. Against this background, the Federal Reserve will have to progressively raise interest rates to move monetary policy back to a neutral stance. The neutral level of short-term interest rates is estimated to be around 4 to 4.5 per cent. Real GDP is set to increase by some 4.5 per cent in 2004, supported by strong domestic demand and exports. The pace of expansion is expected to slow down in the course of 2005, but the annual growth rate should still be close to 4 per cent (table 1.3.1).

In the euro area, the recovery is likely to remain lacklustre in 2004 and 2005. Real GDP is forecast to increase by some 1¾ per cent in 2004 and by 2 per cent in 2005. These modest rates of growth will not lead to any significant improvements in the labour markets. The upswing will continue to be led by exports, which are buoyed by favourable growth in other regions of the world economy. In fact, the strength of exports has been offsetting the dampening effects from the rise in oil prices. Private household consumption is expected to expand only moderately, reflecting depressed consumer confidence and small gains in aggregate wage incomes due to the weak demand for labour. Growth in households' real disposable incomes, moreover, will be reduced by the rise in energy prices, which will tend to dampen spending on non-energy products. Consumer confidence is currently well below its long-term average, reflecting uncertainty about labour market prospects and longer-term concerns about the outlook for pensions and health care. Consequently, the savings propensity in the euro area is very high. The strengthening export performance, in combination with low interest rates, is expected to stimulate business investment in machinery and equipment, which should therefore gather some momentum in 2005.

Among the three largest economies in the euro area, annual GDP growth is forecast to edge up to 2.1 per cent in 2004 in France, a slight increase (of 0.4 percentage points) compared with the spring forecast, which largely reflects the impact of stronger export growth. For the same reason there has also been a small increase (of 0.2 percentage points) in the forecasts for Germany, where real GDP is now expected to rise by 1.7 per cent in 2004. In Italy, real GDP is forecast to increase by slightly more than 1 per cent this year.

Outside the euro area, real GDP in the United Kingdom should increase by some 3 per cent in 2004, above the trend growth rate of 2.5 per cent a year. The recovery is driven by the strong growth of private consumption and government expenditures. Changes in real net exports, however, will constitute a substantial drag

---

[96] Using PPP-based GDP weights to aggregate individual country forecasts.

TABLE 1.3.1

Annual changes in real GDP in Europe, North America and Japan, 2002-2005

(Percentage change over the previous year)

	2002	2003	2004 Forecast	2005 Forecast
France	1.2	0.5	2.1	2.1
Germany	0.2	-0.1	1.7	1.7
Italy	0.4	0.3	1.1	1.8
Austria	1.4	0.7	1.7	2.3
Belgium	0.7	1.1	1.9	2.3
Finland	2.3	1.9	2.7	3.0
Greece	3.9	4.3	4.1	2.9
Ireland	6.9	1.4	3.5	4.4
Luxembourg	1.7	2.1	2.4	3.1
Netherlands	0.2	-0.7	1.1	2.0
Portugal	0.5	-1.2	1.1	2.1
Spain	2.0	2.4	2.8	3.0
Euro area	0.9	0.6	1.7	2.1
Denmark	1.0	0.5	2.0	2.4
Sweden	2.1	1.6	2.8	2.7
United Kingdom	1.8	2.2	3.1	2.6
EU-15	1.1	0.9	2.0	2.2
Cyprus	2.0	2.0	3.4	4.1
Czech Republic	2.0	2.9	3.3	3.7
Estonia	7.2	5.1	5.5	5.6
Hungary	3.5	2.9	3.3	3.7
Latvia	6.4	7.5	6.4	5.8
Lithuania	6.8	9.0	6.7	5.9
Malta	2.3	-1.7	1.4	2.0
Poland	1.4	3.8	5.3	5.0
Slovakia	4.4	4.2	4.4	4.7
Slovenia	3.4	2.3	3.3	3.6
New EU members-10	2.5	3.7	4.5	4.5
EU-25	1.2	1.1	2.2	2.4
Iceland	-0.6	1.9	3.7	5.6
Israel	-0.8	1.3	2.9	3.5
Norway	1.4	0.3	3.4	3.0
Switzerland	0.2	-0.5	1.8	2.0
WECEE	1.2	1.1	2.2	2.4
Canada	3.4	2.0	2.9	3.3
United States	2.2	3.1	4.7	3.8
North America	2.3	3.0	4.6	3.8
Japan	-0.3	2.5	4.1	1.8
Europe, North America and Japan	1.5	2.1	3.4	2.9
Memorandum items:				
CEBS-8	2.5	3.7	4.5	4.5
Western Europe and North America	1.7	2.0	3.3	3.0

Source: Eurostat; OECD national accounts; national statistics; Consensus Economics, *Consensus Forecasts*, 14 June 2004 and *Eastern Europe Consensus Forecasts*, 17 May 2004.

Note: The aggregate "western Europe" comprises the former EU-15 plus Cyprus, Iceland, Malta, Norway and Switzerland. WECEE comprises EU-25 plus Iceland, Norway and Switzerland. Central Europe and Baltic states (CEBS-8) includes the new EU members less Cyprus and Malta. For data on south-east European and European CIS countries see table 1.3.2.

on overall economic activity in 2004, a consequence of the appreciation of the pound and weak demand in the major markets of continental Europe. Growth is forecast to be more balanced in 2005, with exports picking up and the

change in real net exports becoming less of a drag on economic growth. At an average annual rate of 2¾ per cent, economic growth will remain somewhat above trend in 2005, and the gap between actual and potential output will therefore be closed.

Among the other west European countries outside the euro area, economic growth in 2004 is forecast at slightly above the euro area average in Denmark and Switzerland. There will be a more pronounced strengthening of activity in Norway and Sweden, where real GDP is forecast to increase by 3.4 per cent and 2.8 per cent, respectively (table 1.3.1).

For the member states of the European Union as a whole (EU-25), real GDP is forecast to increase by 2.2 per cent in 2004 and by 2.4 per cent in 2005. This modest average masks a significantly better performance in the new EU member states (see below). For the wider aggregate of countries in western, central and eastern Europe the average growth rate will be the same as that for the EU.

The new EU members maintain rapid rate of growth

In the early months of 2004, economic growth in the new EU members accelerated further, led by a strong economic upturn in Poland and a continuing surge in economic activity in the Baltic region. The new EU members are expected to continue to benefit from the general improvement in both global demand and import demand in western Europe. Taken as a whole, in 2004 as well as in 2005, these economies are set to preserve their positive GDP growth difference of some 2 percentage points above that of the EU-15 (table 1.3.1). The rise in world oil prices did not have a notable negative effect on economic activity in central and eastern Europe in the first quarter, but this may just be due to lags in the domestic transmission mechanisms. Some moderation in the pace of industrial output growth in the second quarter may be a sign of the burden of rising costs to local producers. If energy prices remain high throughout 2004, there could be a more significant negative effect on aggregate economic activity in the region.

Economic growth in Poland has been mostly export-driven since 2001. The further weakening of the zloty's effective exchange rate (both in nominal and in real terms) in the early months of 2004 gave an extra boost to manufacturing exports, which are likely to continue to act as a source of growth in the short run. In addition, the strong fiscal-cum-monetary stimulus obviously provided a further boost to the Polish economy both in 2003 and in the first half of 2004. However, this policy now has run its course, especially in view of the need to consolidate the public finances, so Poland will increasingly have to rely on external factors of growth. If the growth of fixed investment continues to strengthen (as most analysts believe), this may give further support to economic activity. In general, given an accumulated momentum, the rate of growth of Polish GDP in 2004 is likely to remain high (and the highest among the central European countries) but some slowdown is expected in 2005.

Hungarian economic performance in the first quarter suggests a shift towards export-led growth coupled with a strong recovery in domestic investment. These changes are in line with the current policy of boosting competitiveness (mostly by curbing the growth of real wages) and the results so far have exceeded expectations. GDP growth in Hungary in 2004 will probably exceed the consensus forecast available at the time of writing this *Survey* (3.3 per cent) and is more likely to be in the range between 3.5 and 4 per cent. In contrast, the projected acceleration of growth in Slovakia in 2004 and 2005 is mostly based on the expected recovery (after stagnation in 2003) of domestic demand as both private consumption and fixed investment should be stimulated by the current monetary easing. At the same time, strong export growth should continue to support economic activity although the rate will probably slow down somewhat from the exceptionally high rates in 2003.

The three Baltic economies are set to remain the fastest growing region in Europe. The continued expansion of their export capacities, in combination with strong domestic demand, are expected to support GDP growth rates at high single-digit rates in both 2004 and 2005. At the same time, the large current account deficits in Estonia and Latvia pose certain macroeconomic risks and may lead to a tightening of macroeconomic policies.

GDP growth in the Czech Republic and Slovenia is expected to be lower than that of the other new EU members in central Europe and the Baltic region (around 3.5 per cent in both countries in 2004 and 2005). In the Czech Republic, this relatively low rate of growth largely reflects the efforts of the government to reduce the public sector deficit to more sustainable levels (table 1.2.20). At the same time, private consumption and fixed investment are expected to remain strong and should partly offset the negative effect of the public sector on aggregate growth. Given its goal of joining ERM-2 in 2004, the Slovenian government has maintained a rather tight macroeconomic policy stance since 2003, seeking to meet all the Maastricht criteria. One negative outcome has been a strong real appreciation of the currency, which has had a negative effect on competitiveness and export performance. The relaxation of monetary policy in the first half of 2004 suggests that this policy course, having achieved its goals, is probably coming to an end. The growth of aggregate output is also expected to pick up, although its rate in the short run will still lag behind that in neighbouring countries.

Strong growth continues in south-east Europe...

Economic growth in south-east Europe is also set to remain fairly strong in the short run. The reform efforts in Bulgaria, Croatia and Romania, related to their goal of joining the EU, seems to be paying off. The progress made in the accession negotiations by Bulgaria and Romania and the expected start of such negotiations by Croatia have made the prospects of EU membership much more realistic. The fact that these countries have become attractive investment sites (not least in view of their expected membership of the EU) is confirmed by the recent surge of inward FDI. In turn, this has undoubtedly contributed to the strengthening of their economic performance.

GDP growth in both Bulgaria and Romania is expected to continue at close to 5 per cent both in 2004 and 2005, supported by strong domestic demand and export growth (table 1.3.2). However, Bulgaria's escalating current account deficit (which reached 8.4 per cent of GDP in 2003 and continued to increase in the first quarter) prompted the authorities to adopt a series of measures in May to curb domestic demand. These included a further tightening of the fiscal stance in 2004 (although Bulgaria's government finances are close to balance) as well as measures to contain the growth of bank credit, which has been supporting domestic demand.[97] This effective tightening of macroeconomic policy may have a negative impact on economic activity in the second half of the year. In contrast, the recent slowdown of inflation in Romania, coupled with more efficient tax collection, has allowed some relaxation of monetary policy (and a further loosening can be expected in the near future) and this should give an additional boost to economic activity through 2005.

The strong economic recovery in Turkey (where GDP is expected to continue to grow at around 5 per cent in both 2004 and 2005) reflects sound economic fundamentals and rising consumer and investor confidence after the successful adjustment efforts which followed the financial crisis. Both domestic demand and exports will continue to provide a strong impetus to the economy in 2004 and 2005. In Croatia, GDP growth is expected to be around 4 per cent and to be largely export led. In 2004 and 2005, the Croatian government envisages a tightening of fiscal policy, in order to curb the country's chronic twin deficits. Thus, while private consumption, investment and exports should preserve their dynamism, the envisaged cuts in public spending will have a negative impact on GDP growth in the short run.

After a slowdown in 2003, economic activity in Serbia and Montenegro has been picking up in the early months of 2004 and this is set to continue throughout the year thanks to a strong recovery of domestic demand. At the same time, the policy of preserving nominal exchange rate stability has resulted in a persistent real appreciation of the exchange rate, with negative effects on the current account balance. In view of the country's foreign debt problem, this is not a

---

[97] In the absence of instruments of direct control over the money supply (under the currency board arrangement) the authorities could only resort to indirect measures such as an increase in the minimum required reserves as well as a tightening of prudential banking regulations.

TABLE 1.3.2

Annual changes in real GDP in south-east Europe and the CIS, 2002-2005

(Percentage change over the previous year)

	2002	2003	2004 Forecast	2005 Forecast
South-east Europe	6.4	5.1	5.0	4.8*
Albania	4.7	6.0	6.0ᵃ	..
Bosnia and Herzegovina	3.7	3.2	4.0*	..
Bulgaria	4.9	4.3	4.7	4.7
Croatia	4.6	4.3	4.0	4.3
Romania	5.0	4.9	4.9	4.9
Serbia and Montenegro ᵇ	3.8	1.5	8.0ᵃ	..
The former Yugoslav Republic of Macedonia	0.9	3.2	–*	..
Turkey	7.8	5.8	5.0	4.8
CIS	5.2	7.7	7.1	6.0*
Armenia	12.9	13.9	7.0ᵃ	..
Azerbaijan	10.6	11.2	8.9	9.7
Belarus	5.0	6.8	9.0ᵃ	6-7ᵃ
Georgia	5.5	11.0	10.0*	..
Kazakhstan	9.8	9.2	8.4	7.8
Kyrgyzstan	-	6.7	4.5ᵃ	4.6ᵃ
Republic of Moldova ᶜ	7.8	6.3	5.2	5.1
Russian Federation	4.7	7.3	6.8	5.7
Tajikistan	9.5	10.2	8.0ᵃ	..
Turkmenistan ᵈ	19.8	17.0	..	..
Ukraine	5.2	9.4	8.1	6.2
Uzbekistan	4.2	4.4	3.8	3.7
Total above	5.6	6.9	6.5	5.6*
Memorandum items:				
South-east Europe without Turkey (SEE-7)	4.6	4.2	5.0	4.8*
CIS without Russian Federation	6.4	8.5	7.8	6.6*
Low-income CIS economies	6.2	7.7	6.1	5.8*
Caucasian CIS countries (CCIS-3)	9.5	11.8	8.8	8.4*
Central Asian CIS countries (CACIS-5)	7.4	7.7	6.9	6.6*
Three European CIS countries (ECIS-3)	5.3	8.6	8.3	6.3

Source: National statistics, CIS Statistical Committee; Consensus Economics, *Eastern Europe Consensus Forecasts*, 17 May 2004; reports by official forecasting agencies.

Note: Aggregates are UNECE secretariat calculations, using PPPs obtained from the European Comparison Programme. Aggregates shown are: south-east Europe (the 8 countries below that line); CIS (the 12 member countries of the Commonwealth of Independent States). Sub-aggregates are: Caucasian CIS countries (CCIS-3): Armenia, Azerbaijan, Georgia; central Asian CIS countries (CACIS-5): Kazakhstan, Kyrgyzstan, Tajikistan, Turkmenistan, Uzbekistan; three European CIS countries (ECIS-3): Belarus, Republic of Moldova, Ukraine. Low-income CIS economies: Armenia, Azerbaijan, Georgia, Republic of Moldova, Kyrgyzstan, Tajikistan and Uzbekistan. Unless otherwise noted, country forecasts shown are those reported in the latest *Eastern Europe Consensus Forecasts* report.

ᵃ Official forecast.

ᵇ Excluding Kosovo and Metohia.

ᶜ Excluding Transdniestria.

ᵈ Figures for Turkmenistan should be treated with caution. In particular, the deflation procedures that are used to compute officially reported growth rates are not well documented and the reliability of these figures is questionable.

sustainable policy course. An eventual reversal of this policy could help to bring about a shift towards a healthier, export-driven type of economic growth in Serbia and Montenegro. In Albania, progress in

consolidating the public finances on the basis of more efficient tax collection has paved the way for an easing of monetary policy and it is believed that there is still room for further relaxation. Expectations are for aggregate output to continue growing at around 6 per cent in 2004 and 2005.

...and in the CIS

The recent surge in world commodity prices and, especially, in the price of oil, has given a considerable boost to the economies of the commodity exporting CIS countries and to the CIS region as a whole. During the first few months of the year economic growth in the region was considerably above expectations and this prompted in many cases the raising of growth forecasts. In the short run, the external environment is likely to remain favourable for commodity exporters and consequently economic growth in the CIS economies can be expected to remain high through 2005.

Russia has benefited considerably not only from high oil prices but also from the strong global demand for oil, and these have been the main factors behind the acceleration of growth from the beginning of 2004.[98] During the first half of the year, Russia's growth forecast for 2004 was being raised literally every month.[99] The consensus forecast at the time of writing this *Survey* was that Russia's GDP would grow by close to 7 per cent in 2004 as a whole; a slowdown by around 1 percentage point was expected for 2005 (table 1.3.2). In fact, some slowdown is already generally expected in the second half of 2004, following an expected moderation in world oil prices. In the short run, macroeconomic policy is likely to maintain a neutral stance: as discussed earlier, the room for manoeuvre in monetary policy is limited due to the surge in capital inflows; on the fiscal side, the general government's balance is comfortably in surplus but most of this is now channelled to the Stabilization Fund.

However, this type of growth, predominantly based on the expansion of commodity exports, is clearly not sustainable in the longer run. The Russian economy is already confronted with some of the negative consequences of this pattern of growth, such as the considerable cumulative real appreciation of the rouble, which is hurting local manufacturers. While the energy sector is likely to remain important in the foreseeable future, the realization of Russia's long-run growth potential hinges on the diversification of the economy and on the acceleration and deepening of systemic and structural reforms.

_____

[98] Extraction and exports of oil in Russia are still on the rise. In June, Russia announced that its oil output in 2004 could reach 450 million tons, an increase of more than 7 per cent over 2003 (according to earlier projections, an increase of just 3 per cent was envisaged in 2004). In 2003 oil extraction rose by some 11 per cent.

[99] Between December 2003 and June 2004, the official GDP growth forecast for 2004 was raised by almost 2 percentage points, to 6.6 per cent.

As in Russia, economic growth in Ukraine during the first half of the year turned out to be much stronger than initially expected thanks to favourable world market conditions for Ukraine's major exports – steel and chemicals. This has prompted major revisions to the growth forecasts for 2004: GDP growth is currently expected be in the high single digits, several percentage points above earlier estimates.[100] In Kazakhstan, another major commodity exporter, GDP growth is also expected to be close to 10 per cent in 2004 and is likely to remain fairly high in 2005 as well. In Belarus, the strong export-led upturn in manufacturing should also contribute to solid GDP growth in 2004 as a whole.

Among the smaller CIS economies, economic growth is expected to remain high in the commodity exporting countries, with GDP growing in most cases at rates in the high single digits in 2004. In Azerbaijan, some new, large-scale oil-extracting capacity is expected to be put into operation in 2005 and subsequent years and this expansion of productive capacity should eventually lead to double-digit rates of growth. In contrast, rates of GDP growth in most of the countries that are not specialized in commodity exports (such as Armenia, Georgia, the Republic of Moldova and Uzbekistan) will generally remain below the CIS average in the short run.

Downside risks and uncertainties remain important

With the recent stabilization of oil prices around $35 p/b, the risks to the short-term outlook from a further rise in oil prices appear to have receded.[101] Uncertainty remains, nevertheless, about possible terrorist attacks on major oil networks in the Middle East, with subsequent upward pressure on prices, including risk premia.

Another risk is a stronger than expected rise of inflationary pressures as a result of the rapid closing of the global output gap, which could lead to a more pronounced tightening of monetary policy than anticipated, especially in the United States. Interest rates in the United States are generally expected to be raised at a measured pace. This assumes that inflationary pressures will be held in check, in part by the higher trend of productivity growth. A faster than expected tightening of monetary policy in the United States would risk adverse effects on United States equity, bond and real estate markets, with negative repercussions on household net worth and domestic financing conditions. There would also be adverse spillovers to the financing conditions available to emerging markets, reflected in widening spreads and dampening effects on economic activity.

---

[100] In May, the Ministry of the Economy raised its forecast for the rate of GDP growth in 2004 from a range of between 4.8 per cent and 8 per cent to 9.5 per cent.

[101] In its growth forecasts for 2004 and 2005, prepared in the spring of 2004, the OECD assumed an oil price of $32 p/b from the second quarter of 2004.

A more general upward pressure on long-term interest rates in the international bond markets could emerge from the increasing awareness that it may prove to be very difficult for governments of the major economies to reverse the recent deterioration of their public finances, even in an environment of sustained and stronger growth. In the absence of determined efforts to ensure fiscal sustainability, bond yields may rise in response to a higher risk premia, with dampening effects on private sector investment.

In China, which has been a major source of regional and global output growth in recent years, there is a risk that the measures introduced by the authorities to slow down the growth of economic activity could have a more abrupt and sharper impact than intended. The highly indebted state owned sector, moreover, is vulnerable to higher interest rates, pointing to the need for a gradual tightening of financing conditions.

The main downside risk, however, remains the huge current account deficit of the United States. It is generally accepted that this imbalance is not sustainable and will therefore need to be reduced to "normal" levels over the medium term. Current economic conditions, however, are not favourable for this process to make significant progress, if any, in 2004 and 2005. The basic requirement for the current account correction is a substantial depreciation of the dollar to reduce domestic absorption in the United States in combination with a stronger growth of foreign demand for United States products. The adjustment of the real effective exchange rate since early 2002, however, has been partly reversed in the first half of 2004. The major adjustment burden has so far fallen on Europe, given the exchange rate policies pursued in the Asian economies. The growth of domestic demand in Japan and the euro area, moreover, is expected to remain weaker than in the United States. Against this background, major disruptions in the pattern of exchange rates cannot be excluded: these could be triggered by sudden changes in market sentiment and investor confidence with concomitant adverse implications for the recovery in Japan and the euro area. In the United Kingdom, another risk to the sustainability of strong economic growth is a possibly sharp fall in house prices which, if it materialized, would have adverse implications for consumer spending.

Monetary policy can remain on hold in the euro area...

In the euro area, the recovery is still relatively fragile relying, as it does, largely on the stimulus from foreign demand. Against this background and in view of the moderate rates of actual and expected inflation, monetary policy should remain on hold until the recovery is more broadly based, a process which requires a sustained strengthening of domestic demand. The surge in oil prices has translated into a general rise in average domestic price levels due to the subsequent rise in the prices of energy products. This is a normal short-term adjustment process reflecting the change in the terms of trade and the concomitant fall in real incomes due to higher oil prices, and there is therefore nothing that monetary policy should do about this. What monetary policy should be concerned about, however, are the so-called indirect, or second-round, effects of higher oil prices, i.e. the impact on costs of production, especially labour costs, which could trigger an upward inflationary spiral. As in the United States, there is so far no evidence for this kind of pass-through process, which, in any case, given the labour market situation, ample margins of spare capacity and intensive international competitive pressures, can be expected to be very limited in extent.

…while fiscal policy should focus on medium-term consolidation

The crisis surrounding the implementation of the Stability and Growth Pact in 2003 has led to an intensive discussion about possible ways to reform it.[102] As yet there are no firm official positions in this matter, a reflection of a lack of consensus among EU member states. But the European Commission has recently outlined the main elements of a possible strengthening and clarification of the Pact which, at the same time, would increase the flexibility of the rules.[103] These include a greater focus on debt and fiscal sustainability in the surveillance process; more incentives for fiscal consolidation in good current times; the need to take into account country-specific circumstances in the formulation of medium-term budget objectives; and consideration of current economic developments when making recommendations for the correction of excessive deficits.[104] The current fiscal position in several euro area member countries, especially the three larger ones, suggests that the room for manoeuvre of fiscal policy has now been virtually reduced to the operation of automatic stabilizers. The main challenge is to design fiscal consolidation strategies that will ensure fiscal sustainability in the medium and longer term without limiting the operation of fiscal stabilizers.

Should we be more optimistic about the euro area's economic performance?

The euro area's economic performance has been rather disappointing since 2001 and current short-term economic prospects are also relatively modest. There appears to be a pervasive feeling of frustration about a perceived lack of economic dynamism. On the supply side this is seen to be mainly due to excessive rigidities in labour and product markets. But the rigidity of the macroeconomic policy framework has also been widely criticized. The ECB has regularly complained about a lack of structural reforms that it considers are required for raising the rate of potential output growth in the euro area.[105] A recent OECD study points to significant statistical relationships between productivity and innovative activity on the one hand and policy and institutional settings in both product and labour markets on the other.[106]

Consumer confidence in the euro area has been quite depressed recently against the background of weak labour markets and uncertainty about the financial implications of proposals to reform pension and health care systems. This uncertainty has held back household spending on consumer goods, the most important item of expenditure, which accounts for some 60 per cent of GDP. It should be recalled in this connexion that the average unemployment rate in the euro area has been at very high levels for such a long time that most members of the current labour force have only a faint memory, if any, of earlier conditions of "full employment". This helps to explain the uneasiness of workers in the face of cyclical downturns, because losing one's job entails a high risk of a long, if not permanent, exclusion from active participation in the labour market, with an associated sharp decline in real incomes. This contrasts with the United States, where unemployment appears to be mainly cyclical. The persistence of high unemployment in Europe, in fact, reinforces the need not only for labour market reforms but also for an effective social security system, possibly supplemented by private precautionary insurance schemes, as a built-in economic and societal stabilizer.[107]

The economic performance of the euro area (and the EU as a whole) is regularly compared with that of the United States, which is often found to be apparently superior. In fact, the Lisbon agenda, which was formulated in 2000, set the United States as a benchmark, when it set the target of making the EU the most competitive economy in the world by the year 2010. On current trends, however, it is unlikely that this objective will be achieved. This may reflect a lack of commitment by governments to implement the range of measures agreed upon, which would not be the first such disillusionment with an EU-wide agenda. But it may also reflect an excessively optimistic view as to the ability of governments to understand and control the sources of long-term economic growth.

---

[102] UNECE, *Economic Survey of Europe, 2004 No. 1,* chap. 1.

[103] Joaquim Almunia, Member of the European Commission responsible for Economic and Monetary Affairs, *Press Conference on Public Finance Report Communication* (Brussels), 24 June 2004 [www.europa.eu.int/rapid/press].

[104] This is in line with recommendations made in UNECE, *Economic Survey of Europe, 2004 No. 1*, chap. 1.

[105] See, for example, ECB, *Monthly Bulletin,* May 2004, p. 6.

[106] OECD, *The Sources of Economic Growth in OECD Countries* (Paris), 2003.

[107] J.-P. Fitoussi, "Une solidarité coûteuse mais indispensable", *Le Monde, Dossiers & Documents,* No. 332, June 2004.

The perception of lagging behind the United States and the need to better respond to the challenges of globalization has led to pressures for reform of the "European economic model", which is seen to put too much emphasis on social and redistributive mechanisms compared with the more liberal market model in the United States. This is very much the view of the corporate sectors on both sides of the Atlantic. There appears, however, to be a significant difference between perceptions and reality in this matter.[108] Apart from ignoring the fact that Europe is not a homogeneous entity and that there are significant variations among countries around the so-called "European economic model", there has, in fact, been steady progress in important reform areas such as the deregulation of product and financial markets throughout Europe. There has also been a progressive increase in labour market flexibility due to changed rules for unemployment insurance and employment protection and tax reforms have improved the conditions for business activity. In other words, over the past decade or so there has been a progressive change in Europe's economic model towards a more liberal free-market economy with a correspondingly reduced scope for governments to pursue social objectives through direct market interventions. It should also be emphasized that institutional choices reflect cultural traditions and preferences, notably as regards income distribution. It may well be the case that more measures are required to strengthen the supply side of the European economies, but the leitmotif should not be rejection but rather reform of the European model, which for the most part is a reflection of the democratically expressed preferences of European electorates.[109]

The euro area's growth performance over the past decade or so has, moreover, been pulled down by weak economic growth in Germany, which accounts for about one third of the euro area's total GDP. This in turn partly reflects the economic consequences of unification including persistently huge transfer payments to the eastern part of the country and massive overinvestment in the construction sector, which has been depressing total fixed investment for many years. Slow progress with structural reforms has also played a role,[110] but the government has adopted and started to implement an ambitious package of reforms (Agenda 2010) which is expected to improve economic growth performance in the longer term.

In addition, Europe's productivity performance, both in the long and short run, compares quite favourably with that of the United States. The significantly lower average level of GDP per capita in the EU compared with the United States is largely explained by the lower number of hours worked per person in Europe or, largely equivalent, a substantially lower employment rate.[111] The current strong export performance despite the strong appreciation of the euro, suggests, moreover, that, on average, the euro area does not have a problem of international competitiveness. Thus, although the balance of economic advantage may have shifted in some aspects in favour of the United States system, "Europe is not a disaster zone faced with an American economic miracle".[112]

It is important to stress that macroeconomic policies and structural reforms are complements and not substitutes. There is evidently a need to put more emphasis on innovation, to raise investment in human capital and boost basic research and reform labour markets further in order to lift the rate of growth of potential output. But all this can be done much more effectively in a context of sustained economic growth, supported by conducive macroeconomic policies.[113] The plans for a more flexible interpretation of the Stability and Growth Pact therefore go in the right direction. The important issue in the short run is whether the export-led recovery will broaden by spilling over to domestic demand. Given that fiscal policy will be focused on the need for consolidation, this points to the important role of monetary policy in ensuring a supportive policy mix.

---

[108] O. Blanchard, *The Economic Future of Europe*, MIT Department of Economics, Working Paper Series, No. 04-04, February 2004.

[109] A. Turner, *Just Capital – The Liberal Economy* (London, MacMillan, 2001), chap. 6. It may also be noted in this context that "structural problems" have been a traditional feature of the European economy, but that this has not prevented more or less extended periods of strong economic growth in the past

[110] H. Sinn, *Ist Deutschland noch zu retten?* [Can Germany still be saved?] (Münich, 2003).

[111] Blanchard argues that this reflects a greater preference for trading off part of the productivity gains against more leisure rather than gains in real incomes in Europe. O. Blanchard, op. cit. But this would imply that the fall in hours worked is indeed largely voluntary, which is not obvious.

[112] A. Turner, op. cit, p. 165.

[113] J. Pisani-Ferry, *La bonne aventure* (Paris, Éditions La Découverte, 2001), p. 255. See also UNECE, *Economic Survey of Europe, 2001 No. 1*, pp. 7-9.

CHAPTER 2

THE COMPETITIVENESS OF NATIONS: ECONOMIC GROWTH IN THE ECE REGION[114]

2.1 Introduction

Why do some countries grow so much faster, and have much better trade performance, than other countries? What are the crucial factors behind such differences? Which policies can governments pursue to improve the relative performance of their economies (and welfare of its citizens)? These are the kind of questions that motivate a concern for the competitiveness of countries. Although the concept as such has been strongly criticized by some theoreticians, the importance of the underlying challenges makes it unlikely that this issue will lose the attention of policy makers soon.[115]

We begin the paper with a few reflections on the concept of competitiveness and its use. First, the concept is applied on several levels. What has been the prime focus of the debate, and what we will focus on here, is when the concept is applied to a country. Second, it is a relative term. What is of interest is not absolute performance, however that may be defined, but how well a country does relative to others. Some dislike this comparative perspective. But, after all, this is a perspective that we find in nearly all aspects of social life, work, sports, business, etc., among individuals as well as collectives. So why not at the level of countries? We see no compelling reason not to use the concept at that level. Third, when applied to a country, it has a double meaning, it relates both to the economic well-being of its citizens, normally measured through GDP per capita, and the trade performance of the country.[116] The underlying assumption, then, is that these things are intimately related. This is perhaps not so controversial in itself, but the precise nature of this relationship may of course be. In the next section we outline an analytical framework, based on Schumpeterian logic, which among other things explains why, in analyses of competitiveness, it is indeed natural to focus on both GDP and trade performance and their mutual relationship.

Arguably, the discussion of the competitiveness issue has been much obscured by a common tendency among many economists to focus on extremely simplified representations of reality that abstracts from the very facts that make competitiveness an important issue for policy makers and other stakeholders in a country. A well-known example of this is the idea of "perfect competition", which among other things presupposes that all agents have access to the same body of knowledge, produce goods of identical quality and sell these in price-clearing markets, so that the only thing left to care about is to get the price right. For a long time this led applied economists and analysts to focus on price as the only aspect of competitiveness. Joseph Schumpeter long ago described the shortcomings of such simplifications. The true nature of capitalist competition, he argued, is not price competition, as envisaged in traditional textbooks, but technological competition:

> "But in capitalist reality as distinguished from its textbook picture, it is not that kind of competition that counts but the competition from the new commodity, the new technology, the new source of supply, the new type of organization (...) – competition which commands a decisive cost or quality advantage and which strikes not at the margins of the profits and the outputs of the existing firms but at their foundations and their very lives."[117]

In this paper we depart from the "perfect competition" approach and the idea of technology as a

[114] This study, prepared by Jan Fagerberg, Mark Knell and Martin Srholec, is the revised version of a paper presented by the authors at the UNECE Spring Seminar on *Competitiveness and Economic Growth in the ECE Region*, held in Geneva, 23 February 2004. Jan Fagerberg is Professor at the Centre for Technology, Innovation and Culture, University of Oslo. Mark Knell and Martin Srholec are Research Fellows at the Centre. For more details about the Seminar programme see www.unece.org/ead.

[115] For a critique of the concept see, for example, P. Krugman, "Competitiveness: a dangerous obsession", *Foreign Affairs*, Vol. 73, 1994, pp. 28-44. For an extended discussion see J. Fagerberg, "Technology and competitiveness", *Oxford Review of Economic Policy*, Vol. 12, 1996, pp. 39-51, reprinted as chap. 16 in J. Fagerberg, *Technology, Growth and Competitiveness: Selected Essays* (Cheltenham, Edward Elgar, 2002).

[116] There are many definitions around, most of which reflect this "double meaning" in one way or another. A typical example is the following: competitiveness is "the degree to which, under open market conditions, a country can produce goods and services that meet the test of foreign competition, while simultaneously maintaining and expanding domestic real income", OECD, *Technology and the Economy: The Key Relationships* (Paris, OECD, 1992), p. 237.

[117] J. Schumpeter, *Capitalism, Socialism and Democracy* (New York, Harper, 1943), p. 84.

public good. Rather, following Dosi and others, we assume that technology is cumulative and context dependent in ways that prevent the economic benefits of innovation to spread more or less automatically.[118] This more realistic approach to the role of technology in economic change does not prevent diffusion from being a powerful factor behind growth and competitiveness in so-called latecomer countries.[119] On the contrary we side with the economic historian Gerschenkron in his suggestion that the technological gap between a frontier and a latecomer country represents "a great promise" for the latter, since it provides the latecomer with the opportunity of imitating more advanced technology in use elsewhere.[120] However, just as he and others have done, we stress the stringent requirements for getting the most out of such opportunities.[121] In fact, this holds not only for latecomer countries, but also for countries closer to or on the frontier, since similar considerations apply for the successful commercialization of all new technologies, independent of where it was first developed. We use the term "capacity competitiveness" for this aspect of the competitiveness of a country, which we suggest be considered in addition to the two other aspects – technology and price competitiveness – mentioned above. Finally, following one of the suggestions in the literature on competitiveness (see the next section), we also take into account the ability of a country to exploit the changing composition of demand, by offering attractive products that are in high demand at home and abroad. We label this (fourth) aspect "demand competitiveness".

2.2 A synthetic framework

We start by developing a very simple growth model based on Schumpeterian logic, which we will subsequently extend and refine.[122] Assume that the GDP of a country (Y) is a multiplicative function of its technological knowledge (Q) and its capacity for exploiting the benefits of knowledge (C), and a constant (A_1):[123]

$$Y = A_1 Q^\alpha C^\beta \qquad (\alpha, \beta > 0) \qquad (1)$$

Its technological knowledge, in turn, is assumed to be a multiplicative function of knowledge diffused to the region from outside (D) and knowledge (or innovation) created in the country (N) and, again, a constant (A_2):

$$Q = A_2 D^\gamma N^\lambda \qquad (\gamma, \lambda > 0) \qquad (2)$$

Assume further, as common in the literature, that the diffusion of external knowledge follows a logistic curve. This implies that the contribution of diffusion of externally available knowledge to economic growth is an increasing function of the distance between the level of knowledge appropriated in the country and that of the country on the technological frontier (for the frontier country, this contribution will be zero by definition). Let the total amount of knowledge, adjusted for differences in size of countries, in the frontier country and the country under consideration, be T_* and T, respectively:

$$d = \phi - \phi \frac{T}{T_*} \qquad (\phi > 0) \qquad (3)$$

By differentiating (2), using small case letters for growth rates, and substituting (3) into it, we arrive at the following expression for the growth of a country's technological knowledge:

$$q = \gamma\phi - \gamma\phi \frac{T}{T_*} + \lambda n \qquad (4)$$

By differentiating (1) and substituting (4) into it we get the country's rate of growth:

$$y = \alpha\gamma\phi - \alpha\gamma\phi \frac{T}{T_*} + \alpha\lambda n + \beta c \qquad (5)$$

Since our primary interest is in "why growth differs" it may be useful to express the rate of growth of the country in relative terms (growth relative to the world average), y_{rel}:[124]

$$y_{rel} = y - w = -\alpha\gamma\phi \frac{T - T_w}{T_*} + \alpha\lambda(n - n_w) + \qquad (6)$$

$$\beta(c - c_w)$$

[118] G. Dosi, "Sources, procedures and microeconomic effects of innovation", *Journal of Economic Literature*, Vol. 26, 1988, pp. 1120-1171.

[119] J. Fagerberg and M. Godinho, "Innovation and catching up", in J. Fagerberg, D. Mowery and R. Nelson (eds.), *Oxford Handbook of Innovation* (Oxford, Oxford University Press, 2004), forthcoming.

[120] A. Gerschenkron, *Economic Backwardness in Historical Perspective* (Cambridge, MA, The Belknap Press, 1962).

[121] See, for example, M. Abramovitz, "Catching up, forging ahead, and falling behind", *Journal of Economic History*, Vol. 46, 1986, pp. 386-406, and M. Abramovitz, "The origins of the postwar catch-up and convergence boom", in J. Fagerberg, B. Verspagen and N. von Tunzelmann (eds.), *The Dynamics of Technology, Trade and Growth* (Aldershot, Edward Elgar, 1994), pp. 21-52.

[122] This section draws on J. Fagerberg, "The dynamics of technology, growth and trade: a Schumpeterian perspective", in H. Hanusch and A. Pyka (eds.), *Elgar Companion to Neo-Schumpeterian Economics* (Cheltenham, Edward Elgar), forthcoming.

[123] Instead of seeing the model (1)-(6) as a model of GDP growth, one might consider it as a model of GDP per capita (worker) growth, in which case all variables would enter on a per capita (worker) basis. The first application of the model was based on the former assumption, applied here, while later applications, for instance on regional growth, have generally assumed the latter. The relationship between the two versions of the model is straightforward. Note, however, that if the latter assumption is chosen, population (or labour force) growth would enter into the determination of GDP growth.

[124] This is based on the assumption that the two countries face the same competitive conditions (elasticities) but vary in other respects.

Hence, following this perspective the rate of growth of a country may be seen as the outcome of three sets of factors:

- The potential for exploiting knowledge developed elsewhere;

- Creation of new knowledge in the country (innovation);

- Growth in the capacity to exploit the potential entailed by knowledge (independently of where it is created).

This model, simple as it is, encompasses many of the empirical models found in the literature. For instance, the empirical models used in the "catching-up" literature can be seen as a version of (5)-(6) in which the innovation term is ignored.[125] Fagerberg applied the above model to a sample of developed and medium income countries. It was shown that countries that caught up very fast also had very rapid growth of innovative activity. The analysis suggested that superior growth in innovative activity was the prime factor behind the huge difference in performance between Asian and Latin American NICs in the 1970s and early 1980s.[126] It has also been shown that the continuing rapid growth of the Asian NICs relative to other country groupings in the decade that followed was primarily caused by the rapid increases in its innovative performance.[127] Moreover, estimations of the model for different time periods indicate that while imitation has become more demanding over time (and hence more costly to undertake), innovation has become a more powerful factor in explaining observed differences in growth performance.[128]

The model opens up for international technology flows but abstracts from flows of goods and services. We will now introduce the latter. For simplicity we do this in a two country framework, in which the other country is labelled "world". Define the share of a country's exports (X) in world demand (W) as $S_x = X / W$, and similarly the share of imports (M) in its own GDP (Y) as $S_m = M / Y$. For the sake of exposition we assume that the market shares of a country are unaffected by the growth of the market, but we will relax this assumption later. Following the Schumpeterian logic outlined in the previous section, we will assume that, apart from a constant term, a country's market share for exports

depends on three factors: its technological competitiveness (its knowledge assets relative to competitors); its capacity to exploit technology commercially (again relative to competitors); and its price (P) competitiveness (relative prices on tradeables in common currency):

$$S_x = A_3 \left(\frac{Q}{Q_W} \right)^{\rho} \left(\frac{C}{C_W} \right)^{\mu} \left(\frac{P}{P_W} \right)^{-\pi} \quad (\rho, \mu, \pi > 0) \qquad (7)$$

Since, by definition, imports in this model are "world" exports, we may model the import share in the same way, using bars to distinguish the coefficients of the two equations:

$$S_M = A_4 \left(\frac{Q_W}{Q} \right)^{\bar{\rho}} \left(\frac{C_W}{C} \right)^{\bar{\mu}} \left(\frac{P_W}{P} \right)^{-\bar{\pi}} \quad (\bar{\rho}, \bar{\mu}, \bar{\pi} > 0) \qquad (8)$$

By differentiating (7) and substituting (4) into it, and similarly for (8), we arrive at the dynamic expressions for the growth in market shares:

$$s_X = -\rho\gamma\phi \frac{T - T_W}{T_*} + \rho\lambda(n - n_w) + \mu(c - c_w) - \qquad (9)$$

$$\pi(p - p_W)$$

$$s_M = -\bar{\rho}\gamma\phi \frac{T_W - T}{T_*} + \bar{\rho}\lambda(n_W - n) + \bar{\mu}(c_W - c) - \qquad (10)$$

$$\bar{\pi}(p_W - p)$$

We see that the growth of the market share of a country depends on four factors:

- The potential for exploiting knowledge developed elsewhere, which depends on the country's level of technological development relative to the world average;

- Creation of new knowledge (technology) in the country (innovation) relative to that of competitors;

- Growth in the capacity to exploit knowledge, independently of where it is created, relative to that of competitors;

- Change in relative prices in common currency.

Following earlier contributions by Thirlwall and Fagerberg we now introduce the requirement that trade in goods and services has to balance (if not in the short run, than in the long).[129] Countries may, however, have foreign debts (or assets). As is easily verified, we may multiply the left or right hand side of (11) with a scalar without any consequence for the subsequent deductions. Hence an alternative way to formulate this restriction might be that the deficit (surplus) used to service foreign

---

[125] See, for example, W. Baumol, S. Batey Blackman and E. Wolff, *Productivity and American Leadership: The Long View* (Cambridge, MA, MIT Press, 1989).

[126] J. Fagerberg, "Why growth rates differ," in G. Dosi et al. (eds.), *Technical Change and Economic Theory* (London, Pinter, 1988), pp. 432-457.

[127] J. Fagerberg and B. Verspagen, "Technology-gaps, innovation-diffusion and transformation: an evolutionary interpretation", *Research Policy*, Vol. 31, 2002, pp. 1291-1304.

[128] J. Fagerberg, "A technology gap approach to why growth rates differ", *Research Policy*, Vol. 16, 1987, pp. 87-99, reprinted as chap. 1 in J. Fagerberg, *Technology, Growth and Competitiveness: Selected Essays* (Cheltenham, Edward Elgar, 2002), and J. Fagerberg and B. Verspagen, loc. cit.

[129] A. Thirlwall, "The balance of payments constraints as an explanation of international growth rate differences", *Banca Nazionale del Lavoro Quarterly Review*, No. 32, 1979, pp. 45-53, and J. Fagerberg, "International competitiveness", *Economic Journal*, Vol. 98, 1988, pp. 355-374, reprinted as chap. 12 in J. Fagerberg, *Technology, Growth and Competitiveness…*, op. cit.

debt (derived from assets abroad) should be a constant fraction of exports (or imports):

$$XP = MP_W \qquad (11)$$

By differentiating (11), substituting S_X and S_M into it and rearranging we arrive at the dynamic form of the restriction:

$$y = (s_X - s_M) + (p - p_W) + w \qquad (12)$$

This assumption has been extensively tested on data for developed economies and found to hold well.[130]

By substituting (9)-(10) into (12) and rearranging we get the reduced form of the model:

$$y_{rel} = -(\rho + \overline{\rho})\gamma\phi \frac{T - T_w}{T_*} + (\rho + \overline{\rho})\lambda(n - n_w) + \qquad (13)$$
$$(\mu + \overline{\mu})(c - c_W) + [1 - (\pi + \overline{\pi})](p - p_W)$$

By comparing this equation with the similar reduced form of the growth model (6) we see that, apart from the last term on the right hand side, the model has the same structure. The only difference is that the coefficients of the basic growth equation now are shown to be sums of coefficients for the similar variables in the market-share equations (for the domestic and world market). Hence, the sensitivity of the markets (or "selection environments") for new technologies clearly matters for growth. The final term is the familiar Marshall-Lerner condition, which states that the sum of the price elasticities for exports and imports (when measured in absolute value) has to be higher than one if deteriorating price competitiveness is going to harm the external balance (and – in this case – the rate of growth of GDP).

We have modelled the market share equations on the assumption that, when not only price, but also technology and capacity have been taken into account as competitive factors, demand may be assumed to have a unitary elasticity. This means, for instance, abstracting from other factors, that if export demand grows by a certain percentage, exports will do the same, so that the market share remains unaffected. However, there are reasons to believe that this assumption, although appealing in its simplicity, does not necessarily hold in reality. For instance, it has been argued that if a country has a pattern of specialization geared towards industries that are in high (low) demand internationally its exports may grow faster (slower) than world demand, quite independently of what happens to other factors.[131] This

way of reasoning, distinctly Keynesian in flavour, places more emphasis on the growth of world demand, and on the "income elasticities of demand" for a country's exports and imports in determining a country's growth performance.[132] The higher the income elasticity of exports relative to that of imports, it is argued, the higher the rate of growth will be, and vice versa. Arguably, this might be expected to be of greatest relevance for small countries, since these are likely to be more specialized in their economic (and trade) structure than large ones. To take this possibility into account we, following Fagerberg, introduce demand in the market shares equations:[133]

$$S_x = A_3 \left(\frac{Q}{Q_w}\right)^{\rho} \left(\frac{C}{C_w}\right)^{\mu} \left(\frac{P}{P_w}\right)^{-\pi} W^{\tau-1} \qquad (\tau > 0) \qquad (7')$$

$$S_m = A_4 \left(\frac{Q_w}{Q}\right)^{\overline{\rho}} \left(\frac{C_w}{C}\right)^{\overline{\mu}} \left(\frac{P_w}{P}\right)^{-\overline{\pi}} Y^{\overline{\tau}-1} \qquad (\overline{\tau} > 0) \qquad (8')$$

By differentiating and substituting we arrive at the following expression for the reduced form:

$$y_{rel} = -\frac{(\rho + \overline{\rho})}{\overline{\tau}}\gamma\phi \frac{T - T_w}{T_*} + \frac{(\rho + \overline{\rho})}{\overline{\tau}}\lambda(n - n_w) + \qquad (13')$$
$$\frac{(\mu + \overline{\mu})}{\overline{\tau}}(c - c_W) + \frac{1 - (\pi + \overline{\pi})}{\overline{\tau}}(p - p_W) + \frac{\tau - \overline{\tau}}{\overline{\tau}} w$$

The first thing to note is that the higher the demand elasticity for imports, the lower the effect on growth of all other factors. The second is, as before, that while the first three terms on the right hand side resemble the basic growth model (6), the two last terms in (13') resemble the model suggested by Thirlwall.[134] Hence, both the basic model (6) and Thirlwall's model can be seen as special cases of a more general, open economy model.[135]

2.3 The competitiveness of the countries of the ECE region 1993-2001: the "stylized facts"

Fagerberg applied the above open economy model to data for developed (OECD) economies.[136] Between

---

[130] J. Fagerberg, "International competitiveness", op. cit., and V. Meliciani, *Technology, Trade and Growth in OECD Countries – Does Specialization Matter?* (London, Routledge, 2001).

[131] A. Thirlwall, loc. cit., and N. Kaldor, "The role of increasing returns, technical progress and cumulative causation in the theory of international trade and economic growth", *Economie Appliqué* (ISMEA), Vol. 34, 1981, pp. 593-617.

[132] The income elasticity of exports is the growth in exports resulting from a 1 per cent increase in world demand, holding relative prices constant (and ignoring cyclical factors). It is similar for imports.

[133] J. Fagerberg, "International competitiveness", op. cit.

[134] A. Thirlwall, loc. cit.

[135] If the demand elasticities are the same in both markets and the Marshall-Learner condition is exactly satisfied (or relative prices do not change), the two last terms vanish, and we are back in a model that for all practical purposes is identical to (6). If, on the other hand, the country's technological level is exactly average and both relative technology and relative capacity keep constant, the three first terms vanish, and only Thirlwall's model remains.

[136] J. Fagerberg, "International competitiveness", op. cit.

1960 and 1983, the results generally confirmed the importance of growth in technological and capacity competitiveness. The impact of price or cost factors was found to be relatively marginal, consistent with the earlier findings by Kaldor (the so-called Kaldor paradox).[137] Recently, Meliciani has applied a similar model to a longer time series, including a more recent time period, with broadly similar results.[138] In this paper we move significantly beyond the previous empirical applications of this perspective. First we consider a much broader sample, 49 countries, characterized by very different development levels and trends, for a more recent (though shorter) time span (1993-2001). The sample consists of all ECE countries for which data were available, supplemented by some Asian and Latin American countries. The non-member countries were included partly for a comparative purpose, but also because some of these countries during the last few decades have become very important players in the global economy. Second, and of even greater importance, we develop much more sophisticated indicators of the various aspects that together determine the overall competitiveness of a country. This is particularly the case for "technology competitiveness" and "capacity competitiveness", both of which are multidimensional in character and consequently hard to measure. But we also develop a new indicator of "demand competitiveness" that in a better way captures the underlying ideas behind the inclusion of this particular dimension.

Chart 2.3.1 presents some basic data on development levels and trends for the countries included in our investigation. While the vertical axis measures average productivity or income over the period (GDP per capita in PPPs in 1997), the horizontal axis reports annual average growth over the period (1993-2001). By combining these two aspects, level and trend, four different quadrants emerge. First, to the upper left we have countries with above average level GDP per capita but relatively slow growth, i.e. countries that "lose momentum". Japan, Switzerland and the United States are the prime examples. In contrast, in the upper left quadrant, we have countries that continue to grow fast despite a high level of GDP per capita ("moving ahead"). The most spectacular example is Ireland; other countries

included in this more dynamic category are Finland, Singapore and Taiwan. However, most developed countries, including all the remaining EU members, cluster on the borderline between "losing momentum" and "moving ahead", indicating a growth performance close to the average of the sample.

Of particular interest is the performance of the poorer economies, those in the lower half of the graph. Here we see a very clear distinction between those that are "catching up" (in the lower right) and those that are "falling further behind" (in the lower left). The former, those that appear to be on a "catching up" trajectory, include all the new EU members (joined by Croatia), three Asian countries (China, Malaysia and the Republic of Korea) and in Latin America (Chile). In sharp contrast to this favourable development, all the countries in our sample that formerly belonged to the Soviet Union (Belarus, the Republic of Moldova, Russia and Ukraine), and Bulgaria and Romania as well, continue to fall further behind. This unfavourable performance is shared with, among others, some of the Asian and Latin American countries included in our sample.

Clearly there is a lot of diversity in how countries perform. Although in each and every case there will be specific factors at work these will not be in focus here. Rather we will attempt, in a better way than in previous analyses, to single out some general factors that may be of interest when discussing the wide differences across countries in economic performance. These are:

- Technology competitiveness;
- Capacity competitiveness;
- Cost competitiveness;
- Demand competitiveness.

Of these the two former are clearly multi-dimensional and therefore more difficult to handle. Our approach here will be to identify the most important dimensions, find reliable indicators, express these in a comparable format and weigh them together, giving each dimension an equal weight in the calculation of the composite indicator.[139] A complete list with definitions and

---

[137] Kaldor showed for a number of countries that over the long term market shares for exports and relative unit costs or prices tend to move together, i.e. that growing market shares and increasing relative costs or prices tend to go hand in hand – see N. Kaldor, *The Effect of Devaluations on Trade in Manufactures, in Further Essays on Applied Economics* (London, Duckworth, 1978). This was, of course, the opposite of what you would expect from the simplistic though at the time widely diffused approach focusing exclusively on the (assumedly negative) impact of increasing relative costs or prices on market shares, hence the term "paradox". Fagerberg has shown that this finding also applies to a more recent time period, see J. Fagerberg, "Technology and competitiveness", loc. cit.

[138] Meliciani also added a "specialization" variable, reflecting the extent to which countries were specialized in technologically progressive sectors, to the market share equations, for which she found empirical support – V. Meliciani, op. cit.

[139] Admittedly, there is an element of arbitrariness involved here. It would of course have been preferable to have prior knowledge about the "true weights" to use. Having no such information, we chose to give each variable an equal weight. Alternatively, one might have weighted variables based on the degree of correlation, reflecting the assumption that correlated variables express aspects of the same underlying phenomenon, in contrast to uncorrelated ones that are assumed to refer to different phenomena (as done in so-called "factor analysis", for instance). Correlation and causation are not the same, however. For instance, in our case ICT use and corruption are highly correlated, without any obvious causal relationship. In contrast, our two measures of technology diffusion, investments and fees/payments for use of proprietary technology, are almost uncorrelated. For an extended discussion see European Commission, *State-of-the-art Report on Current Methodologies and Practices for Composite Indicator Development* (Ispra, European Commission Joint Research Centre, 2002), and M. Freudenberg, *Composite Indicators of Country Performance: A Critical Assessment*, OECD, STI Working Paper 2003/16 (Paris), November 2003.

CHART 2.3.1

Overall competitiveness, 1993-2001

(GDP per capita at current dollar prices and PPPs)

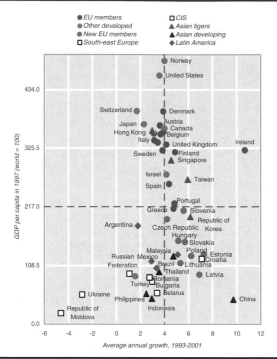

Source: Authors' computations based on World Bank, *World Development Indicators (WDI)*.

Note: Dashed horizontal and vertical lines indicate sample averages.

CHART 2.3.2

Overall and technology competitiveness, 1993-2001

(Average levels)

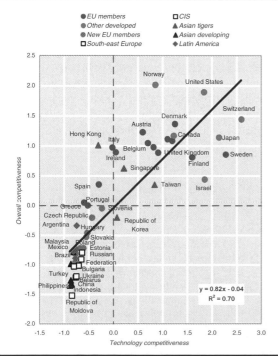

Source: Authors' computations based on World Bank, *World Development Indicators (WDI)*; OECD, *Main Science and Technology Indicators (MSTI)*, and Patent Database; UNESCO; RICYT.

Note: Estimated coefficients are rounded to two digits. See also note to chart 2.3.1

sources for the indicators used is given in the annex. In some cases, missing data had to be estimated. Whenever possible, indicators are defined as activities measured in quantity or constant prices, deflated by population. To further increase comparability we normalize the indicators as follows:

$$\frac{actual\ value\ -\ mean\ value}{standard\ deviation} \qquad (14)$$

In the calculations the mean and standard deviation were fixed to that of the median year (1997). This means that changes over time in the volume of the activities measured by the individual indicators are allowed to spill over to the composite indicator (along with the changes caused by shifts in the position of countries on each individual indicator). For instance, in the early 1990s ICT diffusion was still at a relatively low level. Today ICT technologies are very widely used and are, arguably, of much higher importance to competitiveness than they were a decade ago. The way we calculate the capacity indicator is consistent with this.

(i) Technology competitiveness

Technology (or technological) competitiveness refers to the ability to compete successfully in markets for new goods and services. Hence, this type of competitiveness is closely related to the innovativeness of a country. There is, however, no available data source which measures innovativeness directly. Instead what we have are different data sources reflecting different aspects of the phenomenon. R&D expenditures, for instance, measure some (but not all) of the resources that go into developing new goods and services. Patent statistics, on the other hand, measure the output of (patentable) inventions. This is a very reliable indicator, but the propensity to patent varies considerably across industries, and many innovations are not patentable. So many innovations would not be accounted for by using this indicator only. Taking into account both indicators clearly gives a more balanced picture. To further increase the reliability of the composite indicator we also include a measure of the quality of the science base on which innovation activities depend as reflected in articles published in scientific and technical journals.

Chart 2.3.2 plots technology competitiveness on the horizontal axis against overall competitiveness, as reflected in GDP per capita, on the vertical axis. As is evident from the regression line there is a very close correlation between overall and technological competitiveness. The main deviants are some former centrally planned economies (headed by the Republic of Moldova) and developing countries in Asia, all of which have GDP per capita levels much below what should be expected from their levels of technology competitiveness. But there are also some small advanced countries whose GDP per capita tends to lag behind technological competitiveness (Israel and

Sweden in particular). On the other side of the spectrum, Hong Kong and Norway are examples of countries that have managed to arrive at relatively high levels of productivity and income without a similarly high technology competitiveness.

In chart 2.3.3 the level and trend in technology competitiveness are plotted against each other. When compared with the case of overall competitiveness in chart 2.3.1, the indicator for technological competitiveness displays a much stronger tendency towards divergence. Countries either move ahead of the others or fall further behind, with only a few staying in the middle. Among the countries that move ahead technologically, Finland, Israel, Sweden and Taiwan are most prominent. Those falling further behind include the former centrally planned economies (except Slovenia) and the developing countries in Asia and Latin America.

(ii) Capacity competitiveness

The distinction between technology competitiveness and capacity competitiveness is crucial. For instance, Sony did not develop the transistor, but showed a superior capacity to United States firms when it came to exploiting this new technology in a way that sustained competitiveness. In fact, many of the inroads of Japanese producers on Western markets during most of the post-war period were of this kind. Although the distinction may be clear enough in theory, in practice it may not be all that simple, since resources that are devoted to developing new goods and services may also be beneficial for the ability to exploit such innovations economically and vice versa.[140] Nevertheless, we will focus on four dimensions of capacity competitiveness, as distinct from technology competitiveness. These four dimensions are human capital, ICT infrastructure, diffusion and social and institutional aspects. The importance of a well-developed human capital base for exploiting technological opportunities goes without saying; here we focus on secondary and tertiary education (as reflected in enrolment rates) in particular. Similarly, a well-developed ICT infrastructure is generally acknowledged as a must, we measure this with the help of data on the spread of computers and telecommunication technologies across the population. However, the importance of diffusion – or the ability to quickly put new technologies into use – extends beyond that of ICT. We take this into account in two ways, as embodied in investments and disembodied through payments of royalty or license fees. Finally, we acknowledge that there may be a number of social and institutional factors of importance for the capacity to exploit technological opportunity. Although such factors often defy measurement, at least on a broad cross-

country/cross-temporal basis, there exist survey data on the incidence of corruption across countries, which is relevant to consider.

Chart 2.3.4 plots our estimate of capacity competitiveness (horizontal axis) against overall competitiveness as reflected in GDP per capita (vertical axis). As with technology competitiveness there is a very clear, positive relationship between capacity competitiveness and GDP per capita. The fit is even better than in the previous case, 86 per cent of the differences in GDP per capita across countries can be explained by differences in the capacity to exploit technological opportunity (against 70 per cent for technology competitiveness). Consistent with this close fit there are few obvious deviants, with the possible exception of Ireland, which reports a much higher capacity for exploiting technology than indicated by its GDP per capita.

Chart 2.3.5, which plots the level and trend of capacity competitiveness against each other, confirms the peculiar Irish pattern, with a very high and growing level of capacity for exploiting new technology. Hence, Ireland appears to be an example of a country that has, with considerable success, focused mainly on developing capacity competitiveness at the possible expense of technological competitiveness. This contrasts with the position of a number of other economies, such as Israel, Japan and Switzerland which – although technologically advanced – appear to have less well developed capabilities for exploiting these advantages commercially (chart 2.3.6). While technological competitiveness displays strong signs of divergence, there is more convergence going on in the capacity to exploit technological opportunity. The Baltics, in particular, appear to catch up in capacity competitiveness, while some of the most advanced economies have very slow capacity growth. However, there are also diverging trends at work, with a number of the formerly centrally planned economies reporting below average capacity growth; the same holds for most of the developing Asian and Latin American countries included in our sample.

(iii) Price competitiveness

In one sense price or cost competitiveness should be the easiest dimension to identify. In fact, for a long time economists focused only on price or cost competitiveness, and a well defined indicator – unit labour costs in manufacturing in a common currency – was readily available. We, however, found that indicator to be one of the most problematic in terms of data coverage. The estimates of price or cost competitiveness (unit wage costs in manufacturing) presented here are based on several sources and considerable judgement had to be made in order to improve the coverage (see the annex for further details). Hence the estimates presented should be interpreted with considerable care.

---

[140] W. Cohen and D. Levinthal, "Absorptive capacity: a new perspective on learning and innovation", *Administrative Science Quarterly*, Vol. 35, 1990, pp. 128-152.

CHART 2.3.3

Technology competitiveness, 1993-2001

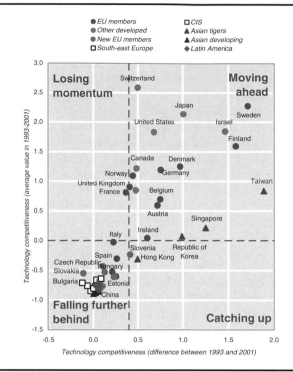

Source: As for chart 2.3.2.
Note: As for chart 2.3.1.

CHART 2.3.5

Capacity competitiveness, 1993-2001

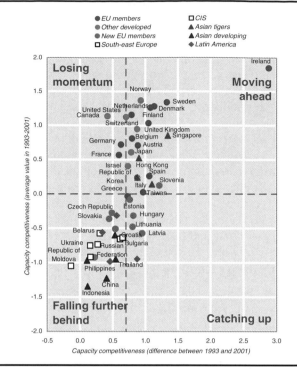

Source: As for chart 2.3.4.
Note: As for chart 2.3.1.

CHART 2.3.4

Overall and capacity competitiveness, 1993-2001
(Average levels)

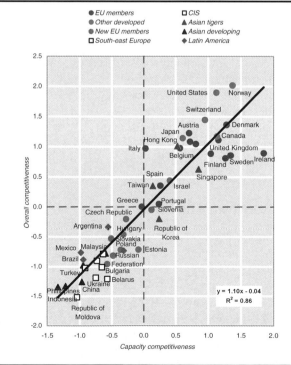

Source: Authors' computations based on World Bank, *WDI;* UNESCO; USAID, Global Education Database; ITU, World Telecommunication Indicators; Transparency International, Corruption Perception Index.

Note: Estimated coefficients are rounded to two digits. See also note to chart 2.3.1

CHART 2.3.6

Technology and capacity competitiveness, 1993-2001
(Average levels)

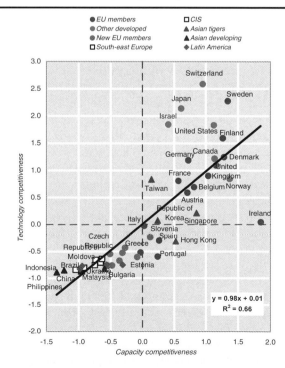

Source: Authors' computations based on World Bank, *WDI;* OECD, *MSTI* and Patent Database; UNESCO; USAID, Global Education Database; ITU, World Telecommunication Indicators; Transparency International, Corruption Perception Index; RICYT.

Note: Estimated coefficients are rounded to two digits. See also note to chart 2.3.1.

CHART 2.3.7

Overall and price competitiveness, 1993-2001

(Average levels)

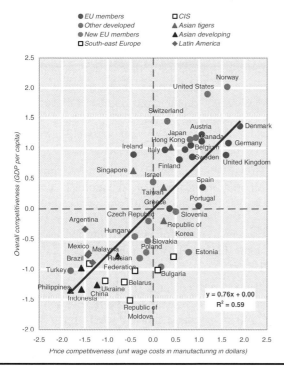

CHART 2.3.8

Overall and price competitiveness, 1993 and 2001

(Percentage change)

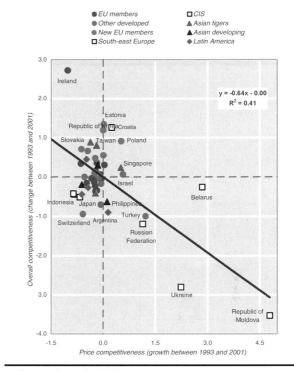

Source: Authors' computations based on World Bank, *WDI*; OECD, STAN Database; ILO, LABORSTA Database; Eurostat, AMECO Database; WIIW, WIIW Industrial Database Eastern Europe.

Note: Estimated coefficients are rounded to two digits. See also note to chart 2.3.1.

Source: As for chart 2.3.7.

Note: Estimated coefficients are rounded to two digits. See also note to chart 2.3.1.

Chart 2.3.7 plots price competitiveness, measured as unit wage costs in manufacturing (horizontal axis) against overall competitiveness, measured through GDP per capita (vertical axis). As is evident from the chart there generally is a positive relationship as should be expected; more advanced (richer) economies, using highly qualified labour, generally pay higher wages per unit produced than do less developed, poorer countries. There is, however, considerable variation around the regression line. For instance, some developed economies, such as Ireland, Norway, Switzerland and the United States, consistently have higher productivity levels than indicated by their price or cost competitiveness, while for some formerly centrally planned economies the situation is the other way around.[141]

The rate of change in price or cost competitiveness is usually considered as more important than the absolute level. Chart 2.3.8 plots the growth of price competitiveness (unit wage costs in manufacturing in common currency) on the horizontal axis against growth of

overall competitiveness (GDP per capita) on the vertical. The regression line has the usual negative slope, which means that on average the higher the growth of price competitiveness, the lower the rate of growth, and vice versa. This, obviously, concurs with the traditional view on competitiveness, which focuses mainly on the damaging effects of excessive wage growth on the economy. Note, however, that the estimated relationship depends to some extent on outliers (Belarus, Ireland, the Republic of Moldova and Ukraine). If these observations are excluded, the regression line becomes much flatter, and the estimated coefficient is no longer significant.

(iv) Demand competitiveness

The relationship between a country production (or trade) structure and the composition of world demand may also be of importance for competitiveness. The better the match, the more favourably the country's economy should develop, and vice versa. We capture this aspect by weighting the growth of world demand (by commodity) by the commodity composition of each country's exports:

$$\sum_{i=1}^{n} w_{ij} g_{iT} \qquad (15)$$

where w is the share of product group in country j exports in the base year, g is the growth of the export market, i is the product group and T is the market total.

---

[141] This may reflect differences in exchange rates. While GDP per capita is measured in PPPs, wages are measured in current exchange rates, which in several countries have been regulated to encourage exports and attract inflows of foreign capital.

CHART 2.3.9

Overall and demand competitiveness, 1993-2001

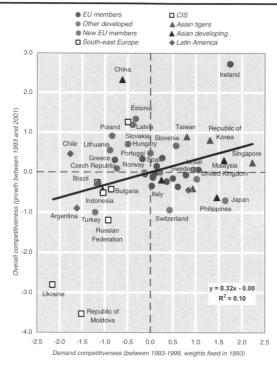

Source: Authors' computations based on World Bank, *WDI* and United Nations COMTRADE Database.

Note: Estimated coefficients are rounded to two digits. See also note to chart 2.3.1.

Chart 2.3.9 plots the relationship between demand competitiveness (horizontal axis), and growth of GDP per capita (vertical axis). It is evident from the regression included in the chart that there is a positive albeit weak relationship between the two variables. Those that appear to have gained most from the composition of demand were Ireland and some Asian economies, while some former centrally planned economies, joined by Chile and Argentina, were the least favourably affected.

2.4 The dynamics of the competitiveness of the countries of the ECE region

Having developed empirical indicators of the different aspects of competitiveness, we will apply these indicators in an analysis of the differing performance of ECE countries. However, the short time period for which (reliable) data are available (especially for many of the former centrally planned economies) puts severe limits on the possibilities for econometric work. We therefore refrained from estimating the entire model, and chose instead to concentrate on its reduced form, as given by equation (13'), according to which the rate of economic growth of a country should be a weighted sum of:

- The potential for diffusion;

- Growth in technological competitiveness;

- Growth in capacity competitiveness;

- Growth in cost competitiveness;

- Demand competitiveness, all relative to that of other countries.

The main purpose of the estimation, then, is to estimate these weights, which in turn will be used to assess the impact of the different aspects of competitiveness on economic growth. To calculate the potential for diffusion we use, as in previous empirical applications of this model, the difference between the level of GDP per capita in the country and average GDP in our sample, deflated by the GDP per capita in the leader country. For the other four variables we used the indicators developed in the previous section.

However, the normalization procedure used in creating the indicators of technology and capacity competitiveness made it difficult to calculate growth rates. We therefore transformed the normalized indicators to a series of positive numbers (by adding a sufficiently high positive number) before calculating the growth rates.[142]

Table 2.4.1 presents the results of the regression analysis. The coefficients for the five variables included in the model all have the expected signs, significantly different from zero at the 1 per cent or 10 per cent level. The explanatory value is high, above 70 per cent. Since the period of estimation was characterized by severe problems for some country groupings (the "Asian crisis" for instance), we also test for the possible impact of this by including dummy variables for relevant country groupings. As is evident from the table none of these dummies were significant at conventional levels of significance, and the impact on the estimates for the other variables was small, although the significance of the estimated coefficients declined in a few cases (particularly for the demand variable).

To illustrate the implications of these estimates, we decomposed the estimated growth of GDP (relative to the average of the sample) for eight different country groups into its constituent parts (as explained by the estimated model and the relevant data). Table 2.4.2 ranks the eight country groups after their initial GDP per capita, from highest to lowest. As is evident from·the table, the model captures most of the qualitative features, although the explanatory power is not perfect, especially not for some

---

[142] Assume a variable A with a constant mean m and a constant standard deviation s, then the normalized indicator i of A is $i = (A-m)/s$. We then define a variable $I = i + n$, which we substitute into the expression for i. Differentiating with respect to time and rearranging we get the following expression for the growth rate of I: $dI/I = dA/(A+s(n-m/s))$. As is easily verifiable, the actual and transformed variable grow at the same rate if $n = m/s$. Since this ratio is unknown, we used the means of similar ratios for the variables included in the calculation of the composite indicators. As a result, in calculating the growth technology competitiveness indicator, n was set to 1 and for capacity competitiveness to 2. However, it turned out that the two series became highly correlated, giving rise to multicollinearity. In an attempt to reduce this problem, we transformed the scale of capacity growth indicator by adding 10 instead of 2 (before calculating the growth of this indicator).

TABLE 2.4.1

Results of OLS regression analysis, 1993-2001

	(1)	(2)	(3)	(4)	(5)
Intercept	0.000	0.044	0.070	-0.069	-0.003
	(0.000)	(0.208)	(0.341)	(-0.309)	(-0.012)
Gap	-0.031	-0.031	-0.033	-0.029	-0.031
	(-3.561)***	(-3.556)***	(-3.759)***	(-3.208)***	(-3.144)***
Technology	0.202	0.196	0.178	0.205	0.201
	(2.755)***	(2.652)***	(2.359)**	(2.779)***	(2.433)**
Capacity	1.077	1.104	1.104	0.983	1.083
	(1.931)*	(1.962)*	(1.991)**	(1.708)*	(1.758)*
Price	-0.567	-0.531	-0.595	-0.562	-0.566
	(-5.572)***	(-4.624)***	(-5.749)***	(-5.474)***	(-5.325)***
Demand	0.425	0.400	0.422	0.444	0.422
	(1.716)*	(1.588)	(1.719)*	(1.772)*	(1.578)
Dummy for CIS countries		-0.716			
		(-0.700)			
Dummy for Balkan countries			-1.150		
			(-1.260)		
Dummy for new EU members				0.422	
				(0.717)	
Dummy for Asian countries					0.017
					(0.024)
R^2	0.708	0.712	0.719	0.712	0.708
Adjusted R^2	0.674	0.670	0.679	0.671	0.667
F-test	20.875	17.272	17.899	17.286	16.992
Observations	49	49	49	49	49

Note: t-statistics are in parentheses. Dependent variable is the annual growth rate of real GDP. The asterisks *, **, and *** denote significance at the 10, 5 and 1 per cent levels (two-tailed tests).

TABLE 2.4.2

Actual and estimated differences in growth vis-à-vis the world average, 1993-2001

Region	GDP per capita (1993)	Actual difference in growth	Estimated difference in growth	Explanatory factors				
				Gap	Technology	Capacity	Price	Demand
Other developed	22 270	-0.2	-0.8	-1.2	-0.1	–	0.2	0.3
EU members	17 826	0.3	0.5	-0.7	0.3	0.3	0.4	0.2
Asian tigers	14 632	2.0	2.4	-0.3	1.6	0.4	0.1	0.6
New EU members	7 621	0.8	0.5	0.5	-0.1	0.1	0.2	-0.2
Latin America	7 276	0.1	0.2	0.6	-0.2	-0.1	0.4	-0.5
South-east Europe	5 180	-1.1	-0.6	0.8	-0.6	-0.4	–	-0.4
CIS	4 633	-5.4	-5.0	0.9	-1.0	-0.7	-3.4	-0.7
Asian developing	3 709	1.7	1.2	1.0	-0.3	-0.4	0.8	0.2

Source: Author's calculations. Data for GDP (in PPP current international dollars) from World Bank, *World Development Indicators (WDI)*.

of the richest countries in our sample (the "other developed" countries). The model predicts that these rich countries should be expected to grow relatively slowly (as they do on average), mainly as a consequence of a lack of diffusion potential and the failure to increase technology and capacity competitiveness sufficiently to make up for this loss. However, the model fails to replicate "the new economy boom" that some of these countries went through in the 1990s, and hence underestimates their average growth during this period. The prediction is better for the EU countries (which also benefit less than many others from the potential for diffusion). However, on average, for the EU countries this is more than counteracted by other factors.[143]

The prediction is also reasonable for the Asian tigers, whose relatively rapid growth is mainly accounted for by growing technological competitiveness. This contrasts with the performance of the poorer country groupings, all of which suffer from deteriorating technology competitiveness (relative to the sample average) and, with the exception of the new EU members, deteriorating capacity competitiveness as well. The poorer economies are also, with the one exception of the developing countries in Asia, hampered by a very unfavourable match between production structure and external demand (which tends to favour the Asian tigers and other advanced economies). These negative factors are especially significant for the former CIS countries, whose negative performance is greatly compounded by very rapidly increasing wage costs per produced unit relative to other countries.

---

[143] Note that the smaller EU member countries, which in many cases improved their technology and capacity competitiveness during this period, as defined here, dominate the EU average. Some of the larger EU countries had a much bleaker performance, however, particularly France and Germany.

CHART 2.5.1

Contribution to change of technology and capacity competitiveness, 1993-2001

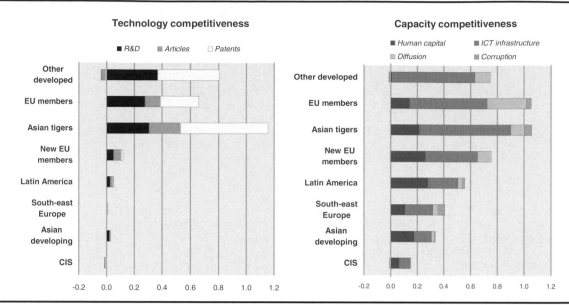

Source: Authors' computations based on World Bank, *WDI*; OECD, *MSTI* and Patent Database; UNESCO; USAID, Global Education Database; ITU, World Telecommunication Indicators; Transparency International, Corruption Perception Index; RICYT.

2.5 Conclusions

The purpose of this paper has been to empirically scrutinize why some countries, with particular emphasis on the ECE region, consistently outperform others. Our search was guided by a theoretical perspective that places emphasis on the role played by four different aspects of competitiveness: technology, capacity, cost and demand. The contribution of the paper is particularly to highlight the two first aspects, which often tend to get lost because of measurement problems.

Our empirical analysis, based on a sample of 49 countries between 1993 and 2001, demonstrated the relevance of both technology and capacity competitiveness. The former is the main explanation behind the continuing good growth performance of the Asian tigers relative to other major country groups. Deteriorating capacity competitiveness, on the other hand, is one of the main factors hampering low income countries in Europe (the formerly centrally planned economies in particular) and Asia in exploiting the potential for catch up in technology and income.

What are the crucial factors behind these developments, and what can governments do in order to improve the relative position of their economies? To better deal with these questions we illustrate in chart 2.5.1 the factors behind the observed changes over time in technology and capacity competitiveness.

The differences across country groups are striking. As for technology competitiveness, there is a clear divide between the advanced countries, with healthy and continuing increases, and the rest of the world, which, with a partial exception for the new EU members, are stagnant at best. The Asian tigers stand out with the best performance. This difference (relative to other developed

countries) is not so much rooted in increases in R&D as in growing innovation (measured by patents) and the development of the scientific infrastructure. A divide of a different sort is clearly visible along the capacity dimension. In this case there actually is some catch up along one dimension, human capital, particularly by the new EU members, and the developing countries in Asia and Latin America. This, however, is more than counteracted by an increasing digital divide (ICT infrastructure), caused by much higher investments in ICT in the already developed economies and among the Asian tigers than elsewhere.

These trends point to the possibility of continuing divergence in the world economy, as emphasized also by other recent studies.[144] However, at any time some countries manage to defy the trend, as the Asian tigers indeed have done in the latter half of the post Second World War period (and Japan before them). In our sample it is the group of the former centrally planned economies that joined the EU in May 2004 that appear to have the best chance in that respect. These favourable prospects contrast with those of a number of other former centrally planned economies, which appear to witness deteriorating competitiveness along all our four dimensions. Clearly, if these countries are ever going to catch up, they will have to find ways to break this vicious circle. Some of the developing countries in Asia are growing fast but this growth has to a large extent been based on exploiting the diffusion potential through a low cost strategy. There is a danger that some of these countries may soon find themselves constrained by lagging technology and capacity competitiveness (unless appropriate action is taken).

_____

[144] See, for example, J. Fagerberg and B. Verspagen, loc. cit.

ANNEX: DATA AND SOURCES

The main sources of data include the World Bank, *World Development Indicators (WDI)*; OECD, *Main Science and Technology Indicators (MSTI)*, Patent Database and STAN Indicators Database; *UNCTAD Handbook of Statistics*; UNESCO Institute for Statistics (UIS); ILO LABORSTA Database; International Telecommunication Union (ITU), World Telecommunication Indicators; United Nations Commodity Trade Statistics Database (COMTRADE); and Transparency International, Corruption Perception Index. The remaining gaps were filled from the Eurostat's Reference Database, NewCronos, and AMECO (Annual Macroeconomic Database); the Ibero-American Network for Science and Technology Indicators (RICYT); WIIW, WIIW Industrial Database Eastern Europe; and the Global Education Database developed by USAID. National sources were only used if necessary for Taiwan and in a few cases for R&D data from other Asian countries.

The selection of subcomponents for composite indicators of technology and capacity competitiveness is based on the theoretical framework, but it is also influenced by the availability of internationally comparable data for a broad range of countries (annex table 2.1). We measure technology competitiveness by three indicators: R&D expenditures (gross domestic expenditure on R&D – GERD), patenting activity (USPTO patent grants) and a number of scientific and technical journal articles (based on the Institute of Scientific Information's Science and Social Science Citation Indexes). We focus on four dimensions of capacity competitiveness, namely human capital, ICT infrastructure, technology diffusion and a broader social or institutional context represented by corruption. In the construction of the composite indicator of capacity competitiveness we applied a two-stage approach using sub-indices of the individual indicators that capture the same dimension. The two-step approach avoids underestimating the influence of those aspects for which fewer indicators are available.

Special care has to be taken for United States patenting performance to suppress the "home country advantage" since the propensity of American residents to register inventions in their own national patent office is higher than that of non-residents. We adjusted the United States performance in its home base downwards based on a comparison between the Japanese and the United States patents registered at the European Patent Office (EPO), which represents a foreign institution both for American and Japanese inventors. We used an estimation proposed by Archibugi and Coco:[145]

*Adjusted US patents at the USPTO = (JAP$_{USA}$ * USA$_{EPO}$)/ JAP$_{EPO}$*

where JAP$_{USA}$ represents patents granted to Japanese residents in the United States, while USA$_{EPO}$ and JAP$_{EPO}$ capture patents granted to Japanese and American residents at the EPO.

Although the selected indicators have broad coverage compared to alternative measures, in some cases there were missing values that had to be dealt with. Depending on the source of the problem we used a linear trend between the nearest neighbours, extrapolated the time series with average annual growth over the available period or used group mean substitution to fill in the missing data points. Out of the total of 3,969 observations (9 indicators, 49 countries and 9 years – Corruption Perception Index excluded – see below), the nearest neighbour substitution was used only for 81 observations (mainly for R&D and education data) and extrapolation for 354 observations (more than two thirds of the latter was due to missing data for the scientific and technical journal articles in 2000-2001 and for secondary and tertiary enrolment in 2001). The coverage of educational data was particularly weak in recent years (in all WDI, UNESCO and USAID databases) due to a recent change of methodology (change from ISCED 76 to ISCED 97). The entire time series were missing in six cases, mainly for the royalty and license fees payments series (for Denmark, Indonesia, Singapore, Switzerland and Taiwan) and for personal computers (Belarus). We used group mean substitution to fill in these gaps using averages for the EU, Asian tigers, other Asian and former CIS countries.

Special treatment was needed for the Corruption Perception Index series as Transparency International publishes this measure only from 1995 onwards and data for most of the former centrally planned economies are reported only for the period 1998-2003. This indicator is the only measure in our composites based on qualitative "soft" data collected by opinion

---

[145] D. Archibugi and A. Coco, "A new indicator of technological capabilities for developed and developing countries (ArCo)", *World Development*, Vol. 32, 2003, pp. 567-724.

ANNEX TABLE 2.1

Composite indicators of technology and capacity competitiveness

Dimension	Subcomponent	Indicator	Scaling	Source
Composite indicator of technology competitiveness				
S&T inputs	R&D expenditure	GERD	Per capita	*WDI*, *MSTI*, RICYT, national sources
S&T outputs	Scientific publications	Scientific and technical journal articles	Per capita	*WDI* (based on ISI)
	Patenting activity	USPTO patent grants (inventor's residence country)	Per capita	OECD Patent Database
Composite indicator of capacity competitiveness				
Human capital	Tertiary education	Tertiary school enrolment	Per cent gross	*WDI*, UNESCO, USAID
	Secondary education	Secondary school enrolment	Per cent gross	*WDI*, UNESCO, USAID
ICT infrastructure	Computers	Personal computers	Per capita	*WDI*, ITU
	Telecommunications	Fixed line and mobile phone subscribers	Per capita	*WDI*, ITU
Diffusion	Embodied technology	Gross fixed capital formation	Per capita	*WDI*
	Disembodied technology	Royalty and license fees: payments	Per capita	*WDI*
Social aspect	Corruption	Corruption Perception Index	Index	Transparency International

surveys. By nature such a measure partly depends on subjective opinions of the respondents, which in a strict sense raises questions about its comparability over time. However, the level of corruption in the economy tends to be rather stable over time in most countries (the mean went down from 6.12 to 5.65 between 1995 and 2003). Hence, we decided to smooth the available series with a linear trend, replace the actual figures with the estimates and extrapolate the missing values at the beginning of the period. This method is robust as the correlation coefficient between the actual and fitted values is 0.9889 for the period 1998-2003.

We used unit wage costs in manufacturing expressed in common currency (dollars) as a measure of price or cost competitiveness (1993-2001, except for the Republic of Moldova (1994-2001)). This indicator was dependent upon data availability defined either as the ratio of total wages to value added or as monthly wages of employees divided by value added per worker. The OECD STAN Indicators Database and Eurostat AMECO Database were used as the main sources of value added, employment and wages for its member and candidate countries, while the WDI and ILO LABORSTA Databases were used for the remaining countries.

The indicator for demand competitiveness was calculated using data from the United Nations COMTRADE Database at the 3-digit level (SITC Rev.3) over the period 1993-1999.

ANNEX TABLE 2.2

Indicators of competitiveness, 1993-2001

	Composite indicators				Unit wage costs in manufacturing (in dollars)		Demand competitiveness (annual average in per cent)
	Technology competitiveness		Capacity competitiveness		Price competitiveness		
	1993	2001	1993	2001	1993	2001	1993-1999
Argentina	-0.78	-0.72	-0.71	-0.37	10.1	11.3	4.6
Austria	0.28	0.99	0.33	1.21	57.1	44.7	7.0
Belarus	-0.78	-0.76	-0.70	-0.40	9.7	32.3	5.1
Belgium	0.34	1.08	0.45	1.24	50.9	46.7	6.6
Brazil	-0.79	-0.73	-1.31	-0.44	11.9	10.4	5.1
Bulgaria	-0.62	-0.74	-0.94	-0.34	46.3	28.3	5.5
Canada	1.02	1.50	0.94	1.36	55.9	41.8	6.7
Chile	-0.76	-0.74	-0.55	0.00	12.7	10.9	4.4
China	-0.87	-0.81	-1.41	-1.01	14.2	7.2	5.8
Croatia	-0.67	-0.59	-0.91	-0.27	30.8	38.8	5.9
Czech Republic	-0.48	-0.37	-0.44	0.05	35.0	32.9	5.6
Denmark	0.80	1.77	0.75	1.89	66.3	61.9	6.4
Estonia	-0.71	-0.49	-0.47	0.29	38.9	43.0	6.1
Finland	0.85	2.43	0.75	1.82	44.9	43.5	6.8
France	0.66	1.02	0.33	0.92	47.0	44.0	6.9
Germany	0.91	1.66	0.47	1.09	62.8	58.9	7.2
Greece	-0.62	-0.41	-0.28	0.44	36.3	40.4	5.6
Hong Kong	-0.54	-0.05	0.07	0.97	40.9	38.8	7.5
Hungary	-0.55	-0.42	-0.67	0.14	32.0	30.3	6.5
Indonesia	-0.89	-0.89	-1.40	-1.29	7.9	6.1	5.3
Ireland	-0.24	0.36	0.62	3.49	36.7	20.8	8.4
Israel	1.29	2.76	0.06	0.78	26.0	38.8	7.5
Italy	-0.12	0.11	-0.39	0.57	39.3	38.1	6.5
Japan	1.72	2.73	0.23	1.00	46.2	48.2	8.3
Korea	-0.40	0.59	-0.20	0.68	40.6	35.0	7.4
Latvia	-0.78	-0.76	-0.95	0.00	33.5	36.6	6.0
Lithuania	-0.81	-0.71	-0.83	-0.03	23.6	25.6	5.4
Malaysia	-0.84	-0.79	-0.82	-0.29	21.8	21.5	8.2
Mexico	-0.85	-0.80	-1.18	-0.72	16.0	12.6	7.4
Republic of Moldova	-0.83	-0.86	-0.96	-1.10	7.7	28.3	4.7
Netherlands	0.87	1.31	0.85	1.62	56.0	48.5	6.6
Norway	0.61	1.09	0.90	1.82	59.7	60.0	6.3
Philippines	-0.88	-0.86	-1.01	-0.91	14.4	16.1	8.1
Poland	-0.71	-0.64	-0.55	-0.11	24.9	36.1	5.5
Portugal	-0.70	-0.45	-0.16	0.71	67.1	45.8	6.3
Romania	-0.80	-0.81	-0.96	-0.81	33.6	24.0	5.3
Russian Federation	-0.66	-0.63	-0.81	-0.54	7.0	10.9	5.4
Singapore	-0.28	0.97	0.19	1.54	20.8	29.4	8.9
Slovakia	-0.49	-0.60	-0.73	-0.20	39.3	28.6	5.9
Slovenia	-0.40	0.01	-0.39	0.82	47.5	38.7	7.1
Spain	-0.41	-0.16	-0.21	0.85	55.6	52.3	6.6
Sweden	1.57	3.28	0.69	2.02	48.9	51.4	7.4
Switzerland	2.39	2.89	0.58	1.44	47.9	35.1	7.0
Taiwan	0.06	1.95	-0.32	0.78	38.3	37.1	7.9
Thailand	-0.88	-0.85	-1.19	-0.65	10.1	8.2	6.8
Turkey	-0.84	-0.76	-1.01	-0.79	6.0	9.3	5.1
Ukraine	-0.71	-0.78	-0.79	-0.64	8.8	21.9	3.9
United Kingdom	0.73	1.13	0.57	1.61	61.7	63.9	7.7
United States	1.59	2.27	0.81	1.50	52.6	55.5	7.6

Source: Author's calculations based on the World Bank, *WDI*; OECD, *MSTI*, STAN and Patent Database; UNESCO; USAID, Global Education Database; ITU, World Telecommunication Indicators; Transparency International, Corruption Perception Index; RICYT; ILO, LABORSTA Database; Eurostat, AMECO Database; United Nations COMTRADE Database.

Note: In the regression analysis, differences between the annual growth rate of the indicator for each country and the sample average as defined in equation (13') were used.

ANNEX TABLE 2.3

Contribution of subcomponents to the composite indicators, 1993-2001

	Technology competitiveness						Capacity competitiveness							
	Contribution to average level during 1993-2001			Contribution to difference between 1993 and 2001			Contribution to average level during 1993-2001				Contribution to difference between 1993 and 2001			
	R&D	Articles	Patents	R&D	Articles	Patents	Human Capital	ICT	Diffusion	Corruption	Human Capital	ICT	Diffusion	Corruption
Argentina	-0.26	-0.27	-0.22	0.01	0.04	0.00	-0.04	-0.20	-0.11	-0.21	0.30	0.21	-0.01	-0.16
Austria	0.27	0.17	0.16	0.32	0.15	0.25	0.12	0.21	0.17	0.21	0.08	0.60	0.13	0.07
Belarus	-0.28	-0.27	-0.23	0.01	0.00	0.01	0.02	-0.23	-0.19	-0.17	0.08	0.08	-0.01	0.15
Belgium	0.29	0.22	0.18	0.34	0.13	0.28	0.43	0.19	0.14	0.06	0.11	0.46	0.11	0.11
Brazil	-0.24	-0.31	-0.23	0.04	0.02	0.00	-0.30	-0.24	-0.17	-0.24	0.51	0.19	0.04	0.13
Bulgaria	-0.28	-0.21	-0.23	-0.04	-0.08	0.00	-0.06	-0.16	-0.21	-0.23	0.23	0.16	0.04	0.19
Canada	0.28	0.49	0.45	0.28	-0.16	0.37	0.32	0.31	0.12	0.38	-0.24	0.48	0.19	-0.01
Chile	-0.26	-0.27	-0.22	0.02	0.00	0.00	-0.18	-0.18	-0.12	0.16	0.15	0.29	0.07	0.05
China	-0.29	-0.33	-0.23	0.04	0.01	0.00	-0.43	-0.30	-0.19	-0.30	0.09	0.12	0.06	0.13
Croatia	-0.23	-0.20	-0.22	0.05	0.02	0.01	-0.15	-0.12	-0.15	-0.22	0.05	0.30	0.10	0.18
Czech Republic	-0.12	-0.10	-0.21	0.09	0.01	0.01	-0.13	-0.06	-0.01	-0.08	0.11	0.51	0.09	-0.22
Denmark	0.41	0.58	0.25	0.47	0.10	0.40	0.26	0.45	0.12	0.45	0.22	0.73	0.18	0.00
Estonia	-0.25	-0.13	-0.22	0.08	0.14	0.01	0.06	-0.04	-0.11	0.01	0.29	0.40	0.11	-0.04
Finland	0.52	0.56	0.51	0.69	0.23	0.65	0.41	0.38	0.05	0.42	0.22	0.60	0.18	0.08
France	0.39	0.21	0.21	0.13	0.09	0.14	0.17	0.21	0.05	0.14	0.02	0.51	0.10	-0.03
Germany	0.45	0.19	0.54	0.24	0.11	0.40	0.09	0.24	0.12	0.27	0.02	0.64	0.06	-0.10
Greece	-0.21	-0.10	-0.22	0.10	0.10	0.01	0.08	0.03	-0.06	-0.09	0.23	0.43	0.12	-0.05
Hong Kong	-0.20	-0.02	-0.08	0.13	0.20	0.17	-0.21	0.31	0.22	0.20	0.01	0.69	0.08	0.12
Hungary	-0.21	-0.12	-0.19	0.05	0.07	0.00	-0.06	-0.10	-0.08	-0.08	0.23	0.40	0.14	0.05
Indonesia	-0.32	-0.34	-0.23	0.00	0.00	0.00	-0.44	-0.33	-0.20	-0.37	0.12	0.03	0.02	-0.06
Ireland	0.06	0.04	-0.06	0.30	0.13	0.17	0.12	0.20	1.24	0.29	0.04	0.65	2.36	-0.17
Israel	0.58	0.72	0.54	0.95	-0.21	0.72	0.02	0.17	0.02	0.20	0.17	0.58	0.05	-0.07
Italy	0.01	0.01	-0.04	0.07	0.10	0.06	0.04	0.12	0.03	-0.16	0.11	0.53	0.09	0.23
Japan	0.65	0.10	1.39	0.27	0.10	0.63	0.07	0.22	0.20	0.11	0.09	0.59	0.05	0.04
Korea	0.14	-0.20	0.14	0.35	0.20	0.44	0.20	0.11	0.06	-0.13	0.28	0.52	0.11	-0.03
Latvia	-0.29	-0.26	-0.22	0.02	-0.01	0.00	-0.02	-0.13	-0.17	-0.25	0.40	0.30	0.10	0.16
Lithuania	-0.27	-0.27	-0.23	0.05	0.04	0.01	-0.05	-0.16	-0.15	-0.12	0.33	0.22	0.03	0.22
Malaysia	-0.29	-0.32	-0.22	0.04	0.01	0.01	-0.33	-0.16	-0.06	-0.04	0.25	0.27	0.04	-0.03
Mexico	-0.29	-0.31	-0.22	0.03	0.02	0.00	-0.32	-0.24	-0.16	-0.26	0.19	0.17	0.02	0.07
Republic of Moldova	-0.31	-0.30	-0.23	-0.01	-0.02	-0.01	-0.19	-0.28	-0.24	-0.33	-0.11	0.06	-0.01	-0.08
Netherlands	0.34	0.48	0.27	0.22	-0.01	0.23	0.28	0.30	0.21	0.36	-0.05	0.68	0.12	0.02
Norway	0.41	0.36	0.08	0.18	0.05	0.24	0.31	0.47	0.24	0.36	0.07	0.74	0.13	-0.01
Philippines	-0.31	-0.33	-0.23	0.02	0.00	0.00	-0.17	-0.31	-0.21	-0.28	0.04	0.10	0.00	-0.03
Poland	-0.24	-0.20	-0.23	0.02	0.04	0.00	0.04	-0.19	-0.13	-0.09	0.30	0.27	0.09	-0.22
Portugal	-0.19	-0.19	-0.22	0.10	0.14	0.01	0.11	0.02	0.01	0.09	0.22	0.47	0.15	0.03
Romania	-0.28	-0.30	-0.23	-0.03	0.03	0.00	-0.21	-0.25	-0.19	-0.27	0.09	0.14	0.03	-0.10
Russian Federation	-0.24	-0.20	-0.22	0.05	-0.02	0.01	0.03	-0.23	-0.18	-0.35	0.14	0.10	0.00	0.02
Singapore	0.11	0.08	0.02	0.44	0.33	0.48	-0.06	0.30	0.23	0.38	0.44	0.75	0.11	0.05
Slovakia	-0.21	-0.12	-0.22	-0.04	-0.08	0.00	-0.15	-0.12	-0.04	-0.20	0.11	0.36	0.09	-0.02
Slovenia	-0.02	-0.03	-0.19	0.15	0.19	0.08	0.06	0.07	-0.03	0.02	0.38	0.63	0.18	0.03
Spain	-0.11	0.00	-0.19	0.10	0.14	0.02	0.22	0.02	0.03	-0.02	0.13	0.45	0.16	0.32
Sweden	0.77	0.78	0.72	0.68	0.08	0.94	0.41	0.50	0.03	0.40	0.40	0.76	0.14	0.02
Switzerland	0.68	0.82	1.08	0.10	0.14	0.26	0.00	0.45	0.15	0.35	0.09	0.75	0.05	-0.02
Taiwan	0.15	-0.06	0.75	0.31	0.16	1.41	-0.10	0.23	0.05	-0.04	0.14	0.76	0.10	0.09
Thailand	-0.31	-0.33	-0.23	0.01	0.00	0.00	-0.27	-0.28	-0.12	-0.27	0.42	0.10	-0.01	0.03
Turkey	-0.29	-0.30	-0.23	0.03	0.04	0.00	-0.36	-0.18	-0.17	-0.21	0.08	0.21	-0.02	-0.06
Ukraine	-0.25	-0.28	-0.23	-0.06	-0.01	0.00	0.06	-0.26	-0.19	-0.36	0.17	0.06	-0.01	-0.06
United Kingdom	0.26	0.48	0.17	0.15	0.04	0.21	0.38	0.28	0.05	0.32	0.31	0.59	0.12	0.02
United States	0.79	0.41	0.62	0.45	-0.16	0.39	0.29	0.47	0.14	0.23	-0.09	0.58	0.22	-0.01

Source: Author's calculations based on the World Bank, *WDI;* OECD, *MSTI* and Patent Database; UNESCO; USAID, Global Education Database; ITU, World Telecommunication Indicators; Transparency International, Corruption Perception Index; RICYT.

STATISTICAL APPENDIX

For the user's convenience, as well as to lighten the text, the *Economic Survey of Europe* includes a set of appendix tables showing time series for main economic indicators over a longer period. The data are presented in two sections: *Appendix A* provides macroeconomic indicators for the market economies in western Europe and the 10 new member states, which joined the European Union at the beginning of May 2004, as well as North America and Japan. *Appendix B* provides comparative macroeconomic indicators for the east European countries (including the eight countries that joined the EU) and the Commonwealth of Independent States. For all countries, national accounts data for more recent years may be subject to revision as more comprehensive benchmark figures become available.

Data were compiled from international and national statistical sources. Details on recent changes in national accounts methodology were provided in chapter 7 of the *Economic Survey of Europe, 2000 No. 1*. Regional aggregates are UNECE secretariat calculations, using PPPs obtained from the 1996 European Comparison Programme. Greece, which became a member of the euro area at the beginning of 2001, has been included in the euro area aggregates for all years shown in the appendix tables in order to ensure continuity of time series.

The figures for 2003 are based on data available in late June 2004.

APPENDIX TABLE A.1

Real GDP in Europe, North America and Japan, 1989-2003

(Percentage change over preceding year)

	1989	1990	1991	1992	1993	1994	1995	1996	1997	1998	1999	2000	2001	2002	2003
France	4.2	2.6	1.0	1.5	-0.9	2.1	1.7	1.1	1.9	3.4	3.2	3.8	2.1	1.2	0.5
Germany [a]	3.9	5.7	5.1	2.2	-1.1	2.3	1.7	0.8	1.4	2.0	2.0	2.9	0.8	0.2	-0.1
Italy	2.9	2.0	1.4	0.8	-0.9	2.2	2.9	1.1	2.0	1.8	1.7	3.0	1.8	0.4	0.3
Austria	4.2	4.7	3.3	2.3	0.4	2.6	1.6	2.0	1.6	3.9	2.7	3.4	0.8	1.4	0.7
Belgium	3.5	3.1	1.8	1.5	-1.0	3.2	2.4	1.2	3.5	2.0	3.2	3.8	0.6	0.7	1.1
Finland	4.8	-0.3	-6.4	-3.8	-1.2	3.9	3.4	3.9	6.3	5.0	3.4	5.1	1.1	2.3	1.9
Greece	3.8	–	3.1	0.7	-1.6	2.0	2.1	2.4	3.6	3.4	3.4	4.4	4.0	3.9	4.3
Ireland	5.8	8.5	1.9	3.3	2.7	5.8	9.9	8.1	11.1	8.6	11.3	10.1	6.2	6.9	1.4
Luxembourg	9.8	5.3	8.6	1.8	4.2	3.8	1.4	3.3	8.3	6.9	7.8	9.0	1.3	1.7	2.1
Netherlands	4.8	4.1	2.4	1.5	0.7	2.9	3.0	3.0	3.8	4.3	4.0	3.5	1.2	0.2	-0.7
Portugal	6.4	4.0	4.4	1.1	-2.0	1.0	4.3	3.5	4.0	4.6	3.8	3.4	1.8	0.5	-1.2
Spain	4.8	3.8	2.5	0.9	-1.0	2.4	2.8	2.4	4.0	4.3	4.2	4.2	2.8	2.0	2.4
Euro area	4.0	3.6	2.6	1.4	-0.8	2.4	2.3	1.5	2.4	2.9	2.9	3.5	1.7	0.9	0.6
Denmark	0.2	1.0	1.1	0.6	–	5.5	2.8	2.5	3.0	2.5	2.6	2.8	1.6	1.0	0.5
Sweden	2.7	1.0	-1.1	-1.3	-2.0	4.2	4.1	1.3	2.4	3.6	4.6	4.3	0.9	2.1	1.6
United Kingdom	2.2	0.8	-1.4	0.2	2.3	4.4	2.9	2.8	3.3	3.1	2.9	3.9	2.3	1.8	2.2
EU-15	3.6	3.0	1.8	1.2	-0.4	2.8	2.5	1.7	2.6	3.0	2.9	3.6	1.8	1.1	0.9
Cyprus	7.9	7.4	0.6	9.8	0.7	5.9	6.1	1.9	2.3	4.8	4.7	5.0	4.0	2.0	2.0
Czech Republic	..	..	-11.6	-0.5	0.1	2.2	5.9	4.3	-0.8	-1.0	0.5	3.3	3.1	2.0	2.9
Estonia	..	..	-10.0	-14.1	-8.5	-1.6	4.5	4.5	10.5	5.2	-0.1	7.8	6.4	7.2	5.1
Hungary	..	..	-11.9	-3.1	-0.6	2.9	1.5	1.3	4.6	4.9	4.2	5.2	3.8	3.5	2.9
Latvia	..	..	-12.6	-32.1	-11.4	2.2	-0.9	3.8	8.3	4.7	3.3	6.9	8.0	6.4	7.5
Lithuania	..	..	-5.7	-21.3	-16.2	-9.8	5.2	4.7	7.0	7.3	-1.7	3.9	6.4	6.8	9.0
Malta	8.2	6.3	6.3	4.7	4.5	5.7	6.2	4.0	4.9	3.4	4.1	6.3	-1.1	2.3	-1.7
Poland	..	..	-7.0	2.6	3.8	5.2	7.0	6.0	6.8	4.8	4.1	4.0	1.0	1.4	3.8
Slovakia	..	..	-14.6	-6.4	-3.7	6.2	5.8	6.1	4.6	4.2	1.5	2.0	3.8	4.4	4.2
Slovenia	..	..	-8.9	-5.5	2.8	5.3	4.1	3.6	4.8	3.6	5.6	3.9	2.7	3.4	2.3
New EU members-10	..	..	-9.6	-2.8	0.1	3.5	5.4	4.7	4.6	3.6	3.0	4.0	2.6	2.5	3.7
EU-25	..	..	0.9	0.8	-0.3	2.8	2.7	1.9	2.7	3.0	2.9	3.6	1.8	1.2	1.1
Iceland	0.3	1.2	0.5	-1.6	0.4	2.2	-0.5	8.3	4.6	5.7	5.4	6.5	3.0	-0.6	1.9
Israel	1.4	6.6	6.1	7.2	3.8	7.0	6.5	5.3	3.0	3.3	2.6	7.5	-0.9	-0.8	1.3
Norway	1.2	2.0	3.6	3.3	2.7	5.3	4.4	5.3	5.2	2.6	2.1	2.8	2.7	1.4	0.3
Switzerland	4.3	3.7	-0.8	–	-0.2	1.1	0.4	0.5	1.9	2.8	1.3	3.7	1.0	0.2	-0.5
Turkey	0.3	9.3	0.9	6.0	8.0	-5.5	7.2	7.0	7.5	3.1	-4.7	7.4	-7.5	7.9	5.8
WECEE	..	..	0.9	0.9	-0.3	2.8	2.7	2.0	2.8	3.0	2.9	3.6	1.8	1.2	1.1
Canada	2.6	0.2	-2.1	0.9	2.3	4.8	2.8	1.6	4.2	4.1	5.5	5.2	1.8	3.4	2.0
United States	3.5	1.8	-0.2	3.3	2.7	4.0	2.5	3.7	4.5	4.2	4.4	3.7	0.5	2.2	3.1
North America	3.4	1.6	-0.3	3.1	2.6	4.1	2.5	3.5	4.5	4.2	4.5	3.8	0.6	2.3	3.0
Japan	5.3	5.2	3.4	1.0	0.2	1.1	1.9	3.4	1.9	-1.1	0.1	2.8	0.4	-0.3	2.5
Europe, North America and Japan	..	..	0.7	1.8	1.0	3.1	2.5	2.8	3.4	2.9	3.2	3.6	1.1	1.5	2.1
Memorandum item:															
CEBS-8	..	..	-9.8	-3.0	0.1	3.5	5.4	4.7	4.6	3.6	2.9	4.0	2.6	2.5	3.7
Western Europe and North America	3.5	2.3	0.7	2.1	1.2	3.4	2.5	2.7	3.6	3.6	3.7	3.7	1.2	1.7	2.0

Source: Eurostat, NewCronos Database; OECD, *National Accounts* (Paris), various issues; national statistics.

Note: All aggregates exclude Israel and Turkey. Growth rates of regional aggregates have been calculated from constant price series, base 2000. (These were computed by summing over all participant countries of the national series rescaled to the price level of the common reference year 2000 and then converted into dollars using 2000 purchasing power parities of GDP.)

[a] West Germany, 1989-1991.

APPENDIX TABLE A.2

Real private consumption expenditure in Europe, North America and Japan, 1989-2003

(Percentage change over preceding year)

	1989	1990	1991	1992	1993	1994	1995	1996	1997	1998	1999	2000	2001	2002	2003
France	2.8	2.5	0.7	0.9	-0.4	1.2	1.2	1.3	0.2	3.4	3.2	2.6	2.7	1.5	1.5
Germany [a]	3.2	4.1	4.6	2.7	0.1	1.1	2.1	1.0	0.6	1.8	3.7	2.0	1.4	-1.0	-0.1
Italy	3.7	2.1	2.9	1.9	-3.7	1.5	1.7	1.2	3.2	3.2	2.6	2.7	0.8	0.5	1.3
Austria	4.3	4.5	2.5	3.0	0.8	2.4	2.6	3.2	1.7	2.7	2.4	3.3	1.4	0.8	1.3
Belgium	3.3	3.2	3.0	1.9	-0.4	2.4	1.6	1.1	2.0	3.1	2.3	3.4	0.8	0.4	1.7
Finland	5.3	-1.1	-3.8	-4.0	-3.8	2.5	4.1	3.7	3.4	4.3	3.5	3.1	1.8	1.5	3.6
Greece	6.3	2.6	2.9	2.3	-0.8	1.9	2.5	2.4	2.7	3.5	2.5	2.0	2.9	2.8	3.5
Ireland	6.5	1.4	1.8	2.9	2.9	4.4	3.6	6.5	7.1	7.2	9.5	8.3	5.3	2.0	2.4
Luxembourg	4.8	3.8	7.0	-2.3	2.1	4.0	1.9	4.3	3.9	6.6	2.6	4.6	5.1	2.7	1.2
Netherlands	3.0	3.8	2.7	0.5	0.3	1.4	3.0	4.0	3.0	4.9	4.8	3.2	1.4	0.8	-1.3
Portugal	2.9	6.4	4.2	4.7	1.1	1.0	0.6	3.0	3.3	5.0	5.1	2.9	1.2	0.7	-0.6
Spain	5.4	3.5	2.9	2.2	-1.9	1.1	1.7	2.2	3.2	4.4	4.7	4.0	2.8	2.6	3.0
Euro area	3.6	3.2	2.8	1.9	-1.0	1.4	1.8	1.6	1.8	3.1	3.5	2.7	1.8	0.6	1.1
Denmark	-0.1	0.1	1.6	1.9	0.5	6.5	1.2	2.5	2.9	2.3	0.7	-0.7	-0.2	0.6	0.8
Sweden	1.2	-0.5	1.1	-1.3	-3.5	1.9	1.0	1.6	2.7	3.0	3.8	5.0	0.4	1.4	1.9
United Kingdom	3.4	1.0	-1.5	0.5	3.0	3.1	1.7	3.6	3.6	3.9	4.4	4.6	2.9	3.3	2.3
EU-15	3.5	2.7	2.0	1.6	-0.4	1.7	1.8	2.0	2.1	3.3	3.6	3.1	1.9	1.1	1.3
Cyprus	6.9	9.0	9.9	3.2	-4.8	5.0	10.3	3.5	3.9	8.6	2.8	8.2	4.6	2.5	2.4
Czech Republic	..	..	-21.4	8.8	1.2	6.9	5.9	7.9	2.4	-1.6	1.7	2.5	3.6	4.0	5.4
Estonia	..	..	..	..	..	0.6	5.0	10.1	10.5	5.2	-2.5	8.6	6.2	10.3	5.7
Hungary	..	..	..	1.4	3.4	0.2	-7.0	-3.7	1.8	4.5	5.5	5.5	5.7	10.2	7.5
Latvia	..	..	-26.0	-43.4	-7.4	3.2	-1.7	10.6	5.0	0.7	4.3	6.3	7.3	7.4	8.6
Lithuania	..	..	..	..	..	..	..	6.5	5.3	4.8	4.1	6.1	3.6	6.1	11.0
Malta	9.2	3.8	3.8	4.3	0.8	2.3	10.5	7.1	1.6	2.5	6.1	7.4	1.7	2.6	0.3
Poland	..	..	6.6	2.5	5.4	3.9	3.2	8.5	6.9	4.8	5.2	2.8	2.0	3.4	3.1
Slovakia	..	..	..	..	1.3	1.0	5.4	7.9	5.5	6.5	3.2	-0.8	4.7	5.3	-0.4
Slovenia	..	..	-10.9	-3.6	13.8	4.0	9.2	2.6	2.5	3.0	5.9	0.4	2.3	0.4	2.9
New EU members-10	..	..	..	..	..	..	..	6.3	5.0	3.6	4.3	3.1	3.3	4.7	4.3
EU-25	..	..	..	..	..	..	..	2.3	2.4	3.3	3.7	3.1	2.1	1.4	1.6
Iceland	-4.2	0.5	2.9	-3.1	-4.7	2.9	2.2	5.4	5.1	10.1	7.3	4.0	-3.0	-1.1	3.6
Israel	0.5	6.0	7.2	7.6	7.2	9.6	7.8	5.6	2.9	4.2	4.2	7.6	3.2	0.1	1.7
Norway	-0.6	0.7	2.3	2.2	2.4	3.3	3.7	6.5	3.2	2.7	3.3	3.9	1.8	3.6	3.7
Switzerland	2.7	1.0	1.7	0.4	-0.6	1.0	0.7	1.0	1.5	2.4	2.3	2.5	2.0	0.7	0.9
Turkey	-0.6	12.0	2.9	3.3	8.6	-5.4	5.2	8.5	7.5	2.1	-0.7	6.4	-9.0	2.9	4.5
WECEE	..	..	..	..	..	..	..	2.3	2.3	3.3	3.7	3.1	2.0	1.5	1.6
Canada	3.4	1.2	-1.6	1.5	1.8	3.0	2.1	2.6	4.6	2.8	3.8	4.0	2.7	3.4	3.1
United States	2.7	1.8	0.2	3.3	3.3	3.7	2.7	3.4	3.8	5.0	5.1	4.7	2.5	3.4	3.1
North America	2.7	1.8	–	3.1	3.2	3.7	2.7	3.4	3.8	4.9	5.0	4.6	2.5	3.4	3.1
Japan	4.8	4.6	2.9	2.6	1.4	2.7	1.8	2.5	0.9	-0.1	0.2	1.0	1.7	0.9	0.8
Europe, North America and Japan	..	..	..	..	..	..	..	2.8	2.8	3.6	3.8	3.5	2.2	2.3	2.3
Memorandum item:															
CEBS-8	..	..	..	..	..	..	..	6.3	5.0	3.5	4.3	3.0	3.3	4.8	4.3
Western Europe and North America	3.0	2.2	1.0	2.4	1.5	2.8	2.3	2.8	3.1	4.2	4.4	3.9	2.2	2.4	2.4

Source: Eurostat, NewCronos Database; OECD, *National Accounts* (Paris), various issues; national statistics.

Note: See appendix table A.1.

[a] West Germany, 1989-1991.

APPENDIX TABLE A.3

Real general government consumption expenditure in Europe, North America and Japan, 1989-2003

(Percentage change over preceding year)

	1989	1990	1991	1992	1993	1994	1995	1996	1997	1998	1999	2000	2001	2002	2003
France	1.6	2.5	2.7	3.8	4.6	0.7	-0.1	2.3	2.1	-0.1	1.5	2.8	2.9	4.6	2.4
Germany [a]	-1.1	3.1	1.9	5.0	0.1	2.4	1.5	1.8	0.3	1.9	0.8	1.0	1.0	1.7	0.9
Italy	0.2	2.5	1.7	0.6	-0.2	-0.9	-2.2	1.0	0.2	0.2	1.3	1.7	3.9	1.9	2.2
Austria	1.7	2.3	3.2	3.5	3.7	3.0	1.3	1.2	-1.5	2.8	3.0	-0.1	-1.4	0.1	0.7
Belgium	1.2	-0.4	3.6	1.5	-0.2	1.4	1.3	2.5	0.2	1.0	3.6	2.7	2.7	1.9	2.8
Finland	2.3	4.2	1.9	-2.5	-4.2	0.8	2.0	2.6	2.9	2.0	1.4	–	2.4	3.8	0.7
Greece	5.4	0.6	-1.5	-3.0	2.6	-1.1	5.6	0.9	3.0	1.7	2.1	2.2	-1.0	5.8	2.9
Ireland	-1.3	5.4	2.7	3.0	0.1	4.1	3.9	3.5	5.8	6.0	8.0	8.4	11.5	10.7	3.0
Luxembourg	8.2	6.7	4.0	3.2	5.2	1.0	4.7	5.6	3.0	1.3	7.3	4.8	6.6	3.2	4.6
Netherlands	1.9	2.2	2.9	2.9	1.6	1.5	1.5	-0.4	3.2	3.6	2.5	2.0	4.2	3.8	2.4
Portugal	6.4	4.2	9.6	-0.9	-0.2	4.3	1.0	3.4	2.2	4.1	5.6	4.1	3.3	2.7	-0.6
Spain	8.3	6.3	6.0	3.5	2.7	0.5	2.4	1.3	2.9	3.7	4.2	5.1	3.6	4.4	4.6
Euro area	1.3	2.9	2.7	2.9	1.5	1.1	0.6	1.6	1.3	1.4	1.9	2.2	2.6	3.1	2.1
Denmark	-0.8	-0.2	0.6	0.8	4.1	3.0	2.1	3.4	0.8	3.1	2.0	0.9	2.7	2.1	1.0
Sweden	3.0	2.5	3.4	1.7	0.1	-0.8	-0.4	0.6	-0.9	3.4	1.7	-1.2	0.9	3.2	0.7
United Kingdom	1.0	2.2	3.0	0.7	-0.7	1.0	1.4	1.3	-0.4	1.2	3.5	2.3	2.6	3.8	3.5
EU-15	1.2	2.7	2.7	2.5	1.2	1.0	0.7	1.6	1.0	1.5	2.1	2.1	2.6	3.2	2.2
Cyprus	1.9	17.4	3.9	13.8	-14.3	4.1	2.9	12.6	4.0	7.3	-7.7	-0.1	10.4	8.5	1.7
Czech Republic	..	..	-12.3	-6.7	3.6	0.2	-4.3	3.6	-4.4	-4.4	2.3	-1.0	5.3	5.7	–
Estonia	..	..	..	..	..	4.0	13.5	-3.1	-1.3	1.7	2.9	1.1	1.8	5.9	5.8
Hungary	..	..	..	-1.1	9.8	-7.4	-5.7	-2.0	3.2	2.6	1.7	2.0	6.0	4.9	1.8
Latvia	..	..	-3.3	8.0	-0.1	-1.2	1.3	1.8	-5.9	13.1	–	-1.9	0.3	2.4	2.5
Lithuania	..	..	..	..	..	..	..	2.5	6.3	6.0	-8.1	3.9	0.3	1.9	5.7
Malta	12.7	5.7	10.9	8.9	6.0	6.4	8.5	8.4	-1.1	-4.0	-0.6	4.9	3.0	2.8	6.0
Poland	..	..	9.6	5.9	3.2	1.2	3.7	2.3	3.3	2.0	1.9	1.3	0.6	0.4	0.4
Slovakia	..	..	-17.8	8.5	-4.3	-10.7	3.6	17.2	-5.4	12.5	-7.1	1.6	4.6	4.7	2.9
Slovenia	..	..	-0.3	-1.7	5.3	2.1	2.5	3.4	2.4	5.4	2.9	2.3	3.9	2.5	1.9
New EU members-10	..	..	..	..	..	..	..	3.1	0.5	2.0	0.7	1.0	3.0	3.0	1.2
EU-25	..	..	..	..	..	..	..	1.7	0.9	1.5	2.0	2.0	2.6	3.1	2.1
Iceland	3.0	4.4	3.1	-0.7	2.3	4.0	1.8	1.2	2.5	3.4	4.6	4.3	3.1	4.0	3.5
Israel	-9.2	7.6	4.6	1.6	4.2	-0.3	-1.0	5.4	1.9	2.2	2.9	2.2	3.4	5.7	-1.8
Norway	2.1	5.3	5.4	5.6	2.7	1.5	1.5	3.1	2.5	3.3	3.2	1.3	5.8	3.1	1.4
Switzerland	5.4	5.4	4.3	1.7	-0.7	2.0	1.0	0.9	-0.1	-0.9	0.3	2.4	4.0	0.8	0.9
Turkey	0.8	8.0	3.7	3.6	8.6	-5.5	6.8	8.6	4.1	7.8	6.5	7.1	-8.5	5.4	-2.4
WECEE	..	..	..	..	..	..	..	1.7	0.9	1.5	2.0	2.0	2.7	3.1	2.1
Canada	2.8	3.5	2.9	1.0	–	-1.2	-0.6	-1.2	-1.0	3.2	2.1	3.1	3.7	2.8	3.8
United States	2.5	2.5	1.3	0.4	-0.3	0.3	0.2	0.4	1.8	1.6	3.1	1.7	2.8	3.6	3.8
North America	2.5	2.6	1.5	0.5	-0.3	0.1	0.1	0.2	1.5	1.8	3.0	1.9	2.9	3.5	3.8
Japan	2.9	3.2	4.1	2.5	3.0	3.2	4.3	2.9	1.0	2.0	4.6	4.9	3.0	2.4	1.0
Europe, North America and Japan	..	..	..	..	..	..	..	1.3	1.1	1.7	2.7	2.3	2.8	3.2	2.6
Memorandum item:															
CEBS-8	..	..	..	..	..	..	..	3.0	0.5	1.9	0.8	1.0	3.0	2.9	1.1
Western Europe and North America	1.9	2.7	2.2	1.6	0.5	0.6	0.4	1.0	1.2	1.6	2.5	2.0	2.8	3.3	2.9

Source: Eurostat, NewCronos Database; OECD, *National Accounts* (Paris), various issues; national statistics.

Note: See appendix table A.1.

[a] West Germany, 1989-1991.

APPENDIX TABLE A.4

Real gross domestic fixed capital formation in Europe, North America and Japan, 1989-2003

(Percentage change over preceding year)

	1989	1990	1991	1992	1993	1994	1995	1996	1997	1998	1999	2000	2001	2002	2003
France	7.3	3.3	-1.5	-1.6	-6.4	1.5	2.0	–	-0.1	7.0	8.3	7.8	1.9	-1.6	-0.8
Germany *a*	6.7	7.7	5.2	4.5	-4.4	4.0	-0.6	-0.8	0.6	3.0	4.1	2.7	-4.2	-6.7	-2.0
Italy	4.2	4.0	1.0	-1.4	-10.9	0.1	6.0	3.6	2.1	4.0	5.0	6.9	1.9	1.2	-2.1
Austria	4.1	6.2	6.6	0.6	-0.9	4.6	1.3	2.2	2.0	3.9	2.1	6.2	-2.3	-2.8	4.3
Belgium	11.8	8.6	-4.1	1.1	-2.5	0.4	3.4	0.9	7.1	3.3	4.4	4.4	0.3	-2.5	1.2
Finland	12.5	-4.6	-18.5	-16.4	-15.2	-3.6	11.2	6.7	13.8	8.4	2.5	4.1	3.9	-3.1	-2.3
Greece	6.1	4.5	4.2	-3.5	-4.0	-3.1	4.1	8.4	6.8	10.6	11.0	8.0	6.5	5.7	15.8
Ireland	10.1	13.4	-7.0	–	-5.1	11.8	15.3	16.8	18.9	14.9	14.0	7.1	0.2	1.5	-4.8
Luxembourg	6.9	3.4	15.8	-15.1	20.6	–	-1.5	3.8	12.7	11.8	14.6	-3.5	10.0	-1.4	-4.0
Netherlands	5.2	2.6	0.3	0.7	-3.2	2.1	4.1	6.3	6.6	4.2	7.8	1.4	-0.1	-4.5	-3.4
Portugal	3.7	7.6	3.3	4.5	-5.5	2.7	6.6	5.7	13.9	11.5	6.4	3.8	0.7	-5.2	-9.7
Spain	12.0	6.5	1.7	-4.1	-8.9	1.9	7.7	2.1	5.0	10.0	8.8	5.7	3.3	1.0	3.0
Euro area	7.0	5.3	1.4	–	-6.4	2.1	3.0	1.7	2.8	5.6	6.2	5.1	0.2	-2.2	-0.6
Denmark	-0.6	-2.2	-3.4	-2.1	-3.8	7.7	11.6	3.9	10.9	10.0	1.4	7.1	4.9	4.5	0.1
Sweden	12.1	0.2	-8.5	-11.3	-14.6	6.6	9.9	4.5	-0.3	7.8	8.2	5.7	-1.0	-3.0	-2.0
United Kingdom	6.0	-2.6	-8.2	-0.9	0.3	4.7	3.1	5.7	6.8	12.7	1.6	3.6	3.6	1.8	2.9
EU-15	6.9	4.0	-0.1	-0.4	-5.8	2.6	3.3	2.3	3.4	6.6	5.5	5.0	0.7	-1.6	-0.1
Cyprus	20.0	-2.8	-1.6	16.2	-12.8	-2.5	-1.7	7.2	-4.1	7.9	-1.0	3.8	3.2	8.0	-3.4
Czech Republic	..	..	-27.3	16.5	0.2	9.1	19.8	8.2	-2.9	0.7	-1.0	5.3	5.5	0.6	3.7
Estonia	..	..	..	..	..	9.2	5.6	9.6	19.9	14.0	-15.6	14.3	13.0	17.2	5.4
Hungary	..	..	..	-2.6	2.0	12.5	-4.3	6.7	9.2	13.2	5.9	7.7	5.0	8.0	3.0
Latvia	..	..	-63.9	-28.7	-15.8	0.8	8.7	22.3	20.7	61.4	-6.8	10.2	11.4	13.0	7.8
Lithuania	..	..	..	..	..	..	..	15.2	24.5	21.8	-6.1	-9.0	13.5	11.1	11.4
Malta	1.0	17.9	–	-0.2	11.1	8.5	17.8	-8.4	-4.5	-3.4	4.0	17.4	-11.1	-13.3	21.2
Poland	..	..	-4.4	2.3	2.9	9.2	16.5	19.7	21.7	14.2	6.8	2.7	-8.8	-5.8	-0.9
Slovakia	..	..	-25.2	-4.4	-4.2	-2.5	0.6	29.1	15.0	11.0	-19.6	-7.2	13.9	-0.9	-1.2
Slovenia	..	..	-11.5	-12.9	10.7	14.1	16.8	11.3	13.5	9.9	21.0	0.6	4.1	2.6	5.4
New EU members-10	..	..	..	..	..	..	..	14.6	11.9	11.2	1.3	3.0	0.2	–	1.8
EU-25	..	..	..	..	..	..	..	3.3	4.1	7.1	5.1	4.8	0.6	-1.4	–
Iceland	-7.9	3.0	3.3	-11.1	-10.7	0.6	-1.1	25.7	10.0	32.8	-3.0	14.8	-7.0	-14.8	7.8
Israel	-2.2	25.3	41.9	5.2	5.3	8.4	6.6	9.1	-1.0	-3.8	0.1	1.7	-4.8	-9.2	-5.0
Norway	-6.9	-10.8	-3.0	-1.1	6.5	5.3	3.9	10.3	15.5	13.1	-5.6	-3.6	-0.7	-3.4	-3.7
Switzerland	5.3	3.8	-2.2	-8.0	-3.0	6.6	4.4	-1.7	2.1	6.6	1.2	4.4	-3.1	-4.8	0.1
Turkey	2.2	15.9	0.4	6.4	26.4	-16.0	9.1	14.1	14.8	-3.9	-15.7	16.9	-31.5	-1.1	10.0
WECEE	..	..	..	..	..	..	..	3.2	4.3	7.2	4.8	4.6	0.5	-1.5	–
Canada	5.6	-4.0	-5.5	-2.7	-2.0	7.5	-2.1	4.4	15.2	2.4	7.3	4.7	4.1	2.4	4.9
United States	..	..	-5.1	4.8	6.0	7.3	5.7	8.1	8.0	9.1	8.2	6.1	-2.3	-2.3	3.9
North America	..	..	-5.1	4.1	5.2	7.3	5.0	7.8	8.6	8.5	8.1	5.9	-1.8	-1.9	4.0
Japan	8.5	7.9	2.3	-2.4	-2.8	-1.5	0.8	6.4	0.9	-3.9	-0.9	2.7	-1.1	-6.2	3.1
Europe, North America and Japan	..	..	..	..	..	..	..	5.6	5.2	5.5	5.1	4.9	-0.7	-2.4	2.1
Memorandum item:															
CEBS-8	..	..	..	..	..	..	..	14.8	12.1	11.2	1.3	3.0	0.2	–	1.8
Western Europe and North America	..	..	-2.4	1.4	-0.9	4.9	4.1	4.9	6.0	7.6	6.7	5.4	-0.7	-1.8	2.0

Source: Eurostat, NewCronos Database; OECD, *National Accounts* (Paris), various issues; national statistics.

Note: See appendix table A.1.

a West Germany, 1989-1991.

APPENDIX TABLE A.5

Real total domestic expenditures in Europe, North America and Japan, 1989-2003
(Percentage change over preceding year)

	1989	1990	1991	1992	1993	1994	1995	1996	1997	1998	1999	2000	2001	2002	2003
France	3.9	2.8	0.5	0.8	-1.6	2.1	1.6	0.7	0.7	4.0	3.6	4.1	2.0	1.5	1.2
Germany [a]	3.2	4.7	4.4	2.8	-1.1	2.3	1.7	0.3	0.6	2.4	2.8	1.8	-0.8	-1.6	0.4
Italy	3.1	2.7	2.1	0.9	-5.1	1.7	2.0	0.9	2.7	3.1	3.2	2.3	1.4	1.3	1.2
Austria	3.7	4.4	3.5	2.3	0.6	3.5	2.6	1.9	1.5	2.9	2.9	2.6	-0.2	–	1.8
Belgium	4.1	3.3	1.7	1.7	-0.9	2.4	2.0	0.9	2.7	2.7	2.5	3.6	0.4	0.8	2.4
Finland	6.3	-0.8	-7.8	-6.1	-5.4	3.0	2.7	3.8	4.8	4.2	2.0	2.5	1.8	0.6	1.8
Greece	5.3	2.2	3.5	-0.5	-1.0	1.1	3.5	3.3	3.5	4.6	3.8	3.7	2.9	3.9	6.2
Ireland	6.9	6.3	0.2	-0.1	1.0	5.1	6.5	7.7	9.7	10.4	7.9	9.1	3.9	2.8	3.4
Luxembourg	6.4	4.7	8.6	-4.1	4.6	2.4	0.7	5.0	6.5	7.3	6.6	5.2	4.3	-0.5	2.7
Netherlands	4.8	3.2	2.0	1.3	-1.6	2.3	3.5	2.8	3.9	4.8	4.3	2.5	1.7	–	-0.4
Portugal	4.9	5.3	6.1	3.4	-2.1	1.5	4.1	3.0	5.1	6.7	5.9	2.9	1.4	-0.5	-2.8
Spain	7.3	4.6	3.0	1.0	-3.3	1.5	3.1	1.9	3.5	5.7	5.6	4.5	3.0	2.6	3.3
Euro area	4.0	3.6	2.5	1.4	-2.3	2.1	2.2	1.1	2.0	3.7	3.6	3.0	1.1	0.6	1.3
Denmark	-0.1	-0.7	-0.1	0.9	-0.3	7.0	4.2	2.2	4.9	4.0	0.1	2.4	1.0	1.9	0.3
Sweden	4.0	0.7	-2.0	-1.5	-5.2	3.2	2.2	0.9	1.1	4.3	3.3	3.6	-0.2	0.8	0.8
United Kingdom	3.0	-0.3	-2.5	0.9	2.1	3.6	1.9	3.2	3.7	5.2	4.1	4.0	3.1	3.1	2.5
EU-15	3.8	2.8	1.5	1.2	-1.7	2.4	2.2	1.5	2.3	3.9	3.6	3.2	1.4	1.0	1.5
Cyprus	9.7	6.3	5.1	9.3	-9.5	7.4	7.8	3.7	2.0	9.0	0.2	5.2	4.2	5.5	1.0
Czech Republic	..	..	-21.4	4.7	2.2	8.4	8.4	7.3	-0.7	-2.4	0.3	4.0	5.1	3.4	4.1
Estonia	..	..	..	..	..	2.0	7.3	7.0	11.8	4.5	-5.1	10.5	7.1	12.2	5.3
Hungary	..	..	..	-2.8	9.0	1.3	-3.8	0.3	4.9	8.2	5.1	4.8	1.9	5.4	5.5
Latvia	..	..	-21.6	-33.1	-22.5	3.9	-1.7	7.6	5.7	11.4	2.9	4.1	10.6	5.6	11.3
Lithuania	..	..	..	..	..	..	..	6.5	10.3	8.0	-0.3	2.0	5.5	6.5	10.4
Malta	8.3	7.6	4.9	0.1	4.8	5.9	9.5	2.8	-0.1	-1.1	5.8	10.7	-5.4	-3.0	5.9
Poland	..	..	0.3	0.5	6.0	4.6	6.8	9.4	9.1	6.3	4.8	2.8	-1.6	0.8	2.4
Slovakia	..	..	-24.6	-4.5	-3.8	-4.5	9.9	18.2	3.7	7.2	-6.3	0.1	7.4	4.3	-2.3
Slovenia	..	..	-9.5	-3.2	12.9	5.5	10.2	3.3	4.7	5.1	8.7	1.3	0.9	2.3	4.2
New EU members-10	..	..	..	..	..	..	..	7.8	5.6	4.9	2.8	3.2	1.7	2.9	3.5
EU-25	..	..	..	..	..	..	..	2.0	2.5	4.0	3.5	3.2	1.4	1.2	1.6
Iceland	-4.4	1.5	4.3	-3.0	-4.2	0.3	I.6	10.5	4.7	12.9	5.4	7.5	-2.8	-2.7	4.2
Israel	-3.3	9.4	12.3	5.5	6.2	6.4	5.6	6.1	1.6	1.8	4.4	3.9	1.6	-0.7	-1.8
Norway	-1.4	–	1.7	2.2	3.2	4.2	4.6	4.4	6.7	5.7	0.3	2.3	1.1	2.3	0.7
Switzerland	4.3	3.8	-1.1	-2.3	-0.8	2.8	1.6	0.2	0.5	4.0	0.3	2.1	1.9	-0.9	-0.1
Turkey	1.4	14.2	-0.6	6.1	13.3	-12.2	11.5	7.3	8.9	0.8	-3.8	9.8	-17.5	9.2	9.1
WECEE	..	..	..	..	..	..	..	2.0	2.6	4.1	3.4	3.1	1.4	1.2	1.6
Canada	4.1	-0.3	-1.9	0.5	1.5	3.3	1.8	1.3	6.1	2.5	4.2	4.7	1.3	3.7	4.6
United States	2.8	1.4	-0.7	3.3	3.2	4.3	2.4	3.7	4.7	5.3	5.3	4.4	0.7	2.8	3.3
North America	2.9	1.3	-0.8	3.0	3.1	4.2	2.3	3.5	4.8	5.0	5.2	4.4	0.7	2.9	3.4
Japan	5.7	5.3	3.0	0.6	0.2	1.3	2.5	3.9	0.9	-1.5	0.2	2.4	1.2	-1.0	1.8
Europe, North America and Japan	..	..	..	..	..	..	..	2.9	3.3	3.7	3.8	3.6	1.1	1.6	2.5
Memorandum item:															
CEBS-8	..	..	..	..	..	..	..	7.8	5.7	4.9	2.8	3.2	1.7	2.9	3.5
Western Europe and North America	3.3	2.0	0.3	2.1	0.7	3.3	2.2	2.5	3.6	4.5	4.4	3.8	1.0	2.0	2.5

Source: Eurostat, NewCronos Database; OECD, *National Accounts* (Paris), various issues; national statistics.

Note: See appendix table A.1.

[a] West Germany, 1989-1991.

APPENDIX TABLE A.6

Real exports of goods and services in Europe, North America and Japan, 1989-2003

(Percentage change over preceding year)

	1989	1990	1991	1992	1993	1994	1995	1996	1997	1998	1999	2000	2001	2002	2003
France	10.0	4.8	5.9	5.4	–	7.7	7.7	3.5	11.8	8.3	4.3	12.6	1.6	1.9	-2.5
Germany [a]	10.3	13.2	12.9	-0.8	-5.5	7.6	5.7	5.1	11.2	7.0	5.5	13.7	5.6	3.4	1.8
Italy	7.8	7.5	-1.4	7.3	9.0	9.8	12.6	0.6	6.4	3.4	0.1	9.7	1.6	-3.4	-3.9
Austria	9.7	7.8	5.2	1.5	-1.4	5.6	3.0	5.2	12.4	8.1	8.5	13.4	7.5	3.7	1.0
Belgium	8.2	4.6	3.1	3.7	-0.4	8.3	5.0	3.0	5.9	6.0	5.1	8.4	1.3	1.0	2.3
Finland	3.0	1.5	-7.4	10.1	16.3	13.6	8.5	5.7	13.7	9.2	6.5	19.3	-0.8	5.1	1.3
Greece	1.9	-3.5	4.1	10.0	-2.6	7.4	3.0	3.5	20.0	5.3	18.1	14.1	-1.0	-7.7	-0.2
Ireland	10.3	8.7	5.7	13.9	9.7	15.1	20.0	12.2	17.4	21.0	15.2	20.6	8.3	6.2	-5.8
Luxembourg	12.6	5.6	9.2	2.7	4.8	7.7	4.6	5.8	14.7	14.1	14.8	17.3	1.8	-0.2	1.9
Netherlands	7.5	5.6	5.6	1.8	4.8	9.7	8.8	4.6	8.8	7.4	5.1	11.3	1.7	0.1	0.1
Portugal	12.2	9.5	1.2	3.2	-3.3	8.4	8.8	7.1	7.1	9.1	2.9	7.8	2.0	2.2	3.9
Spain	1.4	4.7	8.2	7.5	7.8	16.7	9.4	10.4	15.3	8.2	7.7	10.0	3.6	–	4.0
Euro area	8.4	7.6	6.1	3.5	1.2	9.2	8.1	4.4	10.4	7.2	5.2	12.1	3.2	1.2	–
Denmark	4.2	6.2	6.1	-0.9	-1.5	7.0	3.1	4.3	4.1	4.3	12.2	13.4	4.4	4.8	–
Sweden	3.2	1.8	-1.9	2.2	8.3	14.1	11.5	3.7	13.8	8.6	7.4	11.5	0.2	1.2	5.9
United Kingdom	4.5	5.5	-0.1	4.3	4.4	9.2	9.3	8.6	8.4	2.8	4.3	9.4	2.9	0.1	0.1
EU-15	7.6	7.1	5.0	3.5	1.8	9.3	8.2	5.0	10.1	6.6	5.3	11.8	3.1	1.2	0.2
Cyprus	16.8	7.9	-8.4	18.7	-1.3	7.9	4.6	3.6	1.7	–	6.5	9.0	3.4	-5.1	0.3
Czech Republic	..	..	-6.0	9.5	15.8	1.7	16.7	8.2	9.2	10.0	6.1	17.0	11.9	2.8	6.7
Estonia	..	..	..	..	..	3.5	5.3	2.8	28.9	12.0	0.7	28.3	-0.2	0.9	5.7
Hungary	..	..	..	2.1	-10.1	13.7	13.4	12.1	22.3	17.6	12.2	21.0	7.8	3.7	7.2
Latvia	..	..	-32.2	14.9	-22.4	-8.4	4.3	20.2	13.1	4.9	-6.4	12.0	6.9	6.3	4.3
Lithuania	..	..	..	..	..	..	..	19.3	18.7	4.6	-16.8	9.8	21.2	19.5	6.0
Malta	10.7	13.3	7.5	9.7	5.3	7.1	5.4	-5.9	4.0	8.1	8.2	5.6	-4.8	4.7	-2.2
Poland	..	..	-1.7	10.8	3.2	13.1	22.8	12.0	12.2	14.3	-2.6	23.2	3.1	4.8	14.7
Slovakia	..	..	33.4	47.5	-0.2	14.8	4.5	-1.1	17.6	12.8	5.0	13.7	6.3	5.5	22.6
Slovenia	..	..	-20.1	-23.5	0.6	12.3	1.1	2.8	11.3	7.4	1.6	13.0	6.3	6.8	3.1
New EU members-10	..	..	..	..	..	..	..	8.7	14.2	12.3	3.4	18.6	7.4	4.5	10.2
EU-25	..	..	..	..	..	..	..	5.3	10.5	7.2	5.1	12.5	3.6	1.5	1.4
Iceland	2.9	–	-5.9	-2.0	6.5	9.5	-2.3	9.9	–	2.0	4.0	5.0	7.7	3.7	–
Israel	4.1	2.0	-2.8	13.9	10.0	12.9	10.0	5.7	8.6	6.4	12.0	24.0	-11.5	-3.0	6.1
Norway	11.0	8.6	6.1	4.7	3.2	8.4	4.9	10.2	7.7	0.6	2.8	4.0	5.0	0.1	1.2
Switzerland	6.9	2.6	-1.3	3.1	1.3	1.9	0.5	3.6	11.1	3.9	6.5	12.2	0.2	-0.5	-1.4
Turkey	-0.3	2.6	3.7	11.0	7.7	15.2	8.0	22.0	19.1	12.0	-7.0	19.2	7.4	11.1	16.0
WECEE	..	..	..	..	..	..	..	5.4	10.5	7.0	5.1	12.3	3.5	1.5	1.3
Canada	1.0	4.7	1.8	7.2	10.8	12.7	8.5	5.6	8.3	9.1	10.7	8.9	-2.8	1.1	-2.4
United States	11.8	8.7	6.6	6.9	3.2	8.7	10.1	8.4	11.9	2.4	4.3	8.7	-5.2	-2.4	2.0
North America	8.8	7.7	5.4	7.0	5.1	9.7	9.7	7.7	11.0	4.1	6.0	8.8	-4.6	-1.4	0.8
Japan	9.3	6.7	4.1	3.9	-0.1	3.6	4.1	6.4	11.4	-2.4	1.5	12.4	-6.1	8.0	10.1
Europe, North America and Japan	..	..	..	..	..	..	..	6.1	10.7	5.5	5.1	11.3	0.8	1.1	1.7
Memorandum item:															
CEBS-8	..	..	..	..	..	..	..	9.0	14.6	12.6	3.3	18.9	7.5	4.6	10.4
Western Europe and North America	8.0	7.2	5.0	4.5	2.7	9.2	8.4	5.8	10.3	5.7	5.5	10.7	0.7	0.4	0.4

Source: Eurostat, NewCronos Database; OECD, *National Accounts* (Paris), various issues; national statistics.

Note: See appendix table A.1. Data on national accounts basis.

[a] West Germany, 1989-1991.

APPENDIX TABLE A.7

Real imports of goods and services in western Europe, North America and Japan, 1989-2003

(Percentage change over preceding year)

	1989	1990	1991	1992	1993	1994	1995	1996	1997	1998	1999	2000	2001	2002	2003
France	8.0	5.5	3.1	1.8	-3.7	8.2	8.0	1.6	6.9	11.6	6.2	14.6	1.3	2.9	-0.1
Germany *a*	8.5	10.7	12.2	1.5	-5.5	7.4	5.6	3.1	8.3	9.1	8.4	10.5	0.9	-1.7	3.4
Italy	8.9	11.5	2.3	7.4	-10.9	8.1	9.7	-0.3	10.1	8.9	5.6	7.1	0.5	-0.2	-0.6
Austria	8.0	6.9	5.8	1.4	-1.1	8.2	5.6	4.9	12.0	5.7	9.0	11.6	5.9	1.2	3.0
Belgium	9.7	4.9	2.9	4.1	-0.4	7.3	4.7	2.6	5.1	7.3	4.2	8.5	1.1	1.2	4.0
Finland	9.1	-0.6	-12.9	0.5	1.5	12.4	7.4	5.9	11.2	7.9	3.5	16.9	0.2	1.9	0.9
Greece	10.5	8.4	5.8	1.1	0.6	1.5	8.9	7.0	14.2	9.2	15.0	8.9	-3.4	-4.7	8.0
Ireland	13.5	5.1	2.4	8.2	7.5	15.5	16.4	12.5	16.8	25.5	12.1	21.3	6.5	2.3	-5.6
Luxembourg	9.1	5.0	9.1	-3.1	5.2	6.7	4.2	7.6	13.9	15.3	14.6	15.4	3.8	-1.8	2.3
Netherlands	7.7	3.8	4.9	1.5	0.3	9.4	10.5	4.4	9.5	8.5	5.8	10.5	2.4	-0.2	0.6
Portugal	5.9	14.5	7.2	10.7	-3.3	8.8	7.4	4.9	10.0	14.2	8.5	5.5	1.0	-0.5	-0.9
Spain	17.7	9.6	10.3	6.8	-5.2	11.4	11.1	8.0	13.2	13.2	12.6	10.6	4.0	1.8	6.7
Euro area	9.2	8.1	6.1	3.5	-4.3	8.3	7.8	3.3	9.3	10.1	7.6	10.8	1.7	0.3	1.9
Denmark	4.1	1.2	3.0	-0.4	-2.7	12.3	7.5	3.5	10.0	8.9	5.5	13.5	3.4	7.3	-0.6
Sweden	7.7	0.7	-4.9	1.5	-2.2	12.2	7.2	3.0	12.5	11.3	4.9	11.3	-2.5	-1.9	5.4
United Kingdom	7.4	0.5	-4.5	6.8	3.3	5.8	5.6	9.7	9.8	9.3	7.9	9.1	4.9	4.1	1.3
EU-15	8.8	6.6	4.2	3.8	-3.2	8.2	7.5	4.2	9.4	10.0	7.6	10.6	2.0	0.9	1.9
Cyprus	20.4	5.8	2.2	18.2	-18.1	8.2	11.5	6.6	1.2	7.7	-1.6	9.0	3.8	1.5	-1.2
Czech Republic	..	..	-32.8	29.7	23.7	14.7	21.2	13.4	8.1	6.6	5.4	17.0	13.6	4.3	7.6
Estonia	..	..	..	..	..	11.1	6.4	7.5	29.3	12.3	-5.2	28.3	2.1	3.7	11.0
Hungary	..	..	..	0.2	20.2	8.8	-0.7	9.4	23.1	23.8	13.3	19.4	5.1	6.2	10.3
Latvia	..	..	-43.9	8.0	-39.8	-0.7	1.4	28.5	6.8	19.0	-5.2	4.9	12.6	4.5	13.1
Lithuania	..	..	..	..	..	..	..	23.3	25.0	6.2	-12.4	4.7	17.7	17.6	8.8
Malta	11.1	15.7	5.4	3.0	5.9	7.5	10.0	-5.9	-1.7	2.5	10.1	10.4	-9.2	-1.4	6.4
Poland	..	..	29.6	1.7	13.2	11.3	24.3	28.0	21.4	18.5	1.0	15.6	-5.3	2.6	9.3
Slovakia	..	..	-14.7	47.1	-0.7	-4.7	11.6	19.7	14.2	16.5	-6.7	10.5	11.0	5.2	13.8
Slovenia	..	..	-22.4	-22.9	17.6	13.1	11.3	2.3	11.5	10.3	8.0	7.6	3.0	4.8	6.4
New EU members-10	..	..	..	..	..	..	..	16.6	16.1	14.8	2.9	15.3	4.9	4.8	9.4
EU-25	..	..	..	..	..	..	..	5.4	10.2	10.5	7.0	11.2	2.4	1.4	2.8
Iceland	-10.3	1.0	5.3	-6.0	-7.8	4.1	3.9	16.5	–	23.4	4.2	8.0	-9.0	-2.3	6.5
Israel	-5.1	9.5	15.8	8.4	14.1	10.8	7.7	7.7	3.3	1.7	14.9	12.2	-4.5	-2.3	-2.3
Norway	2.2	2.5	0.5	1.6	4.9	5.8	5.7	8.8	12.4	8.5	-1.8	2.7	0.9	2.3	2.2
Switzerland	6.6	2.8	-1.9	-3.8	-0.1	7.7	4.3	3.2	8.3	7.5	4.3	9.5	2.2	-3.1	-0.1
Turkey	6.9	33.0	-5.2	10.9	35.8	-21.9	29.6	20.5	22.4	2.3	-3.7	25.4	-24.8	15.8	27.1
WECEE	..	..	..	..	..	..	..	5.4	10.1	10.4	6.8	11.0	2.4	1.3	2.8
Canada	5.9	2.0	2.5	4.7	7.4	8.0	5.7	5.1	14.2	5.1	7.8	8.1	-5.0	1.4	3.8
United States	3.9	3.8	-0.6	6.9	8.8	11.9	8.0	8.7	13.6	11.6	11.5	13.1	-2.6	3.3	4.0
North America	4.4	3.4	0.1	6.4	8.4	11.0	7.5	7.9	13.7	10.2	10.7	12.1	-3.1	3.0	3.9
Japan	16.9	7.8	-1.1	-0.7	-1.4	7.9	12.5	13.1	1.0	-6.6	3.3	9.2	0.1	2.0	5.0
Europe, North America and Japan	..	..	..	..	..	..	..	6.6	10.5	9.3	7.8	11.3	0.6	1.8	3.2
Memorandum item:															
CEBS-8	..	..	..	..	..	..	..	17.1	16.6	15.0	2.9	15.4	5.1	4.9	9.6
Western Europe and North America	7.3	5.5	2.8	4.3	0.3	9.0	7.4	5.4	10.8	10.0	8.5	11.0	0.2	1.5	2.6

Source: Eurostat, NewCronos Database; OECD, *National Accounts* (Paris), various issues; national statistics.

Note: See appendix table A.1.

a West Germany, 1989-1991.

APPENDIX TABLE A.8

Industrial output in Europe, North America and Japan, 1989-2003
(Percentage change over preceding year)

	1989	1990	1991	1992	1993	1994	1995	1996	1997	1998	1999	2000	2001	2002	2003
France	3.5	1.5	-0.5	-1.5	-3.9	3.9	1.6	-0.2	4.1	3.5	2.5	3.9	1.1	-1.3	-0.2
Germany *a*	4.9	5.2	2.9	-2.3	-7.5	2.9	0.6	0.2	3.2	3.7	1.1	5.6	0.2	-1.0	0.4
Italy	3.9	-1.9	-0.9	-1.0	-2.2	5.9	5.7	-1.7	3.8	1.2	-0.1	4.1	-1.2	-1.3	-0.4
Austria	6.0	7.1	1.7	-1.2	-1.6	4.0	5.1	1.0	6.4	8.2	6.0	9.0	2.8	0.8	1.9
Belgium	3.4	1.5	-1.9	-0.4	-5.1	2.1	6.5	0.5	4.7	3.4	0.9	5.4	-2.2	1.5	–
Finland	2.4	0.4	-8.7	0.8	5.6	11.3	6.1	2.9	8.6	9.3	5.7	11.8	0.1	1.7	0.6
Greece	1.8	-2.4	-1.0	-1.1	-2.9	1.3	1.8	1.2	1.3	7.1	3.9	0.5	1.4	0.4	1.3
Ireland	11.6	4.7	3.3	9.1	5.6	11.9	20.5	8.1	17.5	19.8	14.8	15.4	10.2	7.8	6.3
Luxembourg	7.8	-0.5	0.3	-0.8	-4.3	5.9	1.4	0.1	5.8	-0.1	11.5	4.3	1.8	1.0	2.6
Netherlands	5.2	2.4	1.7	-0.2	-1.2	4.9	2.9	2.4	0.2	2.2	1.4	3.5	0.5	-1.0	-2.1
Portugal	6.7	9.0	–	-2.3	-4.8	-0.2	4.7	5.3	2.6	5.7	3.0	0.5	3.1	-0.5	-0.1
Spain	5.1	-0.4	-0.6	-3.1	-4.7	7.8	4.9	-1.2	7.0	5.4	2.7	4.4	-1.4	0.1	1.4
Euro area	4.7	4.1	1.3	-1.7	-4.7	4.4	3.3	–	4.2	3.8	1.8	5.2	0.4	-0.5	0.4
Denmark	0.4	0.8	0.3	3.0	-3.7	10.3	4.0	1.4	4.9	2.9	0.2	5.4	1.6	1.4	0.4
Sweden	3.7	1.1	-5.2	-2.8	-1.7	11.2	10.5	0.8	5.3	3.5	1.6	6.6	-0.4	0.3	2.8
United Kingdom	2.1	–	-3.3	0.4	2.2	5.3	1.8	1.4	1.4	1.0	1.2	1.9	-1.6	-2.7	-0.4
EU-15	4.1	2.4	0.3	-1.3	-3.3	4.9	3.2	0.2	3.8	3.3	1.6	4.7	–	-0.8	0.3
Cyprus	..	..	..	..	..	..	..	..	..	..	..	4.4	-0.2	0.1	6.9
Czech Republic	..	..	..	..	..	..	..	..	..	..	-3.2	1.5	10.5	4.9	5.9
Estonia	..	..	..	..	..	..	..	..	..	..	-3.9	15.0	8.5	8.5	10.3
Hungary	..	..	..	..	..	..	..	..	..	..	10.1	19.5	3.9	3.3	6.1
Latvia	..	..	..	..	..	..	..	..	6.1	1.8	-9.0	2.7	7.6	6.2	6.9
Lithuania	..	..	..	..	..	..	..	..	..	..	-9.9	2.2	16.0	3.1	16.1
Malta	..	..	..	..	..	..	..	..	..	..	..	..	..	..	..
Poland	..	..	..	..	..	..	..	..	9.8	10.9	4.5	4.7	7.8	0.5	1.6	8.3
Slovakia	..	..	..	..	..	..	..	..	..	..	-2.0	8.5	7.4	6.7	5.5
Slovenia	..	..	..	..	..	..	..	..	..	..	-0.7	8.6	2.0	2.2	-1.8
New EU members-10	..	..	..	..	..	..	..	..	..	..	..	..	..	..	..
EU-25	..	..	0.3	-1.3	-3.3	4.9	3.2	0.4	3.9	3.3	1.7	4.8	0.2	-0.6	0.7
Iceland	..	..	..	..	..	..	..	..	..	..	..	..	..	..	..
Israel	-1.6	8.0	6.8	8.2	6.9	7.4	8.4	5.4	1.8	2.8	1.4	10.1	-5.5	-1.6	-0.4
Norway	9.1	3.3	1.7	5.7	3.9	7.0	5.7	5.3	3.6	-1.2	-0.2	2.9	-1.3	1.0	-4.1
Switzerland	1.5	2.6	0.5	-1.0	-1.8	4.3	2.0	–	4.7	3.6	3.5	8.4	-0.7	-5.1	–
Turkey	3.6	9.5	2.7	5.0	8.0	-6.1	12.7	7.5	11.5	1.2	-3.7	6.1	-8.7	9.5	8.7
WECEE	..	..	..	..	..	..	..	..	..	..	..	..	..	..	..
Canada	-0.3	-2.8	-3.6	1.3	4.8	6.2	4.6	1.2	5.6	3.5	5.8	8.2	-2.9	1.9	0.4
United States	0.9	0.9	-1.5	2.8	3.3	5.4	4.8	4.3	7.4	5.9	4.4	4.4	-3.4	-0.6	0.3
North America	0.8	0.6	-1.7	2.7	3.4	5.5	4.8	4.1	7.2	5.7	4.5	4.7	-3.4	-0.4	0.3
Japan	5.8	4.2	1.9	-5.7	-3.5	1.3	3.3	2.3	3.5	-6.6	0.3	5.4	-6.3	-1.1	3.0
Europe, North America and Japan	..	..	..	..	..	..	..	..	..	..	..	..	..	..	..
Memorandum item:															
CEBS-8	..	..	..	..	..	..	..	..	..	..	..	..	..	..	..
Western Europe and North America	2.6	1.8	-0.5	0.6	–	4.9	4.1	2.2	5.6	4.4	2.9	4.7	-1.8	-0.4	0.5

Source: National statistics; Eurostat, NewCronos Database; OECD, *Main Economic Indicators* (Paris), latest issues; UNECE secretariat estimates.

Note: All aggregates exclude Israel and Turkey. Except for the European Union member countries, industrial output indices for regional aggregates have been calculated as weighted averages of the indices of the constituent countries; the European Union member countries' aggregates are provided by Eurostat. Weights were derived from 2000 value added originating in industry converted from national currency units into dollars using 2000 GDP purchasing power parities.

a West Germany, 1989-1991.

APPENDIX TABLE A.9

Total employment in Europe, North America and Japan, 1989-2003

(Percentage change over preceding year)

	1989	1990	1991	1992	1993	1994	1995	1996	1997	1998	1999	2000	2001	2002	2003
France	1.7	0.8	0.1	-0.6	-1.3	0.1	0.9	0.4	0.4	1.5	2.0	2.7	1.7	0.7	–
Germany *a*	1.8	3.1	2.5	-1.5	-1.4	-0.2	0.2	-0.3	-0.2	1.1	1.2	1.8	0.4	-0.6	-1.0
Italy	0.7	1.6	1.9	-0.5	-2.5	-1.5	-0.1	0.6	0.4	1.0	1.1	1.9	2.0	1.8	1.2
Austria	1.3	1.6	1.4	0.2	-0.6	-0.1	–	-0.6	0.5	1.0	1.4	0.7	0.6	-0.2	0.4
Belgium	1.2	0.9	0.1	-0.5	-0.8	-0.4	4.1	0.3	0.9	1.8	1.4	1.9	1.5	-0.3	0.6
Finland	0.9	-0.4	-5.6	-7.0	-6.0	-1.4	1.8	1.4	3.4	2.0	2.5	2.3	1.5	0.9	-0.4
Greece	0.4	1.3	-1.7	1.4	0.8	1.9	0.9	-0.5	-2.2	7.5	0.1	0.3	-0.3	0.1	0.8
Ireland	–	4.4	-0.3	0.3	1.4	3.2	4.4	3.6	5.6	8.6	6.0	4.7	3.0	1.3	1.4
Luxembourg	3.4	3.9	4.3	2.6	1.5	2.5	2.4	2.8	2.7	4.9	4.6	5.6	5.7	3.2	1.0
Netherlands	2.6	3.0	1.9	1.3	0.3	0.6	2.3	2.3	3.2	2.6	2.6	2.2	1.8	0.9	-0.5
Portugal	2.3	2.2	2.8	-1.6	-2.0	-1.0	-0.2	-5.9	1.7	2.7	1.8	2.3	1.6	0.7	0.2
Spain	3.6	3.8	1.2	-1.4	-2.8	-0.5	1.9	1.3	2.9	3.9	3.5	3.5	2.3	1.5	1.9
Euro area	1.7	2.2	1.4	-0.9	-1.6	-0.3	0.8	0.2	0.8	2.0	1.8	2.2	1.4	0.6	0.2
Denmark	-0.7	-0.7	-0.6	-0.8	-1.5	1.4	1.3	1.0	1.2	1.6	1.2	0.5	0.4	-0.6	-0.6
Sweden	1.5	0.9	-1.5	-4.4	-5.2	-0.9	1.5	-0.9	-1.3	1.5	2.1	2.4	1.9	0.2	-0.3
United Kingdom	2.8	0.4	-3.2	-2.9	-0.8	0.8	0.9	1.6	1.8	1.2	1.5	1.4	0.7	0.2	0.7
EU-15	1.9	1.8	0.4	-1.3	-1.6	-0.1	0.8	0.4	0.9	1.8	1.7	2.0	1.2	0.5	0.2
Cyprus	3.9	2.7	0.3	4.5	-0.1	2.8	4.3	0.4	0.2	1.4	1.8	2.2	2.1	1.0	0.6
Czech Republic	0.6	-0.9	-5.5	-2.6	-1.6	0.8	2.6	0.7	-1.9	-1.3	-2.5	-0.2	0.3	0.4	–
Estonia	2.4	-1.4	-2.3	-5.6	-8.2	-3.4	-6.2	-2.2	-0.3	-1.7	-4.5	-1.2	0.9	1.4	1.5
Hungary	-0.7	-3.3	-10.3	-11.2	-4.9	-2.0	-1.9	-0.8	–	1.4	3.1	1.2	0.3	0.1	1.3
Latvia	-0.5	0.1	-0.8	-7.3	-6.9	-10.1	-3.5	-2.6	4.3	-0.4	-1.8	-2.8	2.2	2.8	1.8
Lithuania	0.2	-2.7	2.4	-2.2	-4.2	-5.8	-1.9	0.9	0.6	-0.8	-2.2	-4.0	-3.3	-7.4	2.4
Malta	0.9	0.8	2.5	1.0	0.5	-1.3	3.3	1.0	1.2	0.8	2.3	8.1	2.1	-0.7	-1.4
Poland	-0.1	-4.2	-5.9	-4.2	-2.4	1.0	1.8	1.9	2.8	2.3	-2.7	-2.3	-0.6	-2.2	-0.7
Slovakia	0.2	-1.8	-12.5	1.1	2.6	-4.2	2.1	3.3	-0.5	-0.3	-3.0	-1.4	1.0	0.2	1.8
Slovenia	-1.3	-3.9	-7.8	-5.5	-2.9	-2.5	-0.2	-0.5	-0.2	0.2	1.8	1.3	1.4	-0.6	–
New EU members-10	–	-3.0	-6.2	-4.6	-3.0	-0.8	0.9	1.1	1.2	1.1	-1.8	-1.4	-0.1	-0.8	–
EU-25	1.5	0.9	-0.7	-1.9	-1.8	-0.2	0.8	0.5	1.0	1.7	1.2	1.5	1.0	0.3	–
Iceland	-1.6	0.1	–	-1.6	-0.8	0.8	0.8	2.4	1.6	3.1	2.3	2.2	2.2	-0.7	1.4
Israel	0.5	2.1	6.1	4.2	6.1	6.9	5.2	2.4	1.4	1.6	3.1	4.0	2.0	0.9	2.0
Norway	-2.8	-0.8	-0.9	-0.2	0.5	1.4	2.1	2.0	3.0	2.5	0.8	0.4	0.3	0.4	-0.6
Switzerland	2.7	3.2	1.9	-1.5	-0.8	-0.7	0.1	–	0.1	1.4	0.8	1.1	1.6	0.6	-0.1
Turkey	2.6	1.7	3.9	0.9	-4.8	7.9	3.7	2.1	-2.5	2.8	2.1	-0.4	-1.0	-0.6	1.7
WECEE	1.5	0.9	-0.7	-1.9	-1.7	-0.2	0.8	0.5	1.0	1.6	1.1	1.5	1.0	0.2	0.2
Canada	2.4	0.6	-1.8	-0.7	1.1	1.8	1.7	0.9	2.1	2.4	2.8	2.4	0.9	2.2	2.2
United States	2.3	1.3	-1.0	0.1	2.0	2.3	2.2	1.7	2.3	2.2	1.9	1.9	-0.1	-0.5	0.8
North America	2.3	1.2	-1.1	–	1.9	2.3	2.1	1.7	2.3	2.2	1.9	2.0	–	-0.3	0.9
Japan	1.5	1.7	2.0	1.1	0.4	0.1	0.2	0.5	1.1	-0.7	-0.8	-0.1	-0.5	-1.3	-0.2
Europe, North America and Japan	1.8	1.1	-0.4	-0.7	-0.1	0.7	1.2	0.9	1.5	1.5	1.1	1.4	0.4	-0.3	0.5
Memorandum item:															
CEBS-8	–	-3.1	-6.3	-4.7	-3.0	-0.8	0.9	1.1	1.2	1.1	-1.9	-1.5	-0.2	-0.9	–
Western Europe and North America	2.0	1.5	-0.2	-0.7	0.1	1.0	1.4	1.0	1.6	2.0	1.8	2.0	0.6	–	0.8

Source: Eurostat, NewCronos Database; OECD, *National Accounts* and *Economic Outlook*, latest issues; national statistics; UNECE secretariat estimates.

Note: All aggregates exclude Israel and Turkey. Total employment is defined as the number of persons engaged in some productive activity within resident production units (national accounts concept). The labour force survey concept (based on resident household surveys) is used for Iceland, Malta and the United Kingdom (up to 1989), Germany (up to 1990) and Turkey (up to 1999).

a West Germany, 1989-1991.

APPENDIX TABLE A.10

Standardized unemployment rates [a] in Europe, North America and Japan, 1989-2003
(Per cent of civilian labour force)

	1989	1990	1991	1992	1993	1994	1995	1996	1997	1998	1999	2000	2001	2002	2003
France	8.9	8.5	9.0	9.9	11.1	11.7	11.1	11.6	11.5	11.1	10.5	9.1	8.4	8.9	9.4
Germany [b]	5.6	4.8	4.2	6.4	7.7	8.2	8.0	8.7	9.7	9.1	8.4	7.8	7.8	8.7	9.6
Italy	9.7	8.9	8.5	8.7	10.1	11.0	11.5	11.5	11.6	11.7	11.3	10.4	9.4	9.0	8.6
Austria	3.1	3.2	3.5	3.6	4.0	3.8	3.9	4.4	4.4	4.5	3.9	3.7	3.6	4.2	4.1
Belgium	7.4	6.6	6.4	7.1	8.6	9.8	9.7	9.5	9.2	9.3	8.6	6.9	6.7	7.3	8.1
Finland	3.1	3.2	6.6	11.7	16.3	16.6	15.4	14.6	12.7	11.4	10.2	9.8	9.1	9.1	9.0
Greece	6.7	6.4	7.1	7.9	8.6	8.9	9.2	9.6	9.8	10.9	11.8	11.0	10.4	10.0	9.3
Ireland	14.7	13.4	14.7	15.4	15.6	14.3	12.3	11.7	9.9	7.5	5.6	4.3	3.9	4.3	4.6
Luxembourg	1.8	1.7	1.6	2.1	2.6	3.2	2.9	2.9	2.7	2.7	2.4	2.3	2.1	2.8	3.7
Netherlands	6.6	5.8	5.5	5.3	6.2	6.8	6.6	6.0	4.9	3.8	3.2	2.9	2.5	2.7	3.8
Portugal	5.2	4.8	4.2	4.3	5.6	6.9	7.3	7.3	6.8	5.1	4.5	4.1	4.1	5.0	6.3
Spain	13.9	13.1	13.2	14.9	18.6	19.8	18.8	18.1	17.0	15.2	12.8	11.3	10.6	11.3	11.3
Euro area	8.2	7.6	7.3	8.5	10.1	10.8	10.5	10.7	10.8	10.2	9.4	8.5	8.0	8.4	8.8
Denmark	6.8	7.2	7.9	8.6	9.6	7.7	6.7	6.3	5.2	4.9	4.8	4.4	4.3	4.6	5.6
Sweden	1.6	1.7	3.1	5.6	9.1	9.4	8.8	9.6	9.9	8.2	6.7	5.6	4.9	4.9	5.6
United Kingdom	7.1	6.9	8.6	9.8	10.0	9.3	8.5	8.0	6.9	6.2	5.9	5.4	5.0	5.1	5.0
EU-15	7.8	7.3	7.4	8.7	10.0	10.4	10.1	10.2	10.0	9.4	8.7	7.8	7.4	7.7	8.1
Cyprus [c]	2.3	1.8	3.0	1.8	2.6	4.1	4.0	4.7	5.2	5.2	5.5	5.2	4.4	3.9	4.4
Czech Republic	..	..	..	..	4.4	4.4	4.1	3.9	4.8	6.4	8.6	8.7	8.0	7.3	7.8
Estonia	..	..	..	..	..	..	..	..	9.6	9.2	11.3	12.5	11.8	9.5	10.1
Hungary	5.3	5.5	6.7	7.4	6.8	6.1	5.6	9.6	9.0	8.4	6.9	6.3	5.6	5.6	5.8
Latvia	..	..	..	..	..	..	..	..	..	14.3	14.0	13.7	12.9	12.6	10.5
Lithuania	..	..	..	..	..	..	..	..	..	11.8	11.2	15.7	16.1	13.6	12.7
Malta [de]	5.7	6.0	5.7	6.3	7.3	6.7	5.9	7.0	7.7	7.8	8.1	7.0	6.7	7.5	8.2
Poland	..	..	..	..	14.0	14.4	13.3	12.3	10.9	10.2	13.4	16.4	18.5	19.8	19.2
Slovakia	..	..	..	..	..	13.7	13.1	11.3	11.9	12.6	16.7	18.7	19.4	18.7	17.1
Slovenia	..	..	..	..	..	..	..	6.9	6.9	7.4	7.2	6.6	5.8	6.1	6.5
New EU members-10	..	..	..	..	..	..	..	..	..	9.7	11.7	13.5	14.4	14.7	14.3
EU-25	..	..	..	..	..	..	..	..	..	9.4	9.2	8.7	8.5	8.8	9.1
Iceland	1.6	1.8	2.6	4.3	5.3	5.4	4.9	3.8	3.9	2.7	2.1	2.3	2.3	3.2	3.4
Israel [f]	8.9	9.6	10.6	11.2	10.0	7.8	6.9	6.7	7.7	8.5	8.9	8.8	9.4	10.3	10.7
Norway	4.9	5.2	5.5	5.9	6.0	5.4	4.9	4.7	4.0	3.2	3.2	3.4	3.6	3.9	4.5
Switzerland	0.5	0.5	1.9	3.0	3.9	3.9	3.5	3.9	4.2	3.6	3.0	2.7	2.6	3.2	4.1
Turkey [ef]	8.7	8.2	7.9	7.9	7.6	8.1	6.9	6.1	6.4	6.8	7.6	6.5	8.3	10.3	9.0
WECEE	..	..	..	..	..	..	..	..	..	9.2	9.0	8.6	8.3	8.7	8.9
Canada	7.6	8.1	10.3	11.2	11.4	10.4	9.4	9.6	9.1	8.3	7.6	6.8	7.2	7.7	7.6
United States	5.3	5.5	6.7	7.4	6.8	6.1	5.6	5.4	4.9	4.5	4.2	4.0	4.8	5.8	6.0
North America	5.5	5.8	7.1	7.8	7.3	6.5	6.0	5.8	5.3	4.9	4.5	4.3	5.0	6.0	6.2
Japan	2.3	2.1	2.1	2.2	2.5	2.9	3.1	3.4	3.4	4.1	4.7	4.7	5.0	5.4	5.3
Europe, North America and Japan	..	..	..	..	..	..	..	..	..	6.9	6.8	6.5	6.7	7.2	7.4
Memorandum item:															
CEBS-8	..	..	..	..	..	..	..	..	..	..	..	..	..	15.0	14.4
Western Europe and North America	6.7	6.5	7.2	8.2	8.7	8.6	8.1	8.1	7.8	7.2	6.7	6.1	6.2	6.9	7.1

Source: OECD, *Main Economic Indicators* and *Quarterly Labour Force Statistics* (Paris), latest issues; Eurostat, NewCronos Database; national statistics; UNECE secretariat estimates.

Note: All aggregates exclude Israel and Turkey. Comparisons with previous years are limited by changes in methodology in Austria (1993), Cyprus (2000), Iceland (1991), Israel (1995), Malta (2000), Norway (1989) and Switzerland (1991).

[a] Eurostat-OECD definition except for Iceland and Switzerland (1989-1990); Austria (1989-1992); Israel (1989-1995); Cyprus and Malta (1989-1999).

[b] West Germany, 1989-1991.

[c] Registered unemployment rate, average of monthly data (1989-1999).

[d] Registered unemployment rate at the end of the year (1989-1999).

[e] Definition follows the Eurostat-OECD standards as of 2000.

[f] Definitions comply with ILO guidelines but do not follow the Eurostat-OECD standards.

APPENDIX TABLE A.11

Consumer prices in Europe, North America and Japan, 1989-2003
(Percentage change over previous year)

	1989	1990	1991	1992	1993	1994	1995	1996	1997	1998	1999	2000	2001	2002	2003
France	3.5	3.2	3.2	2.4	2.1	1.7	1.8	2.0	1.2	0.6	0.5	1.7	1.6	1.9	2.1
Germany [a]	2.8	2.7	4.1	5.1	4.4	2.7	1.7	1.4	1.9	0.9	0.6	1.5	2.0	1.4	1.0
Italy	6.3	6.4	6.3	5.3	4.6	4.1	5.2	4.0	2.0	2.0	1.7	2.5	2.8	2.5	2.7
Austria	2.6	3.3	3.3	4.0	3.6	2.9	2.2	1.9	1.3	0.9	0.6	2.3	2.7	1.8	1.4
Belgium	3.1	3.4	3.2	2.4	2.8	2.4	1.5	2.1	1.6	1.0	1.1	2.5	2.5	1.6	1.6
Finland	6.6	6.2	4.3	2.9	2.2	1.1	0.8	0.6	1.2	1.4	1.2	3.0	2.6	1.6	0.9
Greece	13.7	20.4	19.5	15.9	14.4	10.9	8.9	8.2	5.5	4.8	2.6	3.1	3.4	3.6	3.6
Ireland	4.1	3.3	3.2	3.1	1.4	2.3	2.5	1.7	1.6	2.4	1.6	5.6	4.9	4.7	3.5
Luxembourg	3.4	3.3	3.1	3.2	3.6	2.2	1.9	1.3	1.4	1.0	1.0	3.1	2.7	2.1	2.1
Netherlands	1.1	2.5	3.2	3.2	2.6	2.8	1.9	2.0	2.2	2.0	2.2	2.4	4.2	3.3	2.1
Portugal	12.6	13.4	10.5	9.4	6.7	5.4	4.2	3.1	2.3	2.8	2.3	2.9	4.3	3.6	3.3
Spain	6.8	6.7	5.9	5.9	4.6	4.7	4.7	3.6	2.0	1.8	2.3	3.4	3.6	3.1	3.0
Euro area	4.2	4.4	4.7	4.6	3.9	3.1	2.9	2.5	1.8	1.4	1.2	2.2	2.6	2.2	2.0
Denmark	4.8	2.6	2.4	2.1	1.3	2.0	2.1	2.1	2.2	1.8	2.5	2.9	2.3	2.4	2.1
Sweden	6.6	10.4	9.7	2.6	4.7	2.4	2.9	0.8	0.9	0.4	0.3	1.3	2.6	2.4	2.1
United Kingdom	7.8	9.5	5.9	3.7	1.6	2.5	3.4	2.5	3.1	3.4	1.6	2.9	1.8	1.6	2.9
EU-15	4.9	5.4	4.9	4.2	3.4	2.9	2.9	2.4	2.1	1.8	1.2	2.3	2.4	2.0	2.2
Cyprus	3.8	4.5	5.0	6.5	4.9	4.7	2.6	2.9	3.6	2.2	1.7	4.3	2.0	2.8	4.1
Czech Republic	..	..	..	11.1	20.8	10.0	9.1	8.9	8.4	10.6	2.1	3.9	4.7	1.8	0.2
Estonia	..	..	..	1 078.2	89.6	47.9	28.9	23.1	11.1	10.6	3.5	3.9	5.8	3.5	1.1
Hungary	..	..	..	..	22.6	19.1	28.5	23.6	18.4	14.2	10.1	9.9	9.2	5.4	4.9
Latvia	..	..	..	951.2	109.1	35.7	25.0	17.7	8.5	4.7	2.4	2.8	2.4	1.9	3.0
Lithuania	..	..	..	1 020.5	410.1	72.0	39.5	24.7	8.8	5.1	0.8	1.0	1.5	0.4	-1.2
Malta	0.9	3.0	2.5	1.6	4.1	4.1	4.0	2.1	3.3	2.2	2.1	2.4	2.9	2.2	0.7
Poland	..	..	..	45.3	36.9	33.2	28.1	19.8	15.1	11.7	7.4	10.2	5.5	1.9	0.7
Slovakia	..	..	..	10.2	23.1	13.4	10.0	6.1	6.1	6.7	10.5	12.0	7.0	3.3	8.5
Slovenia	..	..	..	130.7	31.7	21.0	13.5	9.9	8.4	8.1	6.3	9.0	8.6	7.6	5.7
New EU members-10	..	..	..	..	31.0	23.5	20.7	15.8	12.2	10.3	6.3	8.4	5.8	2.9	2.1
EU-25	..	..	..	..	4.2	3.7	3.8	3.2	2.8	2.4	1.7	2.8	2.7	2.1	2.2
Iceland	20.8	15.5	6.8	4.0	4.0	1.6	1.6	2.3	1.8	1.7	3.2	5.1	6.4	5.2	2.1
Israel	20.2	17.2	19.0	12.0	11.0	12.3	10.1	11.3	9.0	5.4	5.2	1.1	1.1	5.7	0.7
Norway	4.5	4.1	3.4	2.4	2.3	1.4	2.4	1.2	2.6	2.3	2.3	3.1	3.0	1.3	2.5
Switzerland	3.1	5.4	5.9	4.0	3.3	0.9	1.8	0.8	0.5	–	0.8	1.6	1.0	0.6	0.6
Turkey	63.3	60.3	66.0	70.1	66.1	105.2	89.1	80.4	85.7	84.6	64.9	54.9	54.4	45.0	25.3
WECEE	..	..	..	..	4.0	3.4	3.5	2.9	2.5	2.2	1.5	2.6	2.6	2.1	2.2
Canada	5.0	4.8	5.6	1.5	1.9	0.2	2.2	1.6	1.6	1.0	1.7	2.7	2.5	2.3	2.8
United States	4.8	5.4	4.2	3.0	2.9	2.6	2.8	2.9	2.3	1.6	2.1	3.4	2.8	1.7	2.2
North America	4.8	5.4	4.3	2.9	2.9	2.4	2.7	2.8	2.3	1.6	2.1	3.4	2.8	1.7	2.2
Japan	2.3	3.1	3.2	1.7	1.3	0.7	-0.1	0.1	1.7	0.7	-0.3	-0.7	-0.7	-0.9	-0.3
Europe, North America and Japan	..	..	..	..	2.9	2.4	2.4	2.3	2.2	1.6	1.4	2.4	2.1	1.4	1.8
Memorandum item:															
CEBS-8	..	..	..	..	34.9	27.9	24.1	17.8	13.6	11.1	6.8	9.2	5.8	2.5	1.6
Western Europe and North America	4.8	5.4	4.6	3.5	3.1	2.6	2.8	2.6	2.2	1.6	1.7	2.9	2.6	1.8	2.2

Source: National statistics.

Note: National definitions of the consumer price index. All aggregates exclude Israel and Turkey. Consumer price indexes for regional aggregates have been calculated as weighted averages of constituent country indices. Weights were derived from 2000 private final consumption expenditure converted from national currency units into a common currency using 2000 purchasing power parities.

[a] West Germany, 1989-1991.

APPENDIX TABLE B.1

Real GDP/NMP in eastern Europe and the CIS, 1980, 1989, 1991-2003

(Indices, 1989=100)

	1980	1989	1991	1992	1993	1994	1995	1996	1997	1998	1999	2000	2001	2002	2003
Eastern Europe	..	100.0	83.3	78.3	77.1	79.8	84.6	88.2	90.5	92.8	94.3	97.9	100.9	104.0	108.1
Albania	79.4	100.0	64.8	60.1	65.9	71.4	80.9	88.2	79.1	89.2	97.1	104.6	111.4	116.6	123.6
Bosnia and Herzegovina	..	..	..	..	..	..	100.0	154.2	210.7	243.1	266.3	280.7	293.3	304.3	314.0
Bulgaria	76.2	100.0	83.3	77.2	76.1	77.5	79.7	72.2	68.2	70.9	72.5	76.4	79.6	83.4	87.0
Croatia	99.0	100.0	73.3	64.7	59.5	63.0	67.3	71.3	76.2	78.1	77.4	79.6	83.2	87.5	91.2
Czech Republic	..	100.0	87.3	86.9	86.9	88.9	94.1	98.2	97.4	96.4	96.9	100.0	102.6	104.1	107.4
Estonia	74.5	100.0	82.7	71.0	65.0	63.9	66.8	69.8	77.2	81.2	81.1	87.5	93.1	99.8	104.9
Hungary	86.3	100.0	85.0	82.4	81.9	84.4	85.6	86.8	90.7	95.1	99.1	104.2	108.3	112.0	115.3
Latvia	68.5	100.0	89.9	61.1	54.1	55.3	54.7	56.8	61.5	64.4	66.6	71.1	76.8	81.8	87.9
Lithuania	64.7	100.0	91.2	71.8	60.2	54.3	57.1	59.8	64.0	68.6	67.4	70.1	74.6	79.6	86.7
Poland	91.1	100.0	82.2	84.4	87.6	92.1	98.6	104.5	111.6	117.0	121.8	126.6	127.9	129.6	134.5
Romania	88.5	100.0	82.2	75.0	76.2	79.2	84.8	88.2	82.8	78.8	77.9	79.6	84.2	88.3	92.6
Serbia and Montenegro [a]	95.7	100.0	81.4	58.7	40.6	41.7	44.2	46.8	50.3	51.5	42.4	45.1	47.6	49.4	50.1
Slovakia	..	100.0	83.3	78.0	75.1	79.7	84.4	89.6	93.7	97.7	99.1	101.1	104.9	109.6	114.2
Slovenia	98.9	100.0	83.7	79.1	81.4	85.7	89.3	92.5	96.9	100.4	105.9	110.1	113.0	116.9	119.5
The former Yugoslav Republic of Macedonia	93.3	100.0	84.3	78.7	72.8	71.6	70.8	71.6	72.6	75.1	78.4	81.9	78.2	78.9	81.4
CIS [b]	77.5	100.0	91.0	78.3	70.7	60.5	57.1	55.1	55.9	54.1	56.9	62.0	65.7	69.2	74.5
Armenia	73.5	100.0	83.5	48.6	44.3	46.7	49.9	52.9	54.6	58.6	60.5	64.1	70.2	80.8	92.1
Azerbaijan	79.6	100.0	87.7	67.9	52.2	41.9	37.0	37.4	39.6	43.6	46.8	52.0	57.1	63.1	70.2
Belarus	65.7	100.0	96.7	87.4	80.8	71.4	63.9	65.7	73.2	79.4	82.1	86.8	91.0	95.5	102.0
Georgia	79.4	100.0	67.0	36.9	26.1	23.4	24.0	26.7	29.5	30.4	31.3	31.8	33.4	35.2	39.1
Kazakhstan	87.0	100.0	88.2	83.5	75.8	66.2	60.8	61.1	62.1	60.9	62.6	68.7	78.1	85.7	93.5
Kyrgyzstan	69.1	100.0	96.5	83.1	70.3	56.2	53.1	56.9	62.5	63.8	66.2	69.8	73.5	73.5	78.4
Republic of Moldova [c]	72.1	100.0	80.5	57.2	56.5	39.0	38.5	36.2	36.8	34.4	33.2	34.0	36.0	38.8	41.3
Russian Federation	78.1	100.0	92.2	78.8	71.9	62.8	60.2	58.1	58.9	55.7	59.2	65.2	68.5	71.7	77.0
Tajikistan	80.8	100.0	91.7	62.1	52.0	40.9	35.8	29.8	30.3	32.0	33.1	35.9	39.5	43.3	47.7
Turkmenistan	80.7	100.0	97.0	82.5	83.7	69.2	64.2	68.5	60.7	65.0	75.8	83.3	90.0	98.1	106.9
Ukraine	75.0	100.0	88.0	79.3	68.0	52.4	46.0	41.4	40.2	39.4	39.3	41.6	45.5	47.9	52.4
Uzbekistan	76.0	100.0	98.7	87.7	85.7	81.2	80.5	81.9	86.1	89.9	93.9	97.6	102.0	106.3	111.0
Total above	..	100.0	88.7	78.3	72.6	66.3	65.4	65.0	66.3	65.7	68.1	72.8	76.3	79.6	84.6
Memorandum items:															
Baltic states (BS-3)	67.8	100.0	89.1	68.2	59.1	56.5	58.3	60.8	65.8	69.8	69.9	73.9	79.0	84.3	90.7
Central Europe (CE-5)	..	100.0	84.1	83.8	85.0	88.6	93.5	98.0	102.3	105.8	109.2	113.4	115.7	118.2	122.3
South-east Europe (SEE-7)	89.0	100.0	80.8	70.7	66.8	69.2	74.4	76.5	74.9	74.6	73.1	75.8	79.5	83.2	86.8
CIS without Russian Federation (CIS-11)	76.4	100.0	88.8	77.3	68.3	56.2	51.1	49.4	50.1	50.9	52.3	55.7	60.4	64.3	69.8
Caucasian CIS countries (CCIS-3)	78.6	100.0	77.7	51.1	39.3	34.3	33.0	34.9	37.3	39.8	41.8	44.7	48.3	53.1	59.4
Central Asian CIS countries (CACIS-5)	81.9	100.0	92.6	82.7	76.9	67.5	63.4	64.2	65.2	66.3	69.6	75.0	82.0	88.1	94.8
Three European CIS countries (ECIS-3)	73.4	100.0	89.1	79.7	69.6	54.9	48.6	45.2	45.4	45.7	46.1	48.7	52.5	55.3	60.0
Former GDR [d]	..	100.0	68.3	73.3	80.1	87.9	91.9	94.9	96.7	97.7	99.0	100.0	99.9	100.0	101.4

Source: UNECE Common Database, derived from national and Interstate Statistical Committee of the CIS statistics.

Note: Data for the east European countries are based on a GDP measure, except where otherwise mentioned. For the countries of the former Soviet Union, NMP data for 1980-1990 were chain-linked to GDP data from 1990. Country indices were aggregated with previous year PPP-based weights obtained from the European Comparison Programme for 1996.

[a] Gross material product (1980-1989 for Croatia, 1980-2000 for Serbia and Montenegro). Serbia and Montenegro: since 1999, without Kosovo and Metohia.

[b] Net material product for 1980-1990 (until 1992 in the case of Turkmenistan).

[c] Excluding Transdniestria since 1993.

[d] Excluding the former east Berlin since 1998.

APPENDIX TABLE B.2

Real total consumption expenditure in eastern Europe and the CIS, 1989-2003

(Indices, 1989=100 or earliest year available thereafter)

	1989	1990	1991	1992	1993	1994	1995	1996	1997	1998	1999	2000	2001	2002	2003
Bulgaria	100.0	100.6	92.3	89.4	86.2	82.3	80.7	74.1	67.1	69.8	75.9	80.2	83.8	86.8	92.5
Croatia	..	..	100.0	87.2	85.3	92.0	106.6	106.5	117.1	117.4	116.1	118.8	120.2	126.0	129.8
Czech Republic	100.0	104.9	85.5	88.4	90.2	94.5	97.2	103.7	104.3	101.8	103.7	105.4	109.7	113.9	118.6
Estonia	..	..	..	..	100.0	101.6	109.3	115.7	123.9	129.1	127.8	136.1	143.0	156.1	165.0
Hungary	100.0	97.3	92.2	92.8	97.9	95.6	89.3	86.4	88.4	91.8	95.8	100.1	105.9	115.1	121.9
Latvia	..	100.0	76.7	49.2	46.5	47.4	47.0	50.7	51.7	53.7	55.4	57.6	60.8	64.5	69.2
Lithuania	..	..	..	..	..	..	100.0	105.4	111.3	117.0	117.8	124.3	127.8	134.3	147.4
Poland	100.0	88.3	94.9	98.2	103.0	107.0	110.5	118.3	125.5	130.7	136.5	139.9	142.3	146.2	149.8
Romania	100.0	108.9	96.0	90.7	91.8	95.3	105.5	112.9	108.1	109.3	106.5	108.1	114.9	117.6	125.7
Slovakia	100.0	103.3	76.9	75.6	74.2	72.3	75.8	83.8	85.7	92.7	92.9	92.7	97.1	102.0	102.5
Slovenia	..	100.0	91.6	88.8	99.1	102.6	110.2	113.3	116.1	120.2	126.4	127.5	131.0	132.3	135.8
The former Yugoslav Republic of Macedonia	..	100.0	93.9	84.2	89.7	95.9	94.3	96.5	98.5	101.8	105.6	114.0	110.0	..	..
Armenia	..	100.0	97.4	84.9	66.4	68.9	74.5	76.8	81.7	85.4	86.6	93.3	100.0	108.2	117.9
Azerbaijan	..	..	..	100.0	77.4	62.2	60.4	65.3	72.2	80.4	88.1	95.7	104.0	113.5	126.8
Belarus	..	100.0	93.5	84.1	78.8	70.0	63.4	65.7	72.3	80.9	87.7	94.2	107.1	115.7	121.9
Georgia	..	100.0	79.2	77.1	45.4	42.4	46.1	..	..	..	..	..	..	..	..
Kazakhstan	..	100.0	96.8	96.2	84.9	67.7	55.0	51.3	51.8	50.4	51.1	52.7	57.7	63.0	67.5
Kyrgyzstan	..	100.0	83.5	72.8	64.3	51.8	43.4	46.2	42.4	48.8	49.3	47.9	48.6	50.3	54.6
Republic of Moldova	..	..	..	..	100.0	82.6	90.3	99.7	111.5	109.3	92.0	107.8	112.5	123.4	139.9
Russian Federation	..	100.0	100.0	94.8	93.9	90.9	88.5	86.1	88.5	86.7	85.6	90.4	96.6	103.7	110.5
Ukraine	..	100.0	94.7	88.7	72.1	65.1	62.7	57.5	56.4	56.4	54.3	55.4	60.5	63.5	71.6

Source: UNECE Common Database, derived from national and Interstate Statistical Committee of the CIS statistics.

APPENDIX TABLE B.3

Real gross fixed capital formation in eastern Europe and the CIS, 1989-2003

(Indices, 1989=100 or earliest year available thereafter)

	1989	1990	1991	1992	1993	1994	1995	1996	1997	1998	1999	2000	2001	2002	2003
Bulgaria	..	100.0	80.0	74.1	61.2	61.9	71.8	56.6	44.7	60.5	73.1	84.4	104.0	112.8	128.4
Croatia	..	..	100.0	88.5	94.5	93.6	108.2	148.8	188.1	192.9	185.4	178.2	190.8	213.7	249.6
Czech Republic	100.0	97.9	71.1	82.8	83.0	90.5	108.5	117.3	113.9	114.7	113.5	119.6	126.2	130.4	140.0
Estonia	..	..	..	..	100.0	109.2	115.3	126.4	151.5	172.7	145.8	166.6	188.3	220.6	232.6
Hungary	100.0	92.9	83.1	81.0	82.6	92.9	88.9	94.9	103.6	117.3	124.2	133.7	140.4	151.6	156.1
Latvia	..	100.0	36.1	25.7	21.6	21.8	23.7	29.0	29.0	35.0	56.5	52.7	58.0	64.7	73.1	78.8
Lithuania	..	..	..	..	..	..	100.0	115.2	143.4	174.7	164.0	149.3	169.5	188.3	209.7
Poland	100.0	75.2	71.9	73.6	75.7	82.6	96.2	115.2	140.1	160.0	170.9	175.6	160.2	150.8	149.4
Romania	100.0	64.4	44.0	48.9	52.9	63.9	68.3	72.2	73.4	69.2	65.9	69.5	76.5	82.9	90.5
Slovakia	..	100.0	74.8	71.5	67.7	66.0	66.4	85.7	98.5	109.3	88.0	81.6	92.9	92.1	91.0
Slovenia	..	100.0	88.5	77.1	85.4	97.4	113.8	126.6	143.6	157.9	191.1	192.3	200.2	205.4	216.5
The former Yugoslav Republic of Macedonia	..	100.0	95.8	79.9	73.6	67.3	74.1	79.0	75.6	73.6	72.5	70.2	64.2	..	..
Armenia	..	100.0	67.0	8.6	7.9	11.5	9.5	10.5	10.7	12.0	12.1	14.0	14.8	19.7	26.3
Azerbaijan	..	..	..	100.0	61.0	115.3	94.5	199.8	333.7	410.5	402.2	412.7	497.7	915.8	1 479.0
Belarus	..	100.0	104.2	84.8	78.3	67.6	47.6	46.1	56.2	61.8	59.3	60.7	59.3	63.3	74.5
Georgia	..	100.0	67.3	49.2	18.5	133.4	219.9	..	..	..	..	..	..	..	..
Kazakhstan	..	100.0	74.2	61.9	44.2	39.2	24.3	18.5	19.1	17.8	17.9	20.7	26.0	28.6	30.9
Kyrgyzstan	..	100.0	89.4	63.2	49.4	35.1	56.4	49.1	34.6	34.0	43.6	55.3	54.3	50.3	49.6
Republic of Moldova	..	..	..	..	100.0	56.5	50.8	63.8	60.4	66.0	50.8	46.4	54.4	57.5	65.1
Russian Federation	..	100.0	100.0	58.5	43.4	32.1	29.7	23.2	21.0	18.4	19.9	23.1	25.7	26.6	29.8
Ukraine	..	100.0	79.1	67.4	46.8	27.6	19.1	14.8	15.1	15.5	15.5	17.4	18.5	19.1	22.1

Source: UNECE Common Database, derived from national and Interstate Statistical Committee of the CIS statistics.

APPENDIX TABLE B.4

Real gross industrial output in eastern Europe and the CIS, 1980, 1989, 1991-2003

(Indices, 1989=100)

	1980	1989	1991	1992	1993	1994	1995	1996	1997	1998	1999	2000	2001	2002	2003
Eastern Europe	82.0	100.0	70.7	58.5	54.2	56.7	60.8	64.0	66.4	67.0	66.6	71.8	74.8	77.5	82.2
Albania	77.0	100.0	50.4	35.2	31.7	25.8	23.9	18.1	18.6	22.7	26.1	29.2	23.4	26.0	28.0
Bosnia and Herzegovina	106.0	100.0	76.9	25.5	2.0	1.7	2.8	5.2	7.0	8.7	9.6	10.5	11.8	12.9	13.5
Bulgaria	71.3	100.0	66.4	54.2	48.8	54.0	56.4	59.3	48.4	44.3	40.7	44.1	44.8	47.7	51.7
Croatia	88.7	100.0	63.4	54.2	51.0	49.6	49.7	51.3	54.8	56.8	56.0	57.0	60.4	63.6	66.2
Czech Republic	81.5	100.0	75.7	69.8	66.1	67.4	73.3	74.8	78.1	79.4	76.9	81.1	86.4	90.5	95.7
Estonia	78.5	100.0	92.8	59.8	48.6	47.1	48.0	49.4	56.6	59.0	57.0	65.3	71.1	76.9	84.5
Hungary	92.9	100.0	74.0	66.8	69.5	76.2	79.7	82.4	91.5	103.0	113.7	134.3	139.1	143.0	152.2
Latvia	72.5	100.0	100.2	65.6	44.6	40.1	38.7	40.8	46.4	47.9	45.3	47.4	51.8	56.1	59.8
Lithuania	70.0	100.0	94.0	65.8	43.2	31.7	33.4	35.0	36.2	40.6	36.5	37.4	43.3	44.7	51.9
Poland	86.3	100.0	69.7	71.7	76.3	85.5	93.8	101.6	113.3	117.3	121.5	129.6	130.4	131.8	142.9
Romania	76.9	100.0	58.8	43.9	44.2	45.6	49.9	53.1	49.3	42.5	41.4	44.4	48.1	51.0	52.6
Serbia and Montenegro	80.0	100.0	72.5	57.0	35.7	36.2	37.6	40.4	44.2	45.8	35.2	39.2	39.2	39.9	38.8
Slovakia	76.7	100.0	75.9	68.6	66.1	69.3	75.1	76.9	77.9	80.9	79.3	85.9	92.5	98.7	103.6
Slovenia	90.3	100.0	78.4	68.1	66.1	70.4	71.8	72.5	73.2	75.9	75.6	80.2	82.6	84.6	85.7
The former Yugoslav Republic of Macedonia	72.1	100.0	74.0	62.3	53.7	48.0	42.9	44.3	45.0	47.0	45.8	47.4	45.9	43.5	45.5
CIS	73.6	100.0	92.7	76.8	66.7	51.9	49.0	47.5	48.5	46.9	51.2	57.3	61.1	64.0	69.4
Armenia	76.3	100.0	85.4	44.2	39.5	41.6	42.2	42.8	43.2	42.3	44.6	47.4	49.9	57.2	65.7
Azerbaijan	76.1	100.0	85.4	59.4	47.7	35.9	28.2	26.3	26.4	27.0	28.0	29.9	31.4	32.6	34.6
Belarus	61.1	100.0	101.1	91.8	83.2	71.0	62.7	64.9	77.1	86.7	95.6	103.0	109.1	114.0	121.8
Georgia	70.6	100.0	73.0	39.6	25.0	15.2	13.2	14.1	15.2	15.0	15.7	16.7	16.5	17.3	19.2
Kazakhstan	72.4	100.0	98.3	84.7	72.2	51.9	47.7	47.8	49.7	48.5	49.8	57.5	65.5	72.4	78.7
Kyrgyzstan	66.7	100.0	99.1	73.5	56.3	35.5	26.7	27.8	38.8	40.9	39.1	41.4	43.7	38.9	45.5
Republic of Moldova	68.7	100.0	91.7	66.9	67.1	48.5	46.6	43.6	43.6	37.0	32.7	35.3	40.1	44.3	50.4
Russian Federation	74.4	100.0	91.9	75.4	64.7	51.2	49.5	47.5	48.5	46.0	51.0	57.1	59.9	62.1	66.5
Tajikistan	72.9	100.0	97.6	73.9	68.1	50.8	43.9	33.4	32.7	35.4	37.4	41.1	47.2	51.1	56.3
Turkmenistan	75.4	100.0	108.2	92.0	95.7	72.1	67.5	81.0	63.1	64.4	74.1	84.4	93.7	103.1	113.4
Ukraine	72.6	100.0	95.1	89.0	81.9	59.5	52.4	49.7	49.6	49.1	51.0	57.8	66.0	70.6	81.8
Uzbekistan	68.5	100.0	103.3	96.4	99.9	101.5	101.6	104.2	108.5	112.4	118.8	125.8	135.4	146.9	156.0
Total above	76.3	100.0	85.8	71.0	62.8	53.4	52.7	52.7	54.1	53.2	56.1	61.8	65.4	68.3	73.4
Memorandum items:															
Baltic states	71.9	100.0	95.3	64.8	44.4	36.1	36.9	38.7	41.8	45.2	41.8	44.1	49.7	52.5	58.9
Central Europe	84.9	100.0	73.4	69.9	70.4	75.9	82.1	86.2	93.0	96.9	99.0	107.1	110.5	113.6	121.3
South-east Europe	80.6	100.0	64.4	46.0	39.3	40.2	42.8	45.3	43.0	39.9	37.6	40.3	42.4	44.6	46.2
CIS without Russian Federation	71.7	100.0	94.6	80.2	71.5	53.7	47.9	47.5	48.6	49.2	51.7	57.7	64.1	68.8	76.5
Caucasian CIS countries	74.3	100.0	81.2	51.3	39.3	29.6	24.6	23.8	24.3	24.5	25.5	27.2	28.2	29.9	32.4
Central Asian CIS countries	72.1	100.0	100.2	85.2	76.2	57.3	52.8	54.6	54.5	54.6	57.2	64.6	72.3	78.7	85.8
Three European CIS countries	70.3	100.0	96.1	88.8	81.6	61.3	54.1	52.4	54.5	55.7	58.7	65.5	73.2	77.8	88.2
Former GDR	75.2	100.0	37.0	34.7	34.9	38.1	39.9	41.7	44.6	48.2	51.7	57.2	59.4	61.8	64.4

Source: UNECE Common Database, derived from national and Interstate Statistical Committee of the CIS statistics.

Note: For the countries of the former Soviet Union, Soviet data for 1980-1990 were chain-linked to national or CIS data from 1990. Country indices were aggregated with previous year PPP-based value added weights on the basis of data obtained from the European Comparison Programme for 1996.

APPENDIX TABLE B.5

Total employment in eastern Europe and the CIS, 1980, 1989-2003

(Indices, 1989=100 or earliest year available thereafter)

	1980	1989	1990	1991	1992	1993	1994	1995	1996	1997	1998	1999	2000	2001	2002	2003
Eastern Europe [a]	95.1	100.0	97.2	93.0	87.6	84.7	84.2	83.7	86.8	87.8	88.0	86.4	85.3	84.7	81.3	..
Albania	77.9	100.0	99.2	97.5	76.0	72.7	80.7	80.4	77.5	76.9	75.4	74.0	74.2	63.9	63.9	64.3
Bosnia and Herzegovina	..	..	..	100.0	38.0	17.0	15.7	17.4	38.8	59.2	62.7	64.6	65.1	64.5	62.5	..
Bulgaria	100.0	100.0	93.9	81.6	75.0	73.8	74.3	75.2	75.3	72.3	72.2	70.7	68.3	68.0	68.2	69.2
Croatia	87.4	100.0	97.1	89.2	79.3	76.6	74.8	73.9	74.5	73.9	86.0	85.1	82.9	82.4	83.1	86.0
Czech Republic	95.3	100.0	99.1	93.6	91.2	89.7	90.4	92.8	93.4	91.6	90.4	88.1	87.9	88.2	87.8	..
Estonia	..	100.0	98.6	96.3	90.9	83.4	80.6	75.6	73.9	73.7	72.4	69.1	68.3	68.9	69.9	70.9
Hungary [b]	104.2	100.0	96.7	86.7	77.0	73.2	71.8	70.4	69.8	69.8	70.7	72.9	73.8	74.0	74.0	75.0
Latvia [c]	97.0	100.0	100.1	99.3	92.0	85.6	77.0	74.3	67.5	70.4	70.1	68.8	66.9	68.4	70.3	71.6
Lithuania [d]	93.4	100.0	97.3	99.7	97.5	93.4	88.0	86.4	87.2	87.7	78.3	76.5	73.4	71.0	73.9	75.6
Poland	102.0	100.0	95.8	90.1	86.3	84.3	85.1	86.7	88.3	90.8	92.9	90.4	88.3	87.8	85.8	85.2
Romania [e]	94.6	100.0	99.0	98.5	95.5	91.9	91.5	86.7	99.9	101.0	99.1	98.4	98.3	97.7	84.4	84.3
Serbia and Montenegro	83.4	100.0	97.0	94.1	90.9	88.3	86.5	85.1	84.8	89.9	89.7	82.4	80.2	80.4	71.9	..
Slovakia [f]	90.8	100.0	98.2	85.9	86.8	87.7	84.0	85.7	88.6	88.1	87.8	85.1	83.9	84.8	84.9	86.4
Slovenia	84.0	100.0	96.1	88.7	83.8	81.3	79.3	79.1	78.7	78.6	78.7	80.2	81.2	82.3	82.8	..
The former Yugoslav Republic of Macedonia	81.2	100.0	98.2	90.7	86.4	81.5	76.6	69.0	65.8	61.8	60.1	61.1	60.3	57.7	54.2	..
CIS	93.8	100.0	100.2	98.8	96.6	94.2	91.4	90.2	89.7	88.3	87.3	87.0	..	..	..	..
Armenia	86.6	100.0	102.4	105.0	99.2	97.0	93.5	92.8	90.2	86.2	84.0	81.6	80.3	79.5	69.5	69.9
Azerbaijan	62.7	100.0	100.9	101.7	101.4	101.2	98.9	98.4	100.5	100.7	100.9	100.9	100.9	101.2	101.5	102.0
Belarus	95.4	100.0	99.1	96.6	94.1	92.9	90.4	84.8	84.0	84.1	85.0	85.5	85.4	85.0	84.3	82.8
Georgia	92.7	100.0	102.3	93.3	73.5	66.4	64.8	64.1	75.4	68.4	64.1	64.2	68.1	69.5	68.1	..
Kazakhstan	86.2	100.0	101.3	100.1	98.3	89.9	85.4	85.0	84.6	84.0	79.5	79.2	80.5	86.9	87.1	90.4
Kyrgyzstan	81.9	100.0	100.5	99.6	105.6	96.6	94.6	94.4	95.0	97.1	98.0	101.5	101.7	102.8	103.9	104.9
Republic of Moldova [g]	97.3	100.0	99.1	99.0	98.0	80.7	80.4	80.0	79.4	78.7	78.5	71.5	72.5	71.7	72.0	65.3
Russian Federation	96.9	100.0	99.6	97.7	95.3	93.7	90.6	87.8	87.2	85.6	84.4	84.6	85.1	85.6	86.5	87.0
Tajikistan	76.7	100.0	103.2	104.9	101.6	98.7	98.7	98.6	92.1	95.3	95.6	92.5	92.9	97.3	98.9	97.6
Turkmenistan	79.8	100.0	103.4	107.0	110.5	114.0	118.5	122.5	124.7	127.2	128.8	133.6	..	..	..	..
Ukraine	99.7	100.0	100.0	98.3	96.4	94.2	90.6	93.3	91.4	88.9	87.9	85.9	83.7	82.7	84.1	84.4
Uzbekistan	75.4	100.0	104.2	108.3	108.5	108.3	109.9	110.8	112.3	113.8	115.4	116.5	117.8	119.8	..	..
Total above [a]	94.2	100.0	99.3	97.1	93.9	91.4	89.3	88.3	88.9	88.2	87.5	86.8	..	..	..	..
Memorandum items:																
Baltic states	75.8	100.0	98.5	98.9	94.3	88.8	82.8	80.1	77.8	79.0	74.3	72.4	70.2	69.7	71.8	73.3
Central Europe	99.7	100.0	96.7	89.8	85.6	83.6	83.5	84.7	85.8	86.8	87.9	86.3	85.2	85.1	84.0	..
South-east Europe [a]	92.3	100.0	97.6	96.5	89.2	85.6	85.5	82.9	89.9	90.9	90.8	89.2	88.2	87.0	79.2	..
CIS without Russian Federation	89.9	100.0	101.0	100.3	98.1	94.8	92.4	93.2	92.8	91.7	90.8	89.9	..	..	..	..
Caucasian CIS countries	77.6	100.0	101.7	99.5	91.5	88.6	86.3	85.7	89.9	86.8	85.0	84.6	85.7	86.1	83.8	..
Central Asian CIS countries	80.5	100.0	102.6	104.0	103.9	99.9	98.9	99.4	99.3	100.4	99.5	100.1	..	..	..	..
Three European CIS countries	98.8	100.0	99.8	98.1	96.1	93.1	89.9	91.1	89.4	87.5	86.8	84.9	83.2	82.3	83.4	82.9

Source: UNECE Common Database, derived from national and Interstate Statistical Committee of the CIS statistics.

[a] Excluding Bosnia and Herzegovina (up to 1990).

[b] End of year, up to 1991; annual average, 1992 onwards.

[c] Labour force survey data since 1996.

[d] Data recalculated since 1998 to correspond to the 2001 population census results.

[e] End of year, up to 1995; annual average, labour force survey data, 1996 onwards.

[f] End of year, up to 1993; annual average, 1994 onwards.

[g] Excluding Transdniestria since 1993.

APPENDIX TABLE B.6

Employment in industry in eastern Europe and the CIS, 1990, 1992-2003

(Indices, 1989=100 or earliest year available thereafter)

	1990	1992	1993	1994	1995	1996	1997	1998	1999	2000	2001	2002	2003
Eastern Europe[a]	95.6	78.7	73.7	71.4	69.7	70.5	69.7	68.6	64.8	62.0	61.1	59.4	..
Albania	..	..	..	100.0	85.6	76.9	79.8	75.6	74.1	52.6	66.6	63.1	60.4
Bosnia and Herzegovina	..	38.7	13.7	15.2	31.1	36.5	44.5	47.9	48.0	48.0	45.7	44.7	..
Bulgaria	91.0	64.8	59.5	57.3	56.0	55.4	53.0	50.8	46.1	43.5	42.9	43.0	43.2
Croatia	102.4	70.3	70.4	67.3	59.5	59.0	56.6	60.0	58.3	56.7	55.9	55.8	..
Czech Republic	95.8	85.1	80.9	76.6	77.0	76.4	76.1	74.9	72.5	71.4	72.0	70.6	..
Estonia	99.0	87.0	73.6	69.5	74.2	70.3	65.2	63.7	59.9	61.5	61.6	58.7	61.0
Hungary	97.0	77.3	69.1	66.0	62.5	61.9	63.0	65.9	66.4	66.0	67.2	66.8	64.1
Latvia	97.0	81.4	69.0	56.3	53.1	51.1	50.9	51.6	47.9	47.9	46.2	47.9	49.1
Lithuania	96.7	91.4	78.0	64.5	59.5	57.0	57.1	56.1	52.3	49.6	48.0	50.1	50.8
Poland	93.7	76.7	74.4	73.8	76.2	75.6	75.8	75.0	69.5	65.3	62.8	59.6	..
Romania [b]	96.5	79.5	73.0	69.4	65.4	71.7	69.9	66.3	62.0	58.1	57.2	55.7	56.0
Serbia and Montenegro	100.9	87.2	85.0	82.7	79.8	78.4	75.8	77.8	70.5	67.1	65.2	60.1	..
Slovakia	95.7	78.7	74.0	71.7	71.6	71.6	70.2	67.3	65.4	63.3	63.9	64.1	..
Slovenia	95.1	84.6	78.1	75.1	72.2	71.5	68.5	67.8	66.7	66.3	66.7	67.3	..
The former Yugoslav Republic of Macedonia	95.3	81.6	77.5	72.9	63.1	59.0	54.4	52.5	55.4	52.9	56.6	51.3	..
CIS	100.0	93.3	89.4	80.4	74.3	70.3	64.7	62.3	61.5	..	..	..	..
Armenia	102.6	84.0	75.2	73.7	62.8	52.9	47.5	43.4	40.5	37.3	35.2	29.7	..
Azerbaijan	97.1	88.9	81.1	77.4	72.9	58.6	50.1	52.0	53.6	51.6	51.1	52.1	52.5
Belarus	98.6	92.1	88.5	84.4	75.2	74.4	74.5	75.5	76.2	75.9	75.0	72.4	69.9
Georgia	104.2	66.0	56.5	51.6	46.8	33.6	30.8	28.1	25.7	27.3	25.9	21.8	..
Kazakhstan	98.5	96.2	83.6	76.9	69.6	66.9	59.0	57.8	57.9	54.7	53.1	52.7	54.3
Kyrgyzstan	99.9	89.5	80.5	72.0	61.2	54.6	51.2	50.1	47.4	44.0	43.8	43.4	42.4
Republic of Moldova [c]	102.4	93.1	55.0	52.1	44.7	43.8	42.9	40.8	35.9	36.1	37.0	38.4	36.8
Russian Federation	100.7	94.1	91.8	82.0	75.7	72.2	65.8	62.5	63.1	64.2	64.8	64.1	..
Tajikistan	102.5	98.2	86.1	81.9	71.9	71.1	62.5	60.1	52.2	47.7	48.2	47.9	48.0
Turkmenistan	104.2	101.0	110.7	110.5	115.4	119.9	132.9	150.2	152.9	..	..	..	..
Ukraine	98.1	92.7	87.9	78.3	72.2	66.8	61.2	59.3	54.4	51.3	56.2	55.0	54.0
Uzbekistan	101.5	96.9	98.6	90.1	92.3	93.5	93.7	94.1	94.9	96.7	98.0	..	..
Total above [a]	98.6	88.5	84.1	77.4	72.9	70.6	66.5	64.5	62.7	..	..	..	..
Memorandum items:													
Baltic states	97.2	87.3	74.2	62.8	60.3	57.7	56.7	56.1	52.4	51.4	50.1	51.1	52.3
Central Europe	94.9	79.1	75.1	73.0	73.6	73.1	73.1	72.6	69.2	66.6	65.7	63.8	..
South-east Europe[a]	96.4	78.3	72.3	70.7	67.4	70.4	68.5	66.7	62.2	58.6	57.8	56.1	..
CIS without Russian Federation	99.1	92.1	85.7	78.1	72.0	67.5	63.0	62.0	59.1	..	..	..	..
Caucasian CIS countries	101.4	79.2	70.4	67.0	60.3	47.8	42.4	40.7	39.4	38.3	37.0	34.1	..
Central Asian CIS countries	100.2	96.1	89.7	82.8	78.7	77.4	73.5	73.6	73.2	..	..	..	..
Three European CIS countries	98.4	92.6	86.6	78.1	71.5	67.0	62.5	61.1	57.1	54.6	58.4	57.0	55.8

Source: UNECE Common Database, derived from national and Interstate Statistical Committee of the CIS statistics.

[a] Up to 1993, excluding Albania; up to 1990, excluding Bosnia and Herzegovina.

[b] End of year, up to 1995; since 1996, annual average, labour force survey data.

[c] Excluding Transdniestria since 1993.

APPENDIX TABLE B.7

Registered unemployment in eastern Europe and the CIS, 1990-2003
(Per cent of labour force, end of period)

	1990	1991	1992	1993	1994	1995	1996	1997	1998	1999	2000	2001	2002	2003
Eastern Europe	..	..	11.7	13.4	13.1	12.3	11.7	11.5	12.3	14.3	14.8	15.3	15.8	15.3
Albania	9.5	9.2	27.0	22.0	18.0	12.9	12.3	14.9	17.6	18.2	16.9	14.6	15.8	15.0
Bosnia and Herzegovina	..	..	..	..	..	..	..	39.0	38.7	39.0	39.4	39.9	42.7	44.1
Bulgaria	1.8	11.1	15.3	16.4	12.8	11.1	12.5	13.7	12.2	16.0	17.9	17.9	16.3	13.5
Croatia	..	14.1	17.8	16.6	17.3	17.6	15.9	17.6	18.6	20.8	22.6	23.1	21.3	19.1
Czech Republic	0.7	4.1	2.6	3.5	3.2	2.9	3.5	5.2	7.5	9.4	8.8	8.9	9.8	10.3
Estonia [a]	..	..	1.6	5.0	5.1	5.0	5.6	4.6	5.1	6.7	7.7	7.7	6.8	6.1
Hungary	1.7	7.4	12.3	12.1	10.9	10.4	10.5	10.4	9.1	9.6	8.9	8.0	8.0	8.4*
Latvia	..	..	2.3	5.8	6.5	6.6	7.2	7.0	9.2	9.1	7.8	7.7	8.5	8.6
Lithuania	..	..	3.5	3.4	4.5	7.3	6.2	6.7	6.9	10.0	12.6	12.9	10.9	9.8
Poland	6.5	12.2	14.3	16.4	16.0	14.9	13.2	10.3	10.4	13.1	15.1	17.5	20.0	20.0
Romania	1.3	3.0	8.2	10.4	10.9	9.5	6.6	8.8	10.3	11.5	10.5	8.8	8.4	7.2
Serbia and Montenegro [b]	..	21.0	24.6	24.0	23.9	24.7	26.1	25.6	27.2	27.4	26.6	28*	26*	28*
Slovakia	1.6	11.8	10.4	14.4	14.8	13.1	12.8	12.5	15.6	19.2	17.9	18.6	17.4	15.6
Slovenia	..	10.1	13.3	15.5	14.2	14.5	14.4	14.8	14.6	13.0	12.0	11.8	11.3	11.0
The former Yugoslav Republic of Macedonia	..	24.5	26.2	27.7	30.0	36.6	38.8	41.7	32.3	44.0	45.1	41.8	45.3	45.3
CIS	..	..	2.7	3.8	4.6	5.8	6.6	7.6	9.0	8.3	7.1	6.4	6.5	6.7
Armenia	..	..	3.5	6.3	6.0	8.1	9.7	11.0	8.9	11.5	10.9	9.8	9.1	9.8
Azerbaijan	..	..	0.2	0.7	0.9	1.1	1.1	1.3	1.4	1.2	1.2	1.3	1.3	1.4
Belarus	..	..	0.5	1.3	2.1	2.7	4.0	2.8	2.3	2.0	2.1	2.3	3.0	3.1
Georgia	..	..	0.3	2.0	3.8	3.4	3.2	8.0	4.2	5.6	..	..	..	..
Kazakhstan	..	..	0.4	0.6	1.0	2.1	4.1	3.9	3.7	3.9	3.7	2.8	2.6	1.8
Kyrgyzstan	..	..	0.1	0.2	0.8	3.0	4.5	3.1	3.1	3.0	3.1	3.1	3.1	3.0
Republic of Moldova	..	..	0.7	0.7	1.0	1.4	1.5	1.7	1.9	2.1	1.8	1.7	1.5	1.2
Russian Federation [c]	..	..	5.2	6.1	7.8	9.0	10.0	11.2	13.3	12.2	9.8	8.7	8.8	8.2
Tajikistan	..	..	0.4	1.1	1.8	1.8	2.4	2.8	2.9	3.1	3.0	2.6	2.7	2.4
Turkmenistan	..	..	..	..	..	..	..	..	..	..	..	..	..	..
Ukraine	..	..	0.3	0.4	0.3	0.6	1.5	2.8	4.3	4.3	4.2	3.7	3.8	3.6
Uzbekistan	..	..	0.1	0.2	0.3	0.3	0.3	0.3	0.4	0.5	0.6	..	..	..
Memorandum items:														
Baltic states			2.1	4.5	5.3	6.6	6.4	6.4	7.3	9.1	10.1	10.2	9.4	8.8
Central Europe	..	9.7	11.3	13.3	12.9	12.0	11.2	9.8	10.3	12.5	13.4	14.7	15.1	15.0
South-east Europe	..	9.3	14.2	15.1	14.6	13.6	13.3	15.0	16.1	17.8	17.8	17.2	16.9	16.2
Russian Federation [d]	..	..	0.8	1.1	2.1	3.2	3.4	2.8	2.7	1.7	1.4	1.6	1.8	2.3
Former GDR	..	..	13.5	15.4	13.5	14.9	15.9	19.4	17.4	17.7	17.2	17.6	18.4	17.9

Source: UNECE Common Database, derived from national and Interstate Statistical Committee of the CIS statistics.

Note: Aggregates for eastern European countries until 1997 exclude Bosnia and Herzegovina.

[a] Job seekers until October 2000, thereafter – registered unemployed as percentage of the labour force.

[b] Since 1999, excluding Kosovo and Metohia.

[c] Based on Russian Federation Goskomstat's monthly estimates according to the ILO definition, i.e. including all persons not having employment but actively seeking work.

[d] Registered unemployment.

APPENDIX TABLE B.8

Consumer price indices in eastern Europe and the CIS, 1990-2003
(Annual average, percentage change over preceding year)

	1990	1991	1992	1993	1994	1995	1996	1997	1998	1999	2000	2001	2002	2003
Albania	..	35.5	193.1	85.0	21.5	8.0	12.7	33.1	20.3	- 0.1	–	3.1	5.3	2.5
Bosnia and Herzegovina	594.0	116.2	64 218.3	38 825.1	553.5	- 12.1	- 21.2	11.8	4.9	- 0.6	1.7	1.8	0.9	0.2
Bulgaria	23.8	338.5	91.3	72.8	96.0	62.1	121.6	1 058.4	18.7	2.6	10.3	7.4	5.8	2.3
Croatia	597.1	124.2	663.6	1 516.6	97.5	2.0	3.6	3.7	5.2	3.5	5.4	4.7	1.8	2.2
Czech Republic	9.9	56.7	11.1	20.8	10.0	9.1	8.9	8.4	10.6	2.1	3.9	4.7	1.8	0.2
Estonia	18.0	202.0	1 078.2	89.6	47.9	28.9	23.1	11.1	10.6	3.5	3.9	5.8	3.5	1.1
Hungary	28.9	35.0	23.0	22.6	19.1	28.5	23.6	18.4	14.2	10.1	9.9	9.2	5.4	4.9
Latvia	10.9	172.2	951.2	109.1	35.7	25.0	17.7	8.5	4.7	2.4	2.8	2.4	1.9	3.0
Lithuania	9.1	216.4	1 020.5	410.1	72.0	39.5	24.7	8.8	5.1	0.8	1.0	1.5	0.4	- 1.2
Poland	585.8	70.3	45.3	36.9	33.2	28.1	19.8	15.1	11.7	7.4	10.2	5.5	1.9	0.7
Romania	5.1	170.2	210.7	256.2	137.1	32.2	38.8	154.9	59.3	45.9	45.7	34.5	22.5	15.4
Serbia and Montenegro	580.0	122.0	8 926.0	2.2E+14	7.9E+10	71.8	90.5	23.2	30.4	44.1	77.5	90.4	19.3	9.6
Slovakia	10.4	61.2	10.2	23.1	13.4	10.0	6.1	6.1	6.7	10.5	12.0	7.0	3.3	8.5
Slovenia	551.6	115.0	207.3	31.7	21.0	13.5	9.9	8.4	8.1	6.3	9.0	8.6	7.6	5.7
The former Yugoslav Republic of Macedonia	596.6	110.8	1 511.0	352.0	126.6	16.4	2.5	0.9	- 1.4	- 1.3	6.6	5.2	2.3	1.1
Armenia	6.9	174.1	728.7	3 731.8	4 964.0	175.5	18.7	13.8	8.7	0.7	- 0.8	3.2	1.0	4.7
Azerbaijan	6.1	106.6	912.6	1 129.7	1 663.9	411.5	19.8	3.6	- 0.8	- 8.6	1.8	1.5	2.8	2.1
Belarus	4.7	94.1	971.2	1 190.9	2 219.6	709.3	52.7	63.9	73.2	293.7	168.9	61.4	42.8	28.5
Georgia	4.2	78.7	1 176.9	4 084.9	22 286.1	261.4	39.4	7.1	3.5	19.3	4.2	4.6	5.7	4.9
Kazakhstan	5.6	114.5	1 504.3	1 662.7	1 880.1	176.3	39.2	17.5	7.3	8.4	13.4	8.5	6.0	6.6
Kyrgyzstan	5.5	113.9	1 246.8	1 086.2	180.7	43.5	32.0	23.4	10.5	35.9	18.7	6.9	2.1	3.1
Republic of Moldova	5.7	101.1	1 308.0	1 751.0	486.4	29.9	23.5	11.8	7.7	39.3	31.3	9.8	5.3	11.7
Russian Federation	5.2	160.0	1 528.7	875.0	309.0	197.4	47.8	14.7	27.8	85.7	20.8	21.6	16.0	13.6
Tajikistan	5.9	112.9	822.0	2 884.8	350.3	682.1	422.4	85.4	43.1	27.5	32.9	38.6	12.2	16.3
Turkmenistan	5.7	88.5	483.2	3 128.4	2 562.1	1 105.3	714.0	83.7	16.8	..	..	..	..	..
Ukraine	5.4	94.0	1 485.8	4 734.9	891.2	376.7	80.2	15.9	10.6	22.7	28.2	12.0	0.8	5.2
Uzbekistan	5.8	97.3	414.5	1 231.8	1 550.0	76.5	54.0	58.8	17.7	29.0	24.9	..	..	..

Source: UNECE Common Database, derived from national statistics.

Note: From 1992 onwards indices derived from monthly data except for Armenia, Georgia, Hungary, Serbia and Montenegro and Slovenia (from 1993); Turkmenistan (from 1995); and Uzbekistan (from 1996).

APPENDIX TABLE B.9

Producer price indices in eastern Europe and the CIS, 1990-2003
(Annual average, percentage change over preceding year)

	1990	1991	1992	1993	1994	1995	1996	1997	1998	1999	2000	2001	2002	2003
Albania	..	..	..	..	..	..	..	..	..	..	4.9	-5.4	6.4	6.2
Bosnia and Herzegovina ..	..	129.5	70 374.7	10 967.6	1 184.8	68.7	-4.8	3.2	3.6	4.3	0.9	2.3	0.7	2.6
Bulgaria	14.7	296.4	56.1	28.3	59.1	50.7	132.7	971.0	16.6	3.3	17.0	3.6	1.3	4.9
Croatia	455.3	146.3	826.0	1 510.4	77.7	0.8	1.3	3.7	-1.5	2.5	9.6	3.4	-0.5	1.9
Czech Republic	2.5	70.4	10.8	9.3	5.1	7.7	4.9	5.1	4.9	1.1	5.1	3.0	-1.0	-1.6
Estonia	19.3	208.4	1 208.0	75.2	36.1	25.5	14.7	8.8	4.1	-1.3	4.9	4.5	0.8	0.2
Hungary	22.0	32.6	12.3	14.1	12.3	28.5	22.3	20.9	11.4	5.0	11.4	5.7	-1.1	2.5
Latvia	..	192.0	1 310.0	117.1	17.0	12.0	13.8	4.3	2.0	-4.0	0.8	1.6	1.0	3.2
Lithuania	..	148.2	1 510.0	391.7	44.7	28.7	16.5	6.0	-3.8	1.7	15.8	-2.9	-2.8	-0.3
Poland	622.4	40.9	28.0	32.6	31.0	26.0	13.4	12.2	7.2	5.7	7.8	1.7	1.1	2.7
Romania	26.9	220.1	184.8	165.0	140.7	35.3	50.0	144.0	33.2	41.2	53.4	41.0	24.6	21.1
Serbia and Montenegro ...	468.0	124.0	8 993.0			75.7	88.8	20.6	25.9	43.3	105.4	84.4	10.9	5.8
Slovakia	5.2	68.9	5.3	17.2	10.0	9.1	4.0	4.6	3.3	3.7	9.8	5.9	2.0	3.4
Slovenia	390.4	124.1	215.7	23.3	17.8	12.4	6.7	6.1	6.0	2.2	7.7	9.0	5.3	2.6
The former Yugoslav Republic of Macedonia ...	394.0	112.0	2 193.5	258.6	88.6	4.7	–	4.0	3.5	–	9.1	2.7	-0.6	–
Armenia	2.0	120.0	947.0	892.0	4 394.4	187.8	36.3	21.7	6.0	4.1	-0.4	1.1	3.6	3.7
Azerbaijan	..	179.5	7 453.6	1 974.0	3 971.6	1 340.1	70.6	11.4	-5.5	-1.3	9.4	-2.6	3.3	18.6
Belarus	2.1	151.1	1 939.2	1 536.3	3 362.1	538.6	35.7	89.4	72.8	355.7	185.6	71.7	40.6	37.4
Georgia	..	..	..	..	..	..	..	..	..	2.2	15.5	5.8	3.6	6.0	2.6
Kazakhstan	..	193.0	2 465.1	1 042.8	2 918.5	139.7	23.8	15.6	0.8	19.0	38.0	0.4	0.3	9.5
Kyrgyzstan	..	160.0	1 664.0	831.0	46.8	15.8	28.4	23.4	8.9	51.1	29.6	9.6	5.5	7.5
Republic of Moldova	..	130.0	1 210.9	1 078.5	711.7	52.2	30.2	14.9	9.7	47.1	33.6	12.6	8.0	8.4
Russian Federation	3.9	240.0	3 280.0	900.0	340.0	237.6	50.8	15.0	7.0	59.1	46.5	19.1	11.8	15.6
Tajikistan	..	163.0	1 316.5	1 080.0	665.5	351.7	340.7	103.7	28.4	45.6	39.0	25.1	9.1	15.3
Turkmenistan	..	211.0	994.0	1 610.0	911.0	893.8	2 974.9	260.6	-30.5	..	..	..	..	..
Ukraine	..	163.4	4 128.5	9 667.5	1 134.5	488.9	52.1	7.8	13.2	31.1	20.8	8.6	3.1	7.8
Uzbekistan	..	147.0	1 296.0	1 119.0	2 162.6	792.5	128.5	53.9	40.0	38.0	61.1	..	..	..

Source: UNECE Common Database, derived from national statistics.

Note: From 1994 onwards indices derived from monthly data except: Bosnia and Herzegovina, Croatia, Czech Republic, Poland, The former Yugoslav Republic of Macedonia (from 1992), Hungary, Romania, Slovakia, Slovenia (from 1993), and Serbia and Montenegro and Turkmenistan (from 1995).

APPENDIX TABLE B.10

Nominal gross wages in industry in eastern Europe and the CIS, 1990, 1992-2003

(Annual average, percentage change over preceding year) [a]

	1990	1992	1993	1994	1995	1996	1997	1998	1999	2000	2001	2002	2003
Albania [b]	..	145.3	73.0	54.9	34.1	34.8	10.7	20.4	10.4	17.7	15.1	14.2	..
Bosnia and Herzegovina [c]	..	..	..	..	..	253.6	50.8	31.1	15.4	12.1	..	..	..
Bulgaria	20.8	132.8	55.1	53.9	57.7	90.4	882.9	34.5	..	..	..	..	..
Croatia [c]	..	350.7	1 435.5	130.6	44.0	11.8	16.3	10.6	10.1	7.9	7.7	..	..
Czech Republic	3.0	21.0	22.6	16.9	18.3	17.7	11.9	10.7	6.7	7.2	7.0	5.5	6.3
Estonia [d]	..	570.3	93.3	72.2	35.7	23.5	19.6	9.9	4.7	15.9	7.9	10.0	9.0
Hungary [b]	27.2	24.3	24.9	23.3	19.1	21.7	21.8	16.6	13.5	15.0	14.4	12.6	9.3
Latvia	..	609.8	112.0	60.0	24.1	14.9	21.6	6.5	4.0	3.2	4.9	6.3	9.1
Lithuania	15.3	632.5	246.1	70.0	43.2	34.0	21.7	12.0	-0.4	-0.7	..	..	..
Poland [c]	365.5	41.2	37.8	39.8	30.1	25.8	19.9	14.1	10.5	9.6	6.8	3.2	..
Romania [c]	9.7	173.5	204.2	135.6	54.7	53.9	98.1	57.9	42.0	43.4	39.8	23.1	..
Serbia and Montenegro [c]	400.0	4 886.4	-62.5	229.6	74.1	74.5	41.7	39.6	24.6	113.5	..	..	..
Slovakia [b]	2.4	16.9	23.1	17.7	15.2	14.6	9.3	9.7	7.9	9.3	10.2	7.3	7.3
Slovenia	361.5	194.6	45.1	27.1	17.1	14.0	12.0	10.7	9.3	11.6	10.9	9.9	..
The former Yugoslav Republic of Macedonia [c]	433.6	1 083.7	454.0	105.8	11.1	3.6	2.3	3.1	1.5	6.2	..	..	..
Armenia	5.9	352.3	739.1	3 640.2	210.9	62.3	41.7	20.5	15.2	19.5	22.3	12.6	31.8
Azerbaijan	4.4	870.4	700.8	575.7	354.8	53.0	58.2	19.8	18.1	33.3	14.6	..	..
Belarus	14.1	910.9	1 073.8	69.6	618.7	58.5	96.8	109.4	323.9	197.1	101.8	48.5	35.8
Georgia	6.0	457.3	2 117.2	23 300.5	112.6	145.4	12.7	26.8	23.2	..	..	..	..
Kazakhstan	11.0	1 053.1	993.1	1 542.5	178.2	30.9	22.5	7.8	21.6	26.1	15.3	10.4	13.0
Kyrgyzstan	0.5	773.1	615.1	176.3	54.8	29.1	60.3	20.0	43.2	0.9	18.1	20.7	3.0
Republic of Moldova	14.2	815.0	773.0	284.4	43.8	32.2	24.9	16.6	22.5	31.8	20.9	21.2	29.1
Russian Federation	13.0	1 065.7	798.2	260.2	131.4	64.3	21.6	14.3	52.2	48.8	46.8	31.4	..
Tajikistan	8.0	550.2	917.5	142.2	145.2	425.3	71.9	96.4	26.4	31.5	51.1	29.7	..
Turkmenistan	..	1 010.1	1 467.7	622.2	686.2	915.3	121.5	27.1	28.6	75.7	53.0	..	..
Ukraine	39.0	1 419.0	2 286.1	737.8	408.5	71.5	13.5	5.9	18.1	42.7	35.2	15.8	21.9
Uzbekistan	..	706.1	1 159.3	806.8	278.4	99.8	76.3	60.3	50.0	..	..	..	..

Source: UNECE Common Database, derived from national statistics.

[a] Calculated from reported annual average wages.

[b] Gross wages in total economy. Hungary for 1990 and 1992, Slovakia for 1990.

[c] Net wages in industry. Poland (for 1990 and 1992).

[d] Manufacturing.

APPENDIX TABLE B.11

Merchandise exports of eastern Europe and the CIS, 1993-2003

(Billion dollars)

	1993	1994	1995	1996	1997	1998	1999	2000	2001	2002	2003
Eastern Europe	66.872	77.261	100.621	107.084	115.895	127.933	125.527	141.885	157.277	178.778	230.688
Albania	0.123	0.139	0.202	0.213	0.137	0.207	0.352	0.261	0.305	0.330	0.446
Bosnia and Herzegovina	..	..	0.024	0.058	0.193	0.352	0.518	0.675	0.752	0.729	1.045
Bulgaria	3.769	3.935	5.345	4.890	4.940	4.194	4.006	4.825	5.113	5.692	7.439
Croatia	3.709	4.260	4.633	4.512	4.171	4.541	4.302	4.432	4.666	4.904	6.164
Czech Republic	14.463	15.882	21.273	22.180	22.779	26.351	26.265	29.052	33.397	38.488	48.723
Estonia	0.802	1.305	1.838	2.079	2.934	3.236	2.938	3.174	3.309	3.428	4.511
Hungary	8.921	10.701	12.867	15.704	19.100	23.005	25.012	28.092	30.498	34.337	42.480
Latvia	1.401	0.988	1.304	1.443	1.673	1.812	1.723	1.865	2.001	2.279	2.877
Lithuania	1.994	2.031	2.705	3.355	3.860	3.711	3.004	3.809	4.583	5.519	7.212
Poland	14.202	17.240	22.887	24.440	25.756	28.229	27.407	31.651	36.085	41.010	53.577
Romania	4.892	6.151	7.910	8.085	8.431	8.302	8.487	10.367	11.385	13.869	17.618
Serbia and Montenegro	..	..	1.531	1.846	2.677	2.858	1.498	1.723	1.903	2.275	2.537
Slovakia	5.458	6.714	8.585	8.822	9.640	10.775	10.277	11.908	12.704	14.478	21.960
Slovenia	6.083	6.828	8.316	8.310	8.369	9.050	8.546	8.732	9.252	10.326	12.737
The former Yugoslav Republic of Macedonia	1.055	1.086	1.204	1.147	1.237	1.311	1.191	1.319	1.323	1.116	1.363
CIS total	..	90.929	113.172	125.647	123.181	106.160	106.030	145.928	144.710	153.336	189.789
of which: non-CIS	52.547	61.751	79.800	88.922	86.539	76.657	83.146	116.681	113.927	122.704	151.644
Armenia	0.156	0.216	0.271	0.290	0.233	0.221	0.232	0.301	0.342	0.505	0.678
Non-CIS	0.029	0.058	0.101	0.162	0.138	0.140	0.175	0.227	0.253	0.409	0.551
Azerbaijan	0.725	0.653	0.637	0.631	0.781	0.606	0.929	1.745	2.314	2.168	2.592
Non-CIS	0.351	0.378	0.352	0.341	0.403	0.374	0.718	1.510	2.091	1.924	2.258
Belarus	..	2.510	4.707	5.652	7.301	7.070	5.909	7.331	7.448	8.021	9.964
Non-CIS	0.789	1.031	1.777	1.888	1.922	1.910	2.287	2.927	2.957	3.637	4.511
Georgia	..	0.156	0.154	0.199	0.240	0.193	0.238	0.330	0.320	0.348	0.444
Non-CIS	0.069	0.039	0.057	0.070	0.102	0.085	0.131	0.198	0.176	0.179	0.229
Kazakhstan	..	3.231	5.250	5.911	6.497	5.436	5.592	9.126	8.639	9.670	12.900
Non-CIS	1.501	1.357	2.366	2.732	3.515	3.266	4.100	6.750	5.995	7.476	9.946
Kyrgyzstan	0.396	0.340	0.409	0.505	0.604	0.514	0.454	0.505	0.476	0.486	0.582
Non-CIS	0.112	0.117	0.140	0.112	0.285	0.283	0.271	0.297	0.308	0.317	0.380
Republic of Moldova	0.483	0.565	0.746	0.795	0.875	0.632	0.464	0.472	0.568	0.644	0.790
Non-CIS	0.178	0.159	0.279	0.252	0.267	0.203	0.211	0.196	0.222	0.293	0.367
Russian Federation [a]	..	67.800	82.419	90.600	86.895	74.444	75.551	105.033	101.900	107.200	134.800
Non-CIS	44.297	52.100	65.400	72.000	67.800	58.700	63.600	90.800	86.600	91.000	114.000
Tajikistan	0.350	0.492	0.749	0.770	0.746	0.597	0.689	0.784	0.652	0.737	0.798
Non-CIS	0.227	0.399	0.497	0.439	0.473	0.394	0.374	0.411	0.440	0.549	0.659
Turkmenistan	..	2.145	1.881	1.682	0.751	0.594	1.190	2.500	2.620	2.616	3.160
Non-CIS	1.049	0.494	0.951	0.610	0.300	0.442	0.700	1.200	1.170	1.178	1.710
Ukraine	7.817	10.272	13.128	14.401	14.232	12.637	11.582	14.573	16.265	17.957	23.080
Non-CIS	3.223	4.653	6.168	6.996	8.646	8.435	8.329	10.075	11.589	13.580	17.032
Uzbekistan	..	2.549	2.821	4.211	4.026	3.218	3.200	3.230	3.166	2.986	..
Non-CIS	0.721	0.966	1.712	3.321	2.689	2.425	2.250	2.090	2.127	2.164	..
Total above	..	168.190	213.793	232.730	239.076	234.093	231.557	287.813	301.987	332.114	424.197
Memorandum items:											
Baltic states	4.197	4.324	5.846	6.877	8.467	8.759	7.665	8.848	9.893	11.226	14.599
Central Europe	49.127	57.365	73.928	79.456	85.644	97.410	97.508	109.436	121.937	138.638	179.476
South-east Europe	..	..	20.848	20.751	21.785	21.764	20.355	23.601	25.447	28.914	36.613
CIS without Russian Federation	..	23.129	30.753	35.047	36.286	31.716	30.479	40.895	42.810	46.136	54.989
Caucasian CIS countries	..	1.025	1.062	1.120	1.253	1.019	1.399	2.376	2.976	3.021	3.714
Central Asian CIS countries	..	8.757	11.110	13.079	12.625	10.358	11.125	16.145	15.553	16.494	17.440
Three European CIS countries	..	13.347	18.581	20.848	22.408	20.339	17.955	22.375	24.281	26.622	33.835

Source: UNECE secretariat calculations, based on national statistical publications and direct communications from national statistical offices.

Note: Trade flows reported include the "new trade" among members of the dissolved federal states: former Czechoslovakia (from 1993) and the former SFR of Yugoslavia (from 1992); and the former USSR: for the Baltic states (from 1992) and for the CIS. Data excluding the "new trade" were shown in earlier issues of this publication. Changes in the method of recording trade are reflected from 1993 in data for the Czech Republic (inclusion of OPT transactions, etc.), from 1995 in Latvia (imports registered c.i.f.) and Lithuania (change from special to general system), from 1996 in Hungary (inclusion of trade flows of free trade zones), from 1997 in Slovakia (inclusion of OPT transactions, etc.) and from 2000 in Estonia (change from general to special trade system). All trade values are expressed in dollars at prevailing market exchange rates.

[a] Russian Goskomstat data including trade flows not crossing the Russian borders such as off-board fish sales and estimates of value of goods exported or imported by individuals within an approved duty-free quota.

APPENDIX TABLE B.12

Merchandise imports of eastern Europe and the CIS, 1993-2003
(Billion dollars)

	1993	1994	1995	1996	1997	1998	1999	2000	2001	2002	2003
Eastern Europe	80.386	91.379	125.033	145.996	159.004	173.259	167.558	185.480	202.090	226.567	288.657
Albania	0.421	0.549	0.650	0.913	0.620	0.795	0.903	1.070	1.317	1.489	1.848
Bosnia and Herzegovina	..	..	0.524	1.204	1.555	2.120	2.431	2.290	2.463	2.700	3.327
Bulgaria	5.120	4.272	5.638	5.074	4.932	4.957	5.515	6.507	7.261	7.903	10.742
Croatia	4.166	5.229	7.510	7.788	9.104	8.383	7.799	7.887	9.147	10.722	14.199
Czech Republic	14.617	17.427	25.265	27.919	27.563	28.789	28.126	32.183	36.472	40.736	51.306
Estonia	0.896	1.659	2.540	3.231	4.441	4.786	4.108	4.252	4.294	4.780	6.471
Hungary	12.648	14.554	15.466	18.144	21.234	25.706	28.008	32.080	33.682	37.612	47.526
Latvia	0.961	1.240	1.818	2.320	2.724	3.189	2.946	3.189	3.507	4.040	5.210
Lithuania	2.244	2.352	3.649	4.559	5.644	5.794	4.834	5.457	6.353	7.769	9.796
Poland	18.758	21.566	29.043	37.137	42.314	47.054	45.911	48.940	50.275	55.113	68.004
Romania	6.522	7.109	10.278	11.435	11.280	11.838	10.557	13.055	15.552	17.857	24.003
Serbia and Montenegro	..	..	2.665	4.113	4.826	4.830	3.296	3.711	4.837	6.320	7.510
Slovakia	6.332	6.634	8.777	11.112	11.622	13.006	11.265	12.660	14.689	16.629	22.604
Slovenia	6.501	7.304	9.492	9.421	9.367	10.098	10.083	10.116	10.148	10.902	13.811
The former Yugoslav Republic of Macedonia	1.199	1.484	1.719	1.627	1.779	1.915	1.776	2.085	2.094	1.995	2.300
CIS: total	..	74.976	95.470	107.587	112.731	95.162	70.542	81.786	94.688	103.952	128.749
of which: non-CIS	33.696	44.899	56.861	63.607	71.815	61.760	44.571	47.881	59.675	69.192	85.743
Armenia	0.255	0.394	0.674	0.856	0.892	0.902	0.811	0.885	0.877	0.987	1.269
Non-CIS	0.087	0.188	0.340	0.578	0.593	0.672	0.624	0.711	0.659	0.685	0.960
Azerbaijan	0.629	0.778	0.668	0.961	0.794	1.077	1.036	1.172	1.431	1.666	2.626
Non-CIS	0.241	0.292	0.440	0.621	0.443	0.673	0.711	0.797	0.986	1.015	1.776
Belarus	..	3.066	5.564	6.939	8.689	8.549	6.674	8.574	8.178	9.092	11.505
Non-CIS	1.119	0.974	1.887	2.369	2.872	2.995	2.385	2.551	2.512	2.797	3.499
Georgia	..	0.338	0.385	0.687	0.944	0.884	0.602	0.651	0.685	0.731	1.058
Non-CIS	0.167	0.066	0.231	0.417	0.603	0.617	0.377	0.423	0.428	0.441	0.699
Kazakhstan	..	3.561	3.807	4.241	4.301	4.350	3.687	5.051	6.446	6.584	8.327
Non-CIS	0.494	1.384	1.154	1.295	1.969	2.290	2.089	2.295	3.137	3.541	4.407
Kyrgyzstan	0.448	0.317	0.522	0.838	0.709	0.842	0.600	0.554	0.467	0.587	0.717
Non-CIS	0.112	0.107	0.168	0.351	0.273	0.401	0.341	0.256	0.210	0.264	0.307
Republic of Moldova	0.628	0.659	0.841	1.072	1.172	1.024	0.587	0.776	0.893	1.039	1.403
Non-CIS	0.184	0.183	0.272	0.420	0.567	0.584	0.345	0.517	0.552	0.630	0.809
Russian Federation [a]	..	50.500	62.603	68.000	71.983	58.015	39.537	44.862	53.764	61.000	75.700
Non-CIS	26.807	36.500	44.300	47.200	53.400	43.700	29.200	31.400	40.700	48.800	60.000
Tajikistan	0.630	0.547	0.810	0.668	0.750	0.711	0.663	0.675	0.688	0.721	0.881
Non-CIS	0.374	0.314	0.332	0.285	0.268	0.265	0.148	0.115	0.150	0.173	0.282
Turkmenistan	..	1.468	1.364	1.011	1.183	1.008	1.500	1.780	2.349	1.857	2.242
Non-CIS	0.501	0.782	0.619	0.450	0.531	0.530	1.000	1.100	1.146	1.103	1.492
Ukraine	9.533	10.745	15.484	17.603	17.128	14.676	11.846	13.956	15.775	16.977	23.021
Non-CIS	2.652	2.907	5.488	6.427	7.249	6.779	5.103	5.916	6.943	8.009	11.513
Uzbekistan	..	2.603	2.748	4.712	4.186	3.125	3.000	2.850	3.135	2.712	..
Non-CIS	0.958	1.202	1.630	3.195	3.047	2.256	2.250	1.800	2.253	1.735	..
Total above	..	166.355	220.503	253.584	271.735	268.421	238.100	267.266	296.778	330.519	417.406
Memorandum items:											
Baltic states	4.101	5.251	8.006	10.110	12.809	13.768	11.888	12.897	14.154	16.590	21.476
Central Europe	58.856	67.485	88.043	103.733	112.100	124.653	123.393	135.979	145.266	160.991	203.251
South-east Europe	..	..	28.984	32.154	34.095	34.838	32.276	36.604	42.670	48.986	63.929
CIS without Russian Federation	..	24.476	32.867	39.587	40.748	37.147	31.005	36.924	40.924	42.952	53.049
Caucasian CIS countries	..	1.510	1.727	2.503	2.630	2.864	2.449	2.708	2.994	3.384	4.953
Central Asian CIS countries	..	8.496	9.251	11.470	11.129	10.034	9.449	10.910	13.085	12.460	12.167
Three European CIS countries	..	14.470	21.889	25.614	26.989	24.249	19.107	23.307	24.846	27.108	35.929

Source: UNECE secretariat calculations, based on national statistical publications and direct communications from national statistical offices.

Note: See appendix table B.11.

[a] Russian Goskomstat data including trade flows not crossing the Russian borders such as off-board fish sales and estimates of value of goods exported or imported by individuals within an approved duty-free quota.

APPENDIX TABLE B.13

Balance of merchandise trade of eastern Europe and the CIS, 1993-2003
(Billion dollars)

	1993	1994	1995	1996	1997	1998	1999	2000	2001	2002	2003
Eastern Europe	-13.514	-14.118	-24.411	-38.913	-43.109	-45.327	-42.031	-43.595	-44.812	-47.790	-57.969
Albania	-0.298	-0.410	-0.448	-0.701	-0.483	-0.589	-0.551	-0.809	-1.012	-1.159	-1.402
Bosnia and Herzegovina	..	..	-0.500	-1.146	-1.362	-1.768	-1.913	-1.615	-1.710	-1.971	-2.282
Bulgaria	-1.352	-0.336	-0.294	-0.184	0.008	-0.763	-1.509	-1.683	-2.148	-2.211	-3.304
Croatia	-0.457	-0.969	-2.877	-3.276	-4.933	-3.842	-3.496	-3.455	-4.481	-5.818	-8.035
Czech Republic	-0.154	-1.545	-3.992	-5.739	-4.784	-2.438	-1.861	-3.131	-3.075	-2.248	-2.583
Estonia	-0.094	-0.353	-0.702	-1.152	-1.507	-1.550	-1.170	-1.078	-0.985	-1.352	-1.960
Hungary	-3.727	-3.853	-2.599	-2.440	-2.134	-2.701	-2.996	-3.988	-3.184	-3.275	-5.047
Latvia	0.440	-0.252	-0.515	-0.877	-1.051	-1.377	-1.223	-1.323	-1.506	-1.761	-2.333
Lithuania	-0.250	-0.322	-0.944	-1.204	-1.784	-2.083	-1.831	-1.647	-1.770	-2.250	-2.584
Poland	-4.555	-4.326	-6.156	-12.697	-16.558	-18.825	-18.504	-17.289	-14.190	-14.103	-14.427
Romania	-1.630	-0.958	-2.368	-3.351	-2.849	-3.536	-2.070	-2.688	-4.167	-3.988	-6.385
Serbia and Montenegro	..	..	-1.134	-2.267	-2.149	-1.972	-1.798	-1.988	-2.934	-4.045	-4.973
Slovakia	-0.874	0.080	-0.192	-2.290	-1.983	-2.231	-0.988	-0.752	-1.985	-2.151	-0.644
Slovenia	-0.418	-0.476	-1.176	-1.111	-0.998	-1.048	-1.537	-1.384	-0.895	-0.576	-1.074
The former Yugoslav Republic of Macedonia	-0.144	-0.398	-0.515	-0.480	-0.542	-0.604	-0.585	-0.766	-0.771	-0.880	-0.937
CIS: total	..	15.953	17.702	18.059	10.450	10.999	35.488	64.142	50.022	49.385	61.040
of which: non-CIS	18.851	16.852	22.939	25.315	14.725	14.897	38.575	68.800	54.252	53.511	65.901
Armenia	-0.099	-0.178	-0.403	-0.566	-0.660	-0.682	-0.580	-0.584	-0.536	-0.482	-0.591
Non-CIS	-0.058	-0.130	-0.239	-0.416	-0.455	-0.532	-0.449	-0.484	-0.406	-0.276	-0.408
Azerbaijan	0.096	-0.125	-0.031	-0.330	-0.013	-0.471	-0.107	0.573	0.883	0.502	-0.034
Non-CIS	0.110	0.086	-0.088	-0.280	-0.040	-0.299	0.007	0.713	1.106	0.909	0.483
Belarus	..	-0.556	-0.857	-1.287	-1.388	-1.480	-0.765	-1.244	-0.730	-1.071	-1.541
Non-CIS	-0.330	0.057	-0.110	-0.481	-0.950	-1.085	-0.098	0.376	0.445	0.839	1.012
Georgia	..	-0.182	-0.231	-0.488	-0.704	-0.692	-0.364	-0.321	-0.365	-0.384	-0.614
Non-CIS	-0.098	-0.027	-0.174	-0.347	-0.501	-0.532	-0.246	-0.226	-0.252	-0.263	-0.470
Kazakhstan	..	-0.330	1.443	1.670	2.196	1.086	1.906	4.075	2.193	3.086	4.574
Non-CIS	1.007	-0.027	1.212	1.437	1.547	0.976	2.011	4.456	2.858	3.935	5.539
Kyrgyzstan	-0.052	0.023	-0.113	-0.333	-0.105	-0.328	-0.146	-0.050	0.009	-0.101	-0.135
Non-CIS	−	0.010	-0.028	-0.239	0.012	-0.118	-0.070	0.041	0.097	0.053	0.074
Republic of Moldova	-0.145	-0.094	-0.095	-0.277	-0.297	-0.392	-0.123	-0.305	-0.325	-0.395	-0.612
Non-CIS	-0.006	-0.024	0.007	-0.168	-0.300	-0.381	-0.134	-0.321	-0.331	-0.336	-0.443
Russian Federation *a*	..	17.300	19.816	22.600	14.912	16.429	36.014	60.171	48.136	46.200	59.100
Non-CIS	17.490	15.600	21.100	24.800	14.400	15.000	34.400	59.400	45.900	42.200	54.000
Tajikistan	-0.280	-0.055	-0.061	0.102	-0.004	-0.114	0.026	0.109	-0.036	0.017	-0.083
Non-CIS	-0.147	0.085	0.165	0.154	0.205	0.129	0.225	0.295	0.290	0.376	0.377
Turkmenistan	..	0.677	0.517	0.670	-0.432	-0.414	-0.310	0.720	0.271	0.759	0.918
Non-CIS	0.548	-0.288	0.332	0.160	-0.231	-0.088	-0.300	0.100	0.024	0.075	0.218
Ukraine	-1.716	-0.473	-2.356	-3.202	-2.896	-2.038	-0.265	0.617	0.490	0.980	0.059
Non-CIS	0.571	1.746	0.680	0.569	1.397	1.657	3.227	4.159	4.646	5.571	5.519
Uzbekistan	..	-0.054	0.073	-0.501	-0.159	0.093	0.200	0.380	0.031	0.274	..
Non-CIS	-0.237	-0.236	0.082	0.126	-0.358	0.169	−	0.290	-0.126	0.429	..
Total above	..	1.835	-6.709	-20.853	-30.658	-34.328	-6.543	20.547	5.209	1.595	3.072
Memorandum items:											
Baltic states	0.096	-0.927	-2.160	-3.232	-4.343	-5.009	-4.224	-4.049	-4.261	-5.363	-6.877
Central Europe	-9.729	-10.120	-14.115	-24.277	-26.456	-27.243	-25.885	-26.543	-23.329	-22.354	-23.775
South-east Europe	..	..	-8.136	-11.403	-12.311	-13.074	-11.922	-13.003	-17.223	-20.073	-27.316
CIS without Russian Federation	..	-1.347	-2.114	-4.541	-4.462	-5.430	-0.526	3.971	1.886	3.185	1.940
Caucasian CIS countries	..	-0.485	-0.665	-1.383	-1.377	-1.845	-1.050	-0.332	-0.017	-0.364	-1.239
Central Asian CIS countries	..	0.261	1.859	1.608	1.496	0.324	1.675	5.235	2.468	4.034	5.273
Three European CIS countries	..	-1.123	-3.308	-4.766	-4.581	-3.909	-1.152	-0.932	-0.565	-0.486	-2.094

Source: UNECE secretariat calculations, based on national statistical publications and direct communications from national statistical offices.

Note: See appendix table B.11.

a Russian Goskomstat data including trade flows not crossing the Russian borders such as off-board fish sales and estimates of value of goods exported or imported by individuals within an approved duty-free quota.

APPENDIX TABLE B.14

Merchandise trade of eastern Europe and the Russian Federation, by direction, 1980, 1990, 1992-2003

(Shares in total trade, per cent)

	1980	1990	1992	1993	1994	1995	1996	1997	1998	1999	2000	2001	2002	2003
Eastern Europe, *to and from:*														
Exports														
World	100.0	100.0	100.0	100.0	100.0	100.0	100.0	100.0	100.0	100.0	100.0	100.0	100.0	100.0
Eastern Europe and the CIS	48.5	38.1	23.0	30.7	28.5	28.6	28.5	28.6	24.7	20.8	20.7	21.4	21.2	21.6
CIS	27.1	22.3	12.4	11.4	10.0	9.8	10.0	10.6	7.4	4.2	4.1	4.7	4.5	4.4
Eastern Europe	21.4	15.8	10.7	19.3	18.5	18.7	18.5	18.0	17.3	16.6	16.6	16.7	16.7	17.2
Developed market economies	35.7	49.5	63.0	57.5	61.9	62.6	63.5	63.6	68.3	73.4	73.1	72.9	72.7	72.8
Developing economies	15.8	12.4	14.0	11.8	9.6	8.8	8.0	7.8	7.0	5.8	6.2	5.7	6.1	5.6
Imports														
World	100.0	100.0	100.0	100.0	100.0	100.0	100.0	100.0	100.0	100.0	100.0	100.0	100.0	100.0
Eastern Europe and the CIS	42.0	26.6	24.7	29.9	26.2	25.8	24.7	23.1	20.0	20.6	23.6	23.2	22.5	22.8
CIS	26.8	18.3	17.9	16.5	14.0	13.0	12.0	11.0	8.6	8.5	11.4	10.8	9.9	9.7
Eastern Europe	18.8	14.3	6.8	13.4	12.2	12.9	12.7	12.1	11.4	12.1	12.2	12.4	12.6	13.1
Developed market economies	38.7	53.3	64.4	61.2	65.2	65.6	66.2	66.7	70.2	69.7	66.7	66.2	65.3	64.4
Developing economies	19.3	20.1	10.9	8.9	8.6	8.5	9.1	10.2	9.8	9.7	9.7	10.6	12.2	12.8
Former Soviet Union/Russian Federation, *to and from:*														
Exports														
World	100.0	100.0	100.0	100.0	100.0	100.0	100.0	100.0	100.0	100.0	100.0	100.0	100.0	100.0
Eastern Europe	34.5	21.8	22.3	18.1	15.1	16.8	18.2	19.5	18.1	17.8	20.0	19.3	17.5	17.0
Developed market economies	42.2	49.5	57.9	59.7	66.6	60.6	58.1	58.6	60.0	57.8	55.6	55.0	55.6	53.3
Developing economies	23.3	28.7	19.8	22.2	18.3	22.6	23.7	21.9	21.9	24.4	24.4	25.7	26.9	29.7
Imports														
World	100.0	100.0	100.0	100.0	100.0	100.0	100.0	100.0	100.0	100.0	100.0	100.0	100.0	100.0
Eastern Europe	31.5	24.7	15.9	10.6	14.1	15.5	12.6	13.7	12.0	9.6	10.9	10.1	10.3	10.9
Developed market economies	46.4	52.9	62.4	60.6	70.3	69.5	67.8	68.3	68.2	68.3	69.3	67.8	65.7	64.8
Developing economies	22.1	22.4	21.7	28.8	15.6	15.0	19.6	18.0	19.8	22.1	19.8	22.1	24.0	24.3

Source: UNECE Common Database, derived from national statistics.

Note: Data for 1980-1990 refer to the east European CMEA countries (Bulgaria, Czechoslovakia, German Democratic Republic, Hungary, Poland and Romania) and to the former Soviet Union. Trade data in national currencies were revalued at consistent rouble/dollar cross-rates (see the note to appendix table B.11). As from 1991, the second panel reflects non-CIS trade of the Russian Federation only. In the first panel, reporting group "eastern Europe" covers Bulgaria, former Czechoslovakia, Hungary, Poland and Romania in 1991-1992; in 1993-1995 it covers Albania, Bulgaria, Croatia, the Czech Republic, Estonia, Hungary, Latvia, Lithuania, Poland, Romania, Slovakia, Slovenia and The Former Yugoslav Republic of Macedonia while Bosnia and Herzegovina and Serbia and Montenegro are included only from 1996.

Partner country grouping has been recently revised with subsequent revisions back to 1980. The "eastern Europe" partner group now covers Albania, Bosnia and Herzegovina, Bulgaria, Croatia, the Czech Republic, Estonia, Hungary, Latvia, Lithuania, Poland, Romania, Serbia and Montenegro, Slovakia, Slovenia and The former Yugoslav Republic of Macedonia.

APPENDIX TABLE B.15

Exchange rates of eastern Europe and the CIS, 1990, 1992-2003

(Annual averages, national currency units per dollar)

	Unit [a]	1990	1992	1993	1994	1995	1996	1997	1998	1999	2000	2001	2002	2003
Albania	lek	8.90	75.03	102.06	94.62	92.70	104.50	148.93	150.63	137.69	143.71	143.48	139.93	121.87
Bosnia and Herzegovina	con. marka [b]	..	..	..	..	1.43	1.50	1.73	1.76	1.84	2.12	2.19	2.08	1.73
Bulgaria	leva [c]	2.36	23.42	27.85	54.13	67.08	177.88	1 681.87	1 760.37	1.84	2.12	2.18	2.08	1.73
Croatia	kuna [d]	11.00	264.30	3 577.42	6.03	5.23	5.43	6.10	6.36	7.11	8.28	8.34	7.87	6.70
Czech Republic	koruna	18.56	28.29	29.15	28.79	26.54	27.14	31.70	32.28	34.57	38.60	38.04	32.74	28.21
Estonia	kroon [e]	..	12.11	13.22	12.99	11.46	12.03	13.88	14.07	14.69	16.98	17.49	16.63	13.86
Hungary	forint	63.21	78.98	91.93	105.16	125.68	152.65	186.79	214.40	237.15	282.18	286.49	257.89	225.14
Latvia	lats [f]	..	0.68	0.67	0.56	0.53	0.55	0.58	0.59	0.59	0.61	0.63	0.62	0.57
Lithuania	litas [g]	..	1.78	4.34	3.98	4.00	4.00	4.00	4.00	4.00	4.00	4.00	3.68	3.06
Poland	zloty [h]	9 500	13 627	18 136	22 723	2.42	2.70	3.28	3.49	3.96	4.35	4.09	4.08	3.89
Romania	leu	22.43	307.95	760.05	1 655	2 033	3 084	7 168	8 876	15 333	21 709	29 061	33 055	33 200
Serbia and Montenegro	dinar [i]	10.65	750.00	..	1.55	4.74	4.96	5.70	11.07	22.84	54.74	67.67	64.19	57.41
Slovakia	koruna	18.56	28.30	30.77	32.05	29.72	30.66	33.62	35.23	41.36	46.04	48.35	45.33	36.77
Slovenia	tolar	11.32	81.29	113.24	128.81	118.52	135.37	159.69	166.13	181.77	222.66	242.75	240.25	207.11
The former Yugoslav Republic of Macedonia	denar [j]	11.32	508.07	23.26	43.26	37.88	39.98	50.00	54.46	56.90	65.90	68.04	64.82	54.32
Armenia	dram	..	..	9.11	288.65	405.91	414.04	490.77	504.92	535.06	539.53	555.08	573.35	578.76
Azerbaijan	manat	..	..	102.33	1 739	4 414	4 301	3 985	3 869	4 120	4 474	4 657	4 861	4 911
Belarus	rouble [k]	..	..	3 160	4 652	11 538.	13 472	26 729	58 971	274 512	882	1 390	1 785	2 054
Georgia	lari [l]	..	..	..	1.66	1.29	1.26	1.30	1.39	2.03	1.98	2.07	2.20	2.14
Kazakhstan	tenge	..	..	..	35.54	60.95	67.30	75.44	78.30	119.52	142.13	146.74	153.30	149.71
Kyrgyzstan	som	..	..	..	10.86	10.82	12.81	17.36	20.84	39.01	47.70	48.38	46.94	43.61
Republic of Moldova	leu	..	..	1.58	4.08	4.50	4.60	4.62	5.37	10.52	12.43	12.87	13.57	13.95
Russian Federation	rouble [m]	0.59	192.75	993.00	2 204	4 559	5 121	5 785	9.71	24.62	28.13	29.17	31.35	30.69
Tajikistan	samoni [n]	..	..	..	..	107.59	293.82	560.64	778.30	1 225.96	1.83	2.39	2.76	3.06
Turkmenistan	manat	..	..	..	14.08	116.67	3 595	4 143	4 592.	5 200	5 200	5 200	5 200	5 202
Ukraine	hryvnia [o]	..	..	4 796	3 170	14 728	1.83	1.86	2.45	4.13	5.44	5.37	5.33	5.33
Uzbekistan	sum [p]	..	..	..	10.69	30.12	40.66	66.02	94.79	124.64	236.58	423.08	774.09	971.97

Source: UNECE Common Database, derived from national, IMF and CIS statistics. Annual averages are unweighted arithmetic averages of monthly values. Change or redenomination of currency is indicated by a vertical bar.

Note: Under the central planning system with its state foreign trade monopoly, exchange rates served primarily statistical and accounting purposes (notably the conversion of foreign trade values for statistics expressed in domestic currency), without direct impact on domestic price formation. Market-based exchange rates and a meaningful link to domestic currency values emerged only with the transformations from 1989 onward. The official exchange rates of the earlier period are therefore not suitable for the conversion to dollars of macroeconomic and other data of these countries expressed in domestic currency.

[a] Currency unit of the last period shown. For prior periods, see footnotes.

[b] BAM (convertible marka), the official rate is pegged to the euro. Prior to January 1999, the official rate was pegged to the deutsche mark at a 1:1 rate.

[c] The leva was redenominated at 1:1,000 from 5 July 1999.

[d] The kuna replaced the Croat dinar on 3 May 1994 at 1:1,000; the 1994 average is shown in kuna terms.

[e] The kroon replaced the Soviet rouble in June 1992 with a peg to the deutsche mark (8:1); the average shown for 1992 refers to June-December.

[f] The lats replaced an earlier Latvian rouble at 1:200 on 18 October 1993; the 1993 average is shown in lats terms.

[g] The litas replaced the earlier talonas at 1:100 on 1 June 1993; the 1993 average is shown in litas terms.

[h] The zloty was redenominated at 1:10,000 from 1 January 1995.

[i] The dinar was further redenominated on 1 July 1992 (1:10), 1 October 1993 (1:1 million), 1 January 1994 (1:1 trillion) and 24 January 1994 (1:13 million). Average annual exchange rates not available for 1993. Estimated market exchange rates for 1998-2000.

[j] The denar (which had replaced the Yugoslav dinar 1:1 on 26 April 1992) was redenominated 1:100 on 1 May 1993; the 1993 average is shown in terms of that unit.

[k] The Belarus rouble was redenominated 1:10 on 10 August 1994; the 1994 average here assumes this applied to the entire year. The Belarus rouble was further redenominated at 1:1,000 since January 2000. Annual averages were calculated from end-of-period monthly rates, and the period average since January 1999.

[l] The lari replaced the lari-kupon on 25 September 1995; the annual average for 1994 is shown in million lari-kupon, and the average for 1995 in lari.

[m] 1980-1991: Soviet rouble/dollar rate used in the conversion of foreign trade data for statistical purposes. The rouble was redenominated at 1:1,000 from 1 January 1998.

[n] A new currency, the samoni, was put into circulation on 30 October 2000 replacing the Tajik rouble at 1:1,000. The average for 2000 is shown in samoni terms.

[o] The hryvnia replaced the former karbovanets on 2 September 1996 at 1:100,000; the average for 1996 is shown in hryvnia terms.

[p] The sum replaced the sum-kupon in June 1994 (1:1,000).

APPENDIX TABLE B.16

Current account balances of eastern Europe and the CIS, 1990, 1992-2003

(Million dollars)

	1990	1992	1993	1994	1995	1996	1997	1998	1999	2000	2001	2002	2003
Eastern Europe	..	..	..	-3 027	-7 377	-18 284	-21 499	-22 280	-26 960	-23 613	-21 484	-26 101	-32 391
Albania	-118	-51	19	31	37	-62	-254	-65	-133	-163	-218	-407	-407
Bosnia and Herzegovina	..	..	..	-177	-193	-748	-1 060	-782	-1 098	-1 028	-1 217	-1 750	-2 095
Bulgaria	-1 710	-360	-1 098	-32	-198	164	1 046	-61	-652	-704	-984	-827	-1 666
Croatia *a*	-621	329	637	711	-1 407	-956	-2 512	-1 453	-1 397	-461	-726	-1 920	-2 099
Czech Republic	-122	-456	456	-787	-1 369	-4 121	-3 564	-1 255	-1 462	-2 718	-3 273	-4 166	-5 570
Estonia	..	36	22	-167	-158	-398	-563	-478	-247	-294	-339	-716	-1 199
Hungary *b*	123	325	-3 455	-3 911	-1 638	-1 764	-2 076	-3 390	-3 773	-4 034	-3 237	-4 675	-7 357
Latvia	..	191	417	201	-16	-279	-345	-650	-654	-493	-732	-647	-956
Lithuania	..	321	-86	-94	-614	-723	-981	-1 298	-1 194	-675	-574	-734	-1 218
Poland *c*	3 067	-3 104	-5 788	954	854	-3 264	-5 744	-6 901	-12 487	-9 998	-5 357	-5 007	-4 085
Romania	-3 337	-1 564	-1 174	-428	-1 774	-2 571	-2 104	-2 917	-1 437	-1 374	-2 228	-1 535	-3 254
Serbia and Montenegro	..	..	..	-400	-1 037	-1 317	-1 279	-660	-716	-350	-648	-1 731	-1 943
Slovakia	-767	173	-532	759	511	-1 960	-1 827	-1 982	-980	-702	-1 746	-1 939	-280
Slovenia *a*	518	926	192	575	-75	56	51	-118	-698	-548	37	314	15
The former Yugoslav Republic of Macedonia *a*	-409	-19	-83	-263	-299	-340	-286	-270	-32	-72	-244	-362	-278
CIS *d*	..	-538	10 266	4 696	3 741	4 934	-6 448	-7 229	23 460	48 175	32 929	30 353	36 999
Armenia	..	-50	-67	-104	-218	-291	-307	-403	-307	-278	-200	-148	-178
Azerbaijan	..	488	-160	-121	-401	-931	-916	-1 365	-600	-168	-52	-768	-2 021
Belarus	..	131	-435	-444	-458	-516	-859	-1 017	-194	-338	-394	-311	-505
Georgia	..	-248	-354	-277	-363	-570	-514	-276	-200	-269	-211	-231	-392
Kazakhstan	..	-1 900	-641	-905	-213	-751	-799	-1 236	-236	563	-1 203	-866	-69
Kyrgyzstan	..	-61	-88	-84	-235	-425	-138	-364	-184	-79	-19	-27	-26
Republic of Moldova	..	-152	-155	-82	-95	-192	-275	-335	-68	-116	-68	-52	-142
Russian Federation *e*	-6 300	1 142	12 792	7 844	6 963	10 847	-80	219	24 616	46 839	33 935	29 116	35 845
Tajikistan	..	-53	-208	-170	-89	-75	-61	-120	-36	-62	-74	-15	-5
Turkmenistan	-308	926	776	84	24	2	-580	-935	..	..	..	..	..
Ukraine	..	-526	-765	-1 163	-1 152	-1 185	-1 335	-1 296	1 658	1 481	1 402	3 173	2 891
Uzbekistan	..	-236	-429	118	-21	-980	-584	-103	-126	216	-113	..	..
Total above *d*	..	..	..	1 669	-3 636	-13 350	-27 946	-29 509	-3 500	24 562	11 445	4 252	4 608
Memorandum items:													
Baltic states	..	548	353	-59	-788	-1 400	-1 890	-2 426	-2 095	-1 462	-1 644	-2 097	-3 373
Central Europe	2 820	-2 137	-9 127	-2 410	-1 717	-11 053	-13 160	-13 646	-19 400	-17 999	-13 575	-15 473	-17 276
South-east Europe	..	..	..	-557	-4 871	-5 830	-6 449	-6 208	-5 465	-4 152	-6 264	-8 531	-11 742
CIS without Russian Federation *d*	..	-1 680	-2 526	-3 148	-3 222	-5 913	-6 368	-7 448	-1 156	1 336	-1 007	1 237	1 154
Caucasian CIS countries	..	190	-581	-502	-983	-1 791	-1 736	-2 043	-1 106	-715	-464	-1 147	-2 590
Central Asian CIS countries *d*	..	-1 324	-590	-957	-534	-2 229	-2 162	-2 757	-1 446	1 024	-1 483	-426	1 501
Three European CIS countries	..	-547	-1 355	-1 689	-1 705	-1 893	-2 469	-2 647	1 396	1 027	939	2 810	2 244

Source: National balance of payments statistics; IMF, *Balance of Payments Statistics* (Washington, D.C.) and IMF country studies; UNECE secretariat estimates.

a Excludes transactions with the republics of the former SFR of Yugoslavia: Croatia (1990-1992), Slovenia (1990-1991) and The former Yugoslav Republic of Macedonia (1990-1992).

b Methodological changes (mainly regarding treatment of reinvested earnings) were introduced in 2003 and 2004; 1995-2003 results have been revised accordingly. For 1990-1994, balance of payments data in convertible currencies only.

c National Bank of Poland started publishing balance of payments results on a transaction basis in 2004; the data have been revised accordingly back to 1990. Balance of payments data published in previous issues of this *Survey* were reported on a cash basis.

d Totals include estimates for Turkmenistan and Uzbekistan.

e 1990-1992 exclude transactions with the Baltic and CIS countries.

APPENDIX TABLE B.17

Inflows of foreign direct investment [a] in eastern Europe and the CIS, 1990, 1992-2002

(Million dollars)

	1990	1992	1993	1994	1995	1996	1997	1998	1999	2000	2001	2002	2003
Eastern Europe	..	..	..	..	..	11 413	15 142	20 043	22 231	23 983	22 866	26 669	18 636
Albania [b]	–	20	68	53	70	90	48	45	41	143	207	135	178
Bosnia and Herzegovina	..	..	..	–	–	–	–	67	177	146	119	268	382
Bulgaria [b]	4	41	40	105	90	109	505	537	819	1 002	813	905	1 419
Croatia	–	16	120	117	114	511	533	932	1 467	1 089	1 559	1 124	1 956
Czech Republic	132	1 004	654	869	2 562	1 428	1 300	3 718	6 324	4 986	5 641	8 483	2 583
Estonia	..	82	162	215	202	151	267	581	305	387	542	284	891
Hungary [c]	311	1 471	2 339	1 146	4 741	3 291	4 166	3 344	3 311	2 777	3 949	2 869	2 519
Latvia	..	29	45	214	180	382	521	357	347	410	164	382	359
Lithuania	..	8	30	31	73	152	355	926	486	379	446	732	179
Poland	89	678	1 715	1 875	3 659	4 498	4 908	6 365	7 270	9 341	5 713	4 131	4 225
Romania	–	77	94	341	419	263	1 215	2 031	1 041	1 037	1 157	1 146	1 840
Serbia and Montenegro [b][c]	..	..	..	..	..	–	740	113	112	50	165	475	1 260
Slovakia	18	100	195	269	308	353	220	684	390	1 925	1 579	4 012	571
Slovenia	4	111	113	117	151	174	334	216	107	136	370	1 645	179
The former Yugoslav Republic of Macedonia	–	–	–	24	9	11	30	128	33	175	442	78	95
CIS [d]	..	1 777	1 876	1 770	4 064	5 313	9 035	6 780	6 749	5 439	7 290	8 982	14 397
Armenia [b]	..	–	1	8	25	18	52	221	122	104	70	111	121
Azerbaijan [b]	..	–	60	22	330	627	1 125	1023	510	130	227	1 392	3 285
Belarus [b]	..	7	18	11	15	105	352	203	444	119	96	247	171
Georgia [b]	..	–	–	8	6	40	243	265	82	131	110	165	338
Kazakhstan	..	100	228	635	964	1 137	1 321	1 152	1 472	1 283	2 835	2 590	2 068
Kyrgyzstan	..	0	10	38	96	47	83	109	44	-2	5	5	46
Republic of Moldova [b]	..	17	14	12	67	24	79	76	38	136	146	117	58
Russian Federation	–	1 454	1 211	690	2 065	2 579	4 865	2 761	3 309	2 714	2 748	3 461	6 725
Tajikistan [b]	..	9	9	12	20	18	18	25	21	24	9	36	32
Turkmenistan [b]	–	11	79	103	233	108	108	62	..	..	..	..	..
Ukraine	..	170	198	159	267	521	623	743	496	595	792	693	1424
Uzbekistan [b]	..	9	48	73	-24	90	167	140	121	75	83	..	..
Total above [d]	..	..	..	..	..	16 726	24 176	26 823	28 979	29 422	30 156	35 651	33 033
Memorandum items:													
Baltic states	..	119	238	460	454	685	1 142	1 863	1 139	1 176	1 152	1 399	1 429
Central Europe	555	3 364	5 015	4 275	11 420	9 744	10 929	14 327	17 402	19 165	17 253	21 140	10 077
South-east Europe	..	..	..	..	..	984	3 070	3 853	3 690	3 642	4 461	4 130	7 130
CIS without Russian Federation [d]	..	323	665	1 080	1 999	2 734	4 170	4 019	3 439	2 725	4 542	5 521	7 672
Caucasian CIS countries	..	-	61	38	361	685	1 419	1 509	715	365	406	1 669	3 744
Central Asian CIS countries [d]	..	129	374	861	1 289	1 400	1 697	1 488	1 747	1 510	3 102	2 796	2 276
Three European CIS countries	..	194	229	181	349	649	1 053	1 022	978	850	1 034	1 057	1 653

Source: National balance of payments statistics; IMF, *Balance of Payments Statistics* (Washington, D.C.) and IMF country studies; UNECE secretariat estimates.

[a] Inflows into the reporting country.

[b] Net of residents' investments abroad. Bulgaria, 1990-1994; Armenia, 1990-2002; Azerbaijan, 1993-1998; Belarus, 1992-1996; Republic of Moldova, 1991-1994.

[c] Excludes Kosovo from 1999; 2003 data for Serbia only.

[d] Totals include estimates for Turkmenistan and Uzbekistan.

OTHER RECENT PUBLICATIONS OF ECONOMIC ANALYSIS FROM THE UNITED NATIONS ECONOMIC COMMISSION FOR EUROPE

- *Economic Survey of Europe, 2004 No. 1*, Sales No. E.04.II.E.7 (May)

  This issue provides a review of macroeconomic developments in the whole of Europe, the CIS and North America in 2003 and discusses the outlook for 2004. In addition, there are special studies dealing with tax reforms in the EU acceding countries, benefits from product differentiation, and poverty in eastern Europe and the CIS.

- *Economic Survey of Europe, 2003 No. 2*, Sales No. E.03.II.E.27 (December)

  In addition to an assessment of the economic situation in the ECE region in the autumn 2003, this issue contains the two papers presented at the UNECE Spring Seminar of March 2003, which focused on *Sustainable Development in the ECE Region*. Theodore Panayotou analyses the relationship between economic growth and the environment and David Newbery examines sectoral dimensions of sustainable development.

- *Economic Survey of Europe, 2003 No. 1*, Sales No. E.03.II.E.26 (April)

  This issue contains the secretariat's review of recent macroeconomic developments in the ECE region and an assessment of the outlook for 2003. Special studies deal, *inter alia*, with corporate governance in the ECE region; progress in systemic reforms in the CIS; the impact of EU enlargement on non-candidate countries in eastern Europe and the CIS; and international trade of the CIS.

- *Economic Survey of Europe, 2002 No. 2*, Sales No. E.02.II.E.8 (December)

  In addition to an assessment of the macroeconomic situation in the ECE region in the autumn of 2002, this issue contains the papers presented at the Spring Seminar of May 2002 on *Labour Market Challenges in the ECE Region*. Included are papers by Tito Boeri, Herbert Brücker, Richard Jackman and Alena Nesporova, together with the comments of the discussants and a summary of the general discussion.

- *Economic Survey of Europe, 2002 No. 1*, Sales No. E.02.II.E.7 (April)

  This issue reviews economic developments in 2001 and discusses the outlook for 2002. Special chapters focus on technological activity in the ECE region during the 1990s; alternative policies for approaching EMU accession by central and east European countries; and new forms of household formation in central and eastern Europe: are they related to newly emerging value orientations?

- *Economic Survey of Europe, 2001 No. 2*, Sales No. E.01.II.E.26 (December)

  In addition to an assessment of the macroeconomic situation in the UNECE region in the autumn of 2001, this issue contains the papers presented at the Spring Seminar of May 2001 on *Creating a Supportive Environment for Business Enterprise and Economic Growth: Institutional Reform and Governance*. Included are papers by William Lazonick, Paul Hare, Shang-Jin Wei, Antoni Kamiński and Bartlomiej Kamiński, together with the comments of the discussants and a summary of the general discussion.

* * * * *

More details about other publications and activities of the United Nations Economic Commission for Europe, which pay special attention to issues concerning the transition economies, can be found at the secretariat's website: http://www.unece.org

* * * * *

To obtain copies of publications contact:

Publications des Nations Unies
Section de Vente et Marketing
Organisation des Nations Unies
CH-1211 Genève 10
Suisse
Tel: (4122) 917 2612 / 917 2606 / 917 2613
Fax: (4122) 917 0027
E-mail: unpubli@unog.ch

United Nations Publications
2 United Nations Plaza
Room DC2-853
New York, NY 10017
USA
Tel: (1212) 963 8302 / (1800) 253 9646
Fax: (1212) 963 3489
E-mail: publications@un.org